ILLINOIS CENTRAL COLLEGE
PA3201.S5 1968
STACKS
Studies in the history of Hellenist

A12900 133796

W9-ASB-114

PA
3201   SIFAKIS   43208
.S5   Studies in
1968   of Hellen

University of London Classical Studies

IV

STUDIES IN THE HISTORY
OF HELLENISTIC DRAMA

Studies in the History
of Hellenistic Drama

G. M. SIFAKIS

Illinois Central College
Learning Resouce Center

UNIVERSITY OF LONDON
THE ATHLONE PRESS

43298

PA
3201
.55
1968

Published by
THE ATHLONE PRESS
UNIVERSITY OF LONDON
at 2 Gower Street, London WC1
Distributed by Constable & Co Ltd
10 Orange Street, London WC2

Canada
Oxford University Press
Toronto

U.S.A.
Oxford University Press Inc
New York

© *G. M. Sifakis*, 1967

First edition, 1967
Reprinted, 1968

485 13704 6

Printed in Great Britain by
WILLIAM CLOWES AND SONS, LIMITED
LONDON AND BECCLES

TO NELLY

gratefully

PREFACE

This book was written in the period 1962–4, and was submitted as a qualification for the degree of Ph.D. at the University of London. During the years of my studies in England I was extremely fortunate in being able to work with Professor T. B. L. Webster. I am deeply grateful to him for his unstinted interest in my work, and much more indebted than can be acknowledged here. I am likewise greatly in debt for many valuable suggestions to my examiners Professor R. E. Wycherley and Professor E. G. Turner, and to Mr D. M. Lewis, Dr N. M. Panayotakis and Dr N. C. Hourmouziades, who read my thesis in typescript, and also to Professor R. P. Winnington-Ingram, Mr E. W. Handley and Mr W. J. Slater, who read parts of it.

The friendly and inspiring surroundings I found at the Joint Library of the Institute of Classical Studies and of the Hellenic and Roman Societies were an invaluable boon to me during my stay in London. My special thanks go to the Librarian, Miss Joyce Southan, who read through my manuscript and improved my English.

I should like to record my gratitude to the Greek State Scholarships Foundation whose assistance made possible my study in England; to the Central Research Funds Committee of the University of London for a grant that enabled me to visit Delos and Delphi in the summer of 1963; and to the Institute of Classical Studies for a generous grant towards the cost of publication of this book.

I am grateful to Professor Turner, then director of the Institute of Classical Studies, for inviting me to read a paper at the Institute on 11 March 1963, which was subsequently published in the *Bulletin of the Institute of Classical Studies* 10 (1963); it now appears in a revised and extended form as Appendix I of this book. Appendix II was published in the *Classical Quarterly* 15 (1965), and is reprinted here by the kind permission of the Delegates of the Clarendon Press.

I have finally to thank the staff of the Athlone Press, who dealt with a particularly difficult manuscript with patience and skill, and saved the book from many blemishes.

G. M. S.

CONTENTS

Part II: Delphi

Appendices

ABBREVIATIONS

A.J.A.	*American Journal of Archaeology*
A.J.P.	*American Journal of Philology*
Ath. Mitt.	*Mitteilungen des deutschen archäologischen Instituts.* Athenische Abteilung.
B.C.H.	*Bulletin de Correspondence Hellénique*
B.I.C.S.	*Bulletin of the Institute of Classical Studies,* University of London
B.S.A.	*Annual of the British School at Athens*
C.A.H.	*The Cambridge Ancient History*
Choix	F. Durrbach, *Choix d'inscriptions de Délos,* Paris, 1921–2
C.I.G.	*Corpus Inscriptionum Graecarum*
C.Q.	*Classical Quarterly*
C.R.	*Classical Review*
C.R.A.I.	*Comptes rendus de l'Académie des Inscriptions et Belles-Lettres*
Délos	*Exploration archéologique de Délos.* Faite par l'École française d'Athènes. . .
F.D.	*Fouilles de Delphes* (École française d'Athènes)
F.Gr.Hist.	F. Jacoby, *Die Fragmente der griechischen Historiker* (1923–)
F.H.G.	C. Müller, *Fragmenta Historicorum Graecorum* (1841–70)
I.D.	*Inscriptions de Délos*
I.G.	*Inscriptiones Graecae*
I. Magn.	O. Kern, *Die Inschriften von Magnesia am Maeander,* Berlin, 1900
I. Perg.	M. Fränkel, *Die Inschriften von Pergamon,* Berlin, 1890–5
I. Pr.	F. Hiller von Gaertringen, *Inschriften von Priene,* Berlin, 1906
Jahresh.	*Jahreshefte des österreichischen archäologischen Institutes*
J.d.I.	*Jahrbuch des deutschen archäologischen Instituts*
J.H.S.	*Journal of Hellenic Studies*
Kock	T. Kock, *Comicorum Atticorum Fragmenta* (1880–8)

Le Bas–Wadd.   Ph. Le Bas, *Voyage archéologique en Grèce et en Asie*
               Mineure, tome iii: Inscriptions grecques et latines par
               Ph. Le Bas et W. H. Waddington, Paris, 1870.

M.A.M.A.   *Monumenta Asiae Minoris Antiqua*

Michel   Ch. Michel, *Recueil d'inscriptions grecques*, Bruxelles,
               1900

M.O.M.C.   T. B. L. Webster, *Monuments Illustrating Old and*
               Middle Comedy, B.I.C.S., Supplement no. 9, 1960

M.N.C.   T. B. L. Webster, *Monuments Illustrating New Comedy*,
               B.I.C.S., Supplement no. 11, 1961

M.T.S.   T. B. L. Webster, *Monuments Illustrating Tragedy and*
               Satyr Play, B.I.C.S., Supplement no. 14, 1962

O.G.I.S.   W. Dittenberger, *Orientis Graeci Inscriptiones Selectae*,
               Leipzig, 1903–5

R.E.   *Real-Encyklopädie der klassischen Altertums-Wissenschaft*

R.É.A.   *Revue des Études Anciennes*

R.É.G.   *Revue des Études Grecques*

S.B.   *Sammelbuch griechischen Urkunden aus Aegypten*

S.E.G.   *Supplementum Epigraphicum Graecum*

S.G.D.I.   H. Collitz, *Sammlung der griechischen Dialekt-Inschriften*,
               Göttingen, 1884–1915

S.I.G.[3]   W. Dittenberger, *Sylloge Inscriptionum Graecarum*, 3rd
               ed., Leipzig, 1915–24

T.A.P.A.   *Transactions and Proceedings of the American Philo-*
               logical Association

INTRODUCTION

Although the Hellenistic rulers failed to achieve the political unity of the Greek world, nevertheless a cultural unity was brought about as a result of the great expansion which took place. This unity is most strikingly reflected in the development of a common form of language, the *koine*.

In the classical age drama was a particularly Athenian form of art, although it was not unknown to other Greeks, in Magna Graecia for instance. Aeschylus and Euripides took some of their productions to Sicily or Macedonia. This early practice was intensified in the fourth century when poets and actors travelled a good deal.[1] Later the theatre kept pace with the wide population movements and the diffusion of Hellenism, and became the most popular kind of entertainment. Even the smallest city had its own theatre, which came to be considered as a necessary public building.[2] Nevertheless, the dramatic performances remained within the frame of the Dionysia which were celebrated in every corner of the Greek world, or became a part of some other religious festival like the Mouseia at Thespiai, Amphiaraia at Oropos, Soteria at Delphi, and so on. Their competitive character was also retained till the end of the ancient world. This expansion made necessary the development of various theatrical professions. Actors, musicians, and poets, organized themselves into professional guilds. Hundreds of new poets from every place tried to respond to the tremendous demand. On the other hand, the playgoers had more opportunities to see revivals of the old classics. Contests of three old tragedies and three old comedies (actually Middle and New comedies) are known to have taken place at Athens in the mid-third century (*Hesperia* 7 [1938], 116–18, n. 22). Inscriptions from many other places show that the contests of old plays held a regular part in the programmes of such festivals as, for

[1] Plat. *Laches* 183 a, *Leg.* 817 a; Dem. 19, Hypoth. II, 2; Athen. XII 538f.
[2] Pausanias X 4, 1; R. Martin, *L'urbanisme dans la Grèce antique*, Paris, 1956, pp. 281ff.; R. E. Wycherley, *How the Greeks Built Cities*, London, 2nd ed., 1962, pp. xix, 160ff.; A. H. M. Jones, *The Greek City from Alexander to Justinian*, Oxford, 1940, p. 233.

example, the Heraia at Argos, Naia at Dodona, Soteria at
Delphi (*S.I.G.*³ 1080, cf. p. 84), the Amphiaraia at Oropos
(*I.G.* vii 416–20), the Sarapieia at Tanagra (*I.G.* vii 541–3;
S.E.G. xix 335, cf. pp. 117–8), the Museia at Thespiai (*I.G.* vii
1760–1), the Heraia in Samos (Michel 901), and so forth. The
satyr play also had a flourishing new era. In Athens instead of
the one satyr play produced at the Dionysia during the fourth
century, contests of three old satyr plays are recorded (*Hesperia*,
loc. cit.), while the composition of new ones also went on.

Our knowledge of the post-Menandrian history of drama
derives mainly from inscriptions, works, or fragments, of
Alexandrian and post-Alexandrian scholars, commentators, and
lexicographers, a considerable number of works of art—
mosaics, sculptures, bronzes, terracottas, etc.—representing
dramatic scenes and characters with their masks, and the
remains of ancient theatres. Unfortunately, these sources provide hints rather than full information. This, added to the ex-
treme scarcity of texts, accounts for the common belief that
Greek drama made little, if any, progress after the end of the
fourth century. This assumption is, I think, debatable. Important innovations such as the introduction of the high stage, a
new role for the chorus, changes of scene and scenery, and a
new kind of dramatic music, developed in the Hellenistic period.
But in order to appreciate these developments we have to date
the evidence as accurately as possible, evaluate, and, on the
whole, regard it from a Hellenistic point of view. Thus properly
utilized our late sources will lead to different and more sound
conclusions than if they are used, as has so frequently been
done, merely to illustrate classical or Latin drama.

It might be suggested that most of these innovations were
technical and external, and not inherent in drama, but on the
other hand it could be argued that the dramatist sets the pace
and the producer follows; and we should remember that the
ancient poet was usually the producer of his own plays.
Furthermore, even if there is no question of a new genus of
drama, we must acknowledge the importance of dramatic by-
products—the various kinds of prose and musical mime and the
pantomime—which flourished in Hellenistic times, outlived the
'serious' drama in the later Roman Empire, and the Middle

Ages, and had a great impact on the development of modern drama.

The present dissertation is mainly concerned with the history of dramatic performances in Delos and Delphi. The evidence collected and discussed covers, in the case of Delos, the period of Independence (314–166 B.C.) and the subsequent Athenian domination of the island down to the mid-first century B.C. In the first half of the first century Delos was twice sacked: in 88 by the troops of Mithridates, and by pirates, also allies of Mithridates, in 69 B.C. By the middle of the century all efforts towards recovery had failed, the trade traffic ceased, and the formerly prosperous colonies of merchants and bankers left the place. The decline was quick and definite. As regards Delphi, roughly the same period is covered by our investigation. Pagan life went on in Delphi for centuries after Christ, but there is almost no evidence for drama after the last Pythaid. Some references to tragic performances dating from the middle of the first century A.D. onwards are very briefly mentioned here (without claim to completeness). Drama in Imperial times needs to be studied in conjunction with mime and lower forms of theatrical entertainment, which are outside the scope of this book.

The reasons for choosing Delos and Delphi are easily explained. The fact that both places were sacred to Apollo determined to some extent their parallel historical fates. They were at first centres of the Delphic and Ionic Amphictyonies respectively. In early Hellenistic times Delos became the centre of the Island League set up by Antigonos Monophthalmos and later placed under the Ptolemies, while the Aitolians imposed their authority on the Delphic Amphictyony. In the second century Delos became an Athenian colony. Athens also maintained excellent relations with Delphi at the same time. The bulk of inscriptional evidence for drama in Delos is contemporaneous with that of Delphi. Many artists gave free performances in both cities as offerings to Apollo. A considerable number of actors and other *technitai* are known to have appeared at both places. Finally, both cities provide us with fairly extensive material.

My aim was to answer the questions: When did dramatic

performances take place in the two cities, what plays were performed, by whom, and how were they produced? The final arrangement of each chapter was, however, determined by the nature of the evidence available in each case.

Though primarily engaged in presenting the Delphian and Delian evidence, and discussing the problems to which this material gives rise, I have brought in evidence from other places as well, in order to illustrate some general aspects of Hellenistic theatre production. The detailed discussion of two extremely interesting questions, namely the high stage and chorus in the Hellenistic theatre, and whether the performances of a festival were assigned as a whole to one Dionysiac guild, would be out of proportion in the chapters on Delos and Delphi respectively. They are, therefore, dealt with in two appendices.

For the dating of the Delphic documents G. Daux's *Chronologie Delphique* (1943) has been followed, unless otherwise stated. The dates of Athenian inscriptions are adjusted according to the list of archons given in *The Athenian Year* (1961) by B. D. Meritt.

PART I
Delos

CHAPTER I

DIONYSIA

ARCHAEOLOGICAL EVIDENCE FOR THE CULT OF DIONYSOS

There is no literary or inscriptional evidence for the cult of Dionysos in Delos before the late fourth century, save Anios' story which connects the god with the island.[1] The archaeologists, however, have located two sites sacred to Dionysos, one of which may go back to archaic times. Its main construction was a Stibadion (a peculiar type of Dionysiac *lieu-saint* or temple) situated outside the eastern part of the peribolos of Apollo's sanctuary, and opposite the eastern side of the stoa of Antigonos.[2] The statues of Dionysos and two *papposilenoi* were discovered inside it. Dionysos is nude, seated on a *proedria* throne; the *papposilenoi* are standing, in theatrical costume, carrying wine-skins. The sculptures, as well as the small edifice, date from the end of the second century B.C., but a big phallus which was pulled out of the foundations of the building 'très grossièrement taillé dans un bloc de lave' dates from the archaic period.[3] Near the temple fragments of three more phalli, a

[1] Anios was the son of Rhoio, daughter of Staphylos and granddaughter of Dionysos. Being with child by Apollo, Rhoio was set adrift by her father in a chest. Coming ashore in Euboea, or according to some, in Delos itself, she bore Anios, whom she named because of the ἀνία she had endured. Anios became 'rex idem hominum Phoebique sacerdos' (Virg., *Aen.* III 80), and had three daughters, Oino, Spermo, and Elais, who could, by grace of Dionysos, command the gifts of wine, corn, and oil. So they were able to supply the host of Agememnon when they passed from Delos on their way to Troy. Lycophron *Alex.* 570 and schol., Diod. Sic., V 62, cf. Ovid, *Met.* XIII 632ff.; H. J. Rose, *A Handbook of Greek Mythology*, p. 276, cf. O. Kern, *Die Religion der Griechen*, ii, pp. 136f., Ch. Vellay, *Les légendes du Cycle troyen*, Monaco, 1957, p. 240, W. Kullmann, *Die Quellen der Ilias*, Hermes Einzelschriften 14 (1960), 222. Anios was worshipped as the hero Archegetes by the people of Delos. On his sanctuary see F. Robert, *Rev. Arch.* 6ᵉ sér. 41 (1953, I), 8–40; G. Daux, *B.C.H.* 86 (1962), 959–63. From the period of the second Athenian domination we have priests of Anios recorded among other Athenian officials in the island, *I.G.* ii² 2336₄₆. ₇₇. ₁₂₆=Dow, *Harvard Class. Stud.* 51 (1940), 116ff., ll. 40, 82, 131.

[2] Ch. Picard, *C.R.A.I.* 1944, 136–41, and *B.C.H.* 68–9 (1944–5), 240–70.

[3] L. Bizard, *B.C.H.* 31 (1907), 502.

fragment of a megarian bowl decorated with a zone of phalli in relief, a poros relief showing Dionysos dressed like Artemis and holding a thyrsus with his panther, and another relief representing Agathos Daimon (who has also been associated with the cult of Stibadion[1]), were excavated.[2] A choregic monument was set up at the south-western corner of the temple: a high base bearing a huge phallus on its top. It was dedicated by Karystios, son of Asbelos, about 300 B.C. Above the inscription of the *choregos* (*I.G.* xi 1148, cf. p. 37, n. 4) a cock-like phallus is carved, and two more reliefs on the lateral faces show Dionysos among members of his *thiasos*.[3] Another similar monument must have been erected at the corresponding north-western corner of the temple. R. Vallois has suggested that the other fragments of phalli found around the temple come from similar monuments, and that, during a certain period, it was the practice of the winning *choregoi* at the Dionysia to commemorate their victories by monuments of this kind.[4] It seems then that our Stibadion is a reconstruction of an earlier temple, which was 'la principale construction conservée d'un péribole dionysiaque, dans une zone de culte affectée au dieu sans doute depuis l'époque archaïque'.[5] An inscription[6] found close by mentions the τόπος...ὁ π[ρὸ]ς τῶι [Διο]νύσωι (4–5), and an altar of Dionysos (22), which was located by Vallois.[7]

A few metres south-west of the theatre Dionysos had another, very big, altar, and shared a temenos with Hermes and Pan.[8] The altar was built, or rebuilt, in 180–79 B.C. (*I.D.* 440 A 87–8, 442 B 231–3, also in 178 B.C.?, 443 Bb 156–7). The principal temple of the temenos is dated after 246 B.C.(?)[9] The sanctuary appears to have been consecrated to Dionysos, Hermes, and

---

[1] Picard, *B.C.H.* 68–9, 265–8.

[2] Bizard, *loc. cit.*, 498–502.

[3] *B.C.H.* 31, 504ff., figs. 18–20.

[4] *B.C.H.* 46 (1922), 100–101. For similar finds in the new temple of Dionysos Eleuthereus at Athens see E. Buschor, 'Ein choregisches Denkmal', *Ath. Mitt.* 53 (1928), 96–108, pls. 29–30.

[5] Picard, *B.C.H.* 68–9, 242, cf. *C.R.A.I.* 1944, 138–9.

[6] Published by N. Kontoleon, 'Αρχ. Δελτ. 14 (1931–2), 84–9.

[7] *Les constructions antiques de Délos*, pl. I, 29, cf. *Architecture*, p. 75. Cf. *B.C.H.* 71–2 (1947–8), 408–9.

[8] Vallois, *Les constructions*, pl. I, A, G.

[9] Vallois, *Architecture*, p. 110, cf. p. 105.

Pan, during the Athenian period.[1] Whether it was sacred to
Dionysos in the time of free Delos (314–166 B.C.) we do not
know.

CELEBRATION OF THE FESTIVAL

During the Independence the festival of Dionysos was celebrated once a year in the month Galaxion, which corresponds
to the Attic Elaphebolion, the month of the City Dionysia at
Athens.[2] The main event of the celebration, besides the
theatrical performances, was a procession escorting the *agalma*
of Dionysos. Martin Nilsson[3] was the first to understand that
the *agalma*, whose construction was repeated every year, was
actually a phallus.[4] René Vallois, in 1922, re-examined the
passages of the ' tabulae hieropoeorum' recording the expenses on
purchase of materials, and making of the *agalma*, and suggested
that the object in question was a winged phallus, or rather a
bird-like phallus like the one represented on the front of the
monument of Karystios. In fact, claimed Vallois, the relief is a
faithful copy of the real object of the procession.[5]

The bird-phallus was not carried by feasters like the phallus-
poles of the well-known Attic cup in Florence.[6] It was drawn in
a car referred to as ἅμαξα or φαλλαγωγεῖον, which was made a
little before 301 B.C. (*I.G.* xi 144 A 34–5), and had to be
repaired from time to time (*I.G.* xi 158 A 71, 282 B.C.; 161 A 91,

[1] Two inscriptions on bases of statues dedicated to the three deities, dated
127/6 B.C. (*I.D.* 1907), and 97/6 B.C. (*I.D.* 2400), were found in the sanctuary.
The joint priesthood of Dionysos, Hermes, and Pan goes back to 159/8 B.C.,
Roussel, *D.C.A.*, 233ff. Among the three gods Dionysos was predominant; the
priest is frequently referred to as ἱερεὺς Διονύσου, Roussel, *ibid.*

[2] Th. Homolle, *B.C.H.* 14 (1890), 493.

[3] *Griech. Feste*, p. 281.

[4] There is no real reason for connecting the procession at Delos with the description of *phallophoroi* by Semos of Delos (Athen. XIV 622 a–d = F. Gr. Hist. iii B 396,
24), as has occasionally been done (Bethe, *Prolegomena zur Geschichte des griechischen
Theaters*, p. 54; Wilamowitz, *Aristophanes, Lysistrate*, Berlin, 1927, p. 11, n. 2). The
Delian origin of Semos alone is no evidence, and the fragment in question comes
from his work *On Paeans* and not from his *Deliaca*. Cf. Jacoby, *ibid.*, Kommentar;
Webster in Pickard-Cambridge, *Dithyramb, Tragedy, and Comedy*[2], p. 142; Lesky,
Geschichte der griechischen Literatur[2], p. 264.

[5] 'L' "agalma" des Dionysies de Délos', *B.C.H.* 46 (1922), 94–112.

[6] Florence 3897; Webster, *Greek Theatre Production*, no. F2, pl. 2; Pickard-
Cambridge, *Dithyramb, Tragedy, and Comedy*[2], no. 15, pl. IV.

278 B.C.; 287 A 52, 250 B.C.). The construction of this vehicle is recorded in the oldest inscription mentioning the *phallagogia*, but this does not necessarily imply that it was an innovation introduced at the end of the fourth century.

The *pompe* of Delos seems to combine two different elements of the Dionysiac festivals of Athens: the carrying of a phallus, which was a feature of the Rural Dionysia[1] and the City Dionysia,[2] and the car in which Dionysos was led at the procession of the Anthesteria.[3] In Athens the car was shaped like a ship on wheels representing the arrival of Dionysos from overseas,[4] and there is evidence for similar shipcars at Smyrna[5] and Klazomenai.[6] The Delian documents give no description of the *hamaxa*. We know, however, that a road was specially paved,[7] or rather laid with planks,[8] for it. There are also recorded payments to workmen 'who ballasted the car' or 'took the lead to and from the car'.[9] Now this furnishing of the car with ballast would make sense only if it was to be really floated,[10] and one would not be far from the truth if one recognizes here another shipcar, in the true sense of the word this time.

---

[1] Aristoph. *Ach.* 241–79; Pickard-Cambridge, *Festivals*, p. 41; H. Jeanmaire, *Dionysos*, Paris, 1951, p. 40; H. Herter, *R.E.* xix 1666, 1675, 1703.

[2] Pickard-Cambridge, *op. cit.*, p. 60; Herter, *loc. cit.*, 1704.

[3] M. P. Nilsson, *Studia de Dionysiis atticis*, Diss. Lund, 1900, pp. 125ff.; *Gr. Feste*, pp. 268ff.; *Gesch. d. gr. Rel.*, i, p. 550 (2nd ed., p. 583); L. Deubner, *Attische Feste*, Berlin, 1932, p. 102; Jeanmaire, *op. cit.*, p. 50; Pickard-Cambridge, *Festivals*, p. 11; cf. G. van Hoorn, *Choes and Anthesteria*, Leiden, 1951, p. 25. On the other hand, the car has been connected with the City Dionysia by A. Frickenhaus, *J.d.I.* 27 (1912), 61ff.; cf. A. Rumpf, *Bonner Jahrbücher*, 161 (1961), 211ff.

[4] Cf. the famous Attic kylix by Exekias at Munich (2044), *Bilder griech. Vasen*, Heft 9, pl. 5; Deubner, *Attische Feste*, p. 110, pl. 14/1; E. Buschor, *Griech. Vasenmalerei*, fig. 94; Rumpf, *Mal. u. Zeich.*, pl. 12/6; and the fragment n. 63 of the comic poet Hermippos, Kock, i, p. 243.

[5] Philostr. *Vita Soph.*, I, 25, 1; Aristides, XV, p. 373, XXII, p. 440, Dind.

[6] Fragments of a Klazomenian amphora at Oxford (1924.264) show that the ship had no wheels but was carried by comasts, *Corpus vasorum* IId, pl. 10.24, Pickard-Cambridge, *Dith. Trag. Com.²*, list of monuments no. 82, fig. 4.

[7] *I.G.* xi 203 A 37; 219 A 20 (ὁδοποίησις, στρῶσις ὁδοῦ).

[8] *I.D.* 372 A 102: τοῖς τὴν ὁδὸν στρώσασι τεῖ δωδεκάτει καὶ ξύλα ἐνέγκασι καὶ ἀπενέγκασι Δ.

[9] *I.D.* 372 A 101: τοῖς τὴν ἅμαξαν ἑρματίσασιν καὶ ἀπαγαγοῦσ[ιν -. τ]όμ μόλυβδον ἐνέγκασιν καὶ ἀνενέγκασιν ΓΗΗΙΙΙ. *I.D.* 444 A 30: [ἐρ]γάταις τοῖς τὸν μόλυ[βδο]ν ἐπὶ τὴν ἅμαξαν ἐνέγκασιν καὶ ἀπενέγκασιν ΓΙ.... Cf. *I.D.* 316.119, 338 Aa 57–8, 440 A 33–4, 442 A 199, 447.12–13.

[10] Cf. Vallois, *B.C.H.* 46 (1922), 106, who also finds it probable that the car was submerged in the water so that the bird looked as if floating on the surface.

But where would the shipcar be set afloat? In 269 B.C. somebody called Philokrates was paid five drachmai to clean the
river of Leukothion and Leukothion, i.e. the temenos of
Leukothea, and this work is recorded among the expenses of
the *agalma* and the procession (*I.G.* xi 203 A 37–8). About
260 B.C. Philokrates cleaned Leukothion again, and his reward
is registered immediately after the expenses of the procession
(*I.G.* xi 219 A 21). Another cleaning of Leukothion, which
comes in a small fragment (*I.G.* xi 175 Aa 4), does not seem to
have any connection with the Dionysia, while a second cleaning
of the temenos and the river in 269 B.C., six months after the
celebration of Dionysia, in the month Bouphonion, is puzzling
(*I.G.* xi 203 A 53). In any case, Vallois did not doubt that it
was the river of Leukothion into which the Delians launched
their shipcar, and assuming that the procession set off from the
sanctuary of Apollo and went toward the theatre area, he
associated the river of Leukothion with Inopos, which, about
the middle part of its course, formed 'une série de bassins
naturels dont les Déliens ont tiré parti pour le canaliser'. The
cult of Leukothea would have been associated with one of
those basins.

But the site of Leukothion has been disputed. F. Robert
identified it with some ruins which survive at the east coast of
the bay of Phourni, a long way to the south of the city.[1] His
argument is very simple: the river of Leukothion needed to be
frequently cleaned, which means the alluvia that encumbered
the region round its mouth had to be removed. This river then
must have been a 'rivière torrentielle',[2] a long ravine dry for
the greater part of the year, the current of which was not strong
enough during the season of rain to sweep along the alluvia into
the sea. Delos has three torrents of this kind, and of these only
one happens to have unidentified ruins of a sanctuary on the
left of its mouth. Besides, we should expect to find the sanctuary
of Leukothea, a marine goddess, near the sea.

Robert based his theory on the presupposition that cleaning
a river means (necessarily?) removing alluvia from its mouth,
and did not explain why the work at Leukothion sometimes

[1] *Délos* xx, pp. 109ff.
[2] Robert refers to L. Cayeux, *Délos* iv. 1, pp. 211–12, cp. note 2, p. 12.

occurs in passages recording the expenditure on Dionysia.
Ch. Picard accepted Robert's location of Leukothion, which
makes impossible any relation of it to the Dionysia (but see
Vallois' reservations, *Architecture*, p. 99), and suggested that the
procession moved between the Stibadion and the theatre without mentioning the inscriptional passages which refer to the
ballasting of the car.[1] The route proposed by Picard is actually
parallel to the course of Inopos but, I think, the main difficulty
is that neither Inopos nor any other of the torrents or 'rivières
torrentielles' of Delos would probably have enough water in
Galaxion (March–April)[2] to carry a boat which must have
been of considerable size and weight.[3] Perhaps one of the basins
and/or canals of Inopos could be used, but then why should the
shipcar need to be ballasted if it were to be floated on the smooth
water of a small reservoir?

According to Vallois the word ποταμός could also apply to a
canal fed by the sea. I do not know how true this can be for
Delos but I think that if we do not wish to give up the assumption of a floating Dionysiac ship, which is attractive and,
furthermore, based on a sound interpretation of inscriptions,
we have to consider whether our shipcar could not be made to
travel a certain distance in the sea. This is of course pure
speculation, but would such a κατάπλους not be more con-
sistent with the idea of Dionysos' epiphany? For the whole pro-
cedure of making a new *agalma* of Dionysos every year, no
matter if it was not a representation of the god but a symbol,
suggests this idea of the god's epiphany, the same idea which the
shipcars generally imply.[4] The procession would start off then
from the shore, probably from a point east of the Hieron of
Apollo.

[1] *B.C.H.* 58–9 (1944–5), 269.

[2] L. Cayeux, *Délos* iv. 1, p. 211: 'Disons-le immédiatement, la surface de Délos
est beaucoup trop restreinte et sa topographie trop accidentée pour que, en se
réunissant, les eaux météoriques puissent donner naissance à d'importants cours
d'eau. Toutes choses considérées, il ne peut y avoir à Délos que de torrents ou des
rivières torrentielles . . . La région du Cynthe et de Kato-Vardhia est la seule qui
soit dotée, de nos jours, d'un réseau hydrographique bien défini. Il consiste en
cours d'eau essentiellement temporaires.'

[3] About the end of the third century the car was drawn at the procession by
salaried workmen, *B.C.H.* 46 (1922), 103.

[4] Nilsson, *Gr. Feste*, p. 270, *Gesch. d. griech. Religion*, i, p. 550 (2nd ed., p. 583).
Cf. L. R. Farnell, *The Cults of the Greek States*, v, pp. 191–2, on the ship of Smyrna.

The *pompe* must have been somewhat similar to corresponding ceremonies performed at other places. Vallois imagined the *hamaxa* leading the procession and being followed by the priest, *kanephoroi*, *pompostoloi*, and the feasting crowd.[1] But in fact neither the basket-bearers nor the *pompostoloi*[2] occur in any document dating from the time of Independence. They belong to the second Athenian period[3] and were most probably introduced by the cleruchs in imitation of the procession of the Great Dionysia at Athens, where we also find *kanephoroi* and *pompostoloi* in inscriptions of the second and first century.[4] Therefore in the Athenian period the Dionysiac *pompe* would rather resemble the procession of the City Dionysia of Athens than that of free Delos. Furthermore, no sign of the *phallagogia* is found after 166 B.C.

It is likely that the procession took place on the 12th of Galaxion,[5] and it seems to have been the opening event of the festival. Perhaps a sacrifice to Dionysos on the big altar outside the theatre followed the procession. After that the performances would begin in the theatre.

The 'tabulae archontum' (or choregic inscriptions) which are discussed in another chapter (see p. 19), show that the theatrical performances included dithyrambs, comedies and tragedies. The dithyrambs were performed by choruses of boys. Their *choregoi* are recorded before those of dramas, and if we are allowed to draw parallels between Delos and Athens[6] we may suppose that the boys competed for the dithyrambic victory on the first day of the festival, after the procession was over. Two

---

[1] Cp. Ch. Picard, *Manuel d'archéologie grecque, La sculpture*, iv.2, Paris, 1963, p. 1202.

[2] Roussel, *D.C.A.*, p. 235, takes the *pompostoloi* of Delos to be 'jeunes gens chargés d'escorter les victimes', cp. note 4.

[3] *Pompostoloi* of Dionysia, *I.D.* 2609, and perhaps *I.D.* 2631 (cf. Roussel, *D.C.A.*, p. 235, n. 2). *Kanephoroi* of Dionysia, *I.D.* 1873, 2061; of Dionysia and Lenaia, *I.D.* 1870, 1907.

[4] *Kanephoroi*, *I.G.* ii² 896 (c. 186/5 B.C.), 3489 (after 86 B.C.). Πομποστολήσαντες Διονυσίοις, *I.G.* ii² 971 (140/39 B.C.), cf. 2949 (after 150 B.C.). The substantive πομποστόλος does not occur. The meaning of πομποστολέω given in Liddell-Scott-Jones is 'conduct a procession'. But 30 *pompostoloi* of Zeus (*I.D.* 2607), and at least 25 of Dionysos (*I.D.* 2609) can hardly be considered as conductors of processions. Cp. note 2, and F. Durrbach, *B.C.H.* 26 (1902), 530ff.

[5] Vallois, *B.C.H.* 46 (1922), 103.

[6] Pickard-Cambridge, *Festivals*, p. 64.

pairs of *synchoregoi* and, consequently, two choruses took part in the Dionysia, as was the case at the Apollonia, which did not include dramatic performances. As regards the dithyrambs performed, our information is confined to simply knowing that new poets of dithyramb occasionally contested in Delos. We have only one name of a poet, Ἡράκων, who presented his poems in the island in 236 B.C. (*I.G.* xi 1205₁₋₂).

The dramatic performances followed on the second day. From the fact that the *choregoi* of comedy usually precede those of tragedy in the records of the archons it may be deduced that the comedies were played before the tragedies. The same inscriptions reveal that the performances assumed the form of a contest (see p. 31); two teams of *synchoregoi* and, in consequence, two companies of artists competed for the comic prize(s), and groups of *choregoi* and artists of the same number for the tragic. It seems probable that each of the tragic groups produced three tragedies (see p. 36), and it must be taken for granted that the comedy groups, too, produced more than one play each. It is not certain whether contests of poets were organized during the Independence (see p. 24).

The Delians used to announce the honours they had conferred on different persons during the year at the Apollonia (*I.G.* xi 514, 542, 559, 565, etc.), but the Athenians transferred the announcements to the Dionysia according to the custom of the metropolis. The priest of Dionysos was to take care of the proclamations (*I.D.* 1505, 1507).

In the Athenian period the Dionysia was administered by an *agonothetes*, as at Athens. Well-known Athenian figures such as Sarapion, son of Sarapion,[1] occasionally held the office of *agonothesia* at the Delian Dionysia.[2]

The Athenian cleruchs observed the Lenaia as well. It is possible that dramatic performances were given, though there is no evidence whatever. A procession was conducted, in which basket-bearing maidens played a part, as in the Dionysia (*I.D.* 1870, 1907).

---

[1] Kirchner, *P.A.* 12564; *I.G.* ii² 2336, com. on l. 55; Ferguson, *Hellenistic Athens*, pp. 425–6, 436.

[2] S. Dow, *Harvard Class. Studies* 51 (1940), p. 122, l. 211.

CHAPTER II

FESTIVALS OF THE ISLAND LEAGUE

ANTIGONEIA, DEMETRIEIA

Among the many festivals of Delos there are three, the so-called
'federal' Antigoneia, Demetrieia, and Ptolemaia, for which we
have indications of theatrical performances in addition to those
at the Dionysia. These festivals were actually instituted not by
the Delians but by the League of the Islanders (τὸ κοινὸν
τῶν νησιωτῶν). The League was founded in, or soon after,
314 B.C. by Antigonos Monophthalmos who, being the master
of Asia after he had disposed of Eumenes in 315 B.C., sent his
fleet into the Aegean against Cassander, and posed as
'liberator' of the Greeks.[1] The *koinon* comprised the islands of
Ionian blood, i.e. the majority of the Cyclades and a few others
like Amorgos and Herakleia, being thus in appearance a revival
of the original Ionic Amphictyony. But in reality it rather re-
sembled the Athenian confederacies of the fifth and fourth
centuries, for, though the islands enjoyed a certain degree of
independence and self-administration, they had no policy
armed forces, or currency of their own, and paid taxes to their
protector, whom they honoured as a god. Delos was always the
religious centre of the Ionians and the Aegean sea. It was then
the obvious place where the islanders would exercise the federal
worship.[2] It seems that the institution of the Antigoneia was
one of the first acts of the League, and the celebration of the
fête one of its main activities.

Some years later, most probably when Antigonos' son Demetrios was raised to royalty after his victory at Salamis in Cyprus
(306 B.C.), the islands did not fail to introduce him into their
pantheon, and founded a festival, the Demetrieia, in his honour:

[1] Diod. Sic. XIX 62, 9; W. W. Tarn, *Antigonos Gonatas*, pp. 72ff., and in *C.A.H.*
vi (3rd ed. 1953), p. 490; Durrbach, *Choix*, p. 19.
[2] Tarn, *J.H.S.* 44 (1924), 141–57, settled the question about the supposed
neutrality of Delos.

because, says the decree of the foundation of the festival, the League wished to honour him to the best of its power. From this decree (*I.G.* xi 1036 = *Choix* 13) we learn that the *panegyreis* of Antigoneia and Demetrieia were to be held in alternate years (*trieterides*). The proceedings of the new festival were to be the same as those of the Antigoneia: sacrifices, contests, and *synodos*.[1] The cities had to send their councillors (*synedroi*), and see that victims were provided for the sacrifices, the contests organized, and artists hired. The prizes of the contests to be given at the Demetrieia came from the 'common money' according to the arrangement which had been made for the Antigoneia. The *synedroi* coming to celebrate the first Demetrieia had to bring with them an amount of money equal to that fixed for the Antigoneia, and deliberate how the money would be raised in the future. Finally, the decree was to be set up 'by the altar of the kings'.[2]

The Antigoneia occurs in another inscription, the temple account of 296 B.C.: τοῖς Ἀντιγονείοις δᾷδες εἰς τὸν χορὸν ϜϜ..·| ῥυμὸς καὶ ξύλα Ϝ· τοῖς τὴν σκηνὴν κατενέγκασι εἰς τὸ ἱερὸν ΗΗΗ (*I.G.* xi 154 A 42–3). The chorus mentioned here is the chorus of Delian maidens, the Deliades, celebrated by the Homeric hymn to Apollo (156ff.; Thuc. III 104, 5, cf. Eurip., *H.F.* 687–90, *Hec.* 462–5, Callim. *in Del.* 302–9). Therefore the Deliades adorned the festival of Antigonos, and undoubtedly that of Demetrios, like many other fêtes in Delos (cf. p. 22).[3] But they had nothing to do with the contests and the *technitai* whose μίσθωσις is provided for by the decree of the Demetrieia.

---

[1] Cp. the similar honours which Antigonos received from the city of Skepsis: θυσία, ἀγών, στεφανηφορία, πανήγυρις, and in 311 B.C. τέμενος, βωμός, ἄγαλμα, *O.G.I.S.* 6. We have no evidence for a temple in Delos. As regards the place of the altar and statues of Antigonos and Demetrios see Vallois, *B.C.H.* 53 (1929), 248; E. Will, *Délos* xxii, pp. 170ff.

[2] Will, *loc. cit.*, discusses and rejects Durrbach's restoration [τῶν βασιλέω]ν (*I.G.* xi 1036 = *Choix* 13), and proposes [τῶν Σωτήρω]ν. Subsequently, he argues that the altar in question was identical with that of Zeus Soter-Polieus and Athena Soteira situated at the south-eastern corner of the sanctuary of Apollo (Vallois, *Architecture*, pp. 42–5, *Constructions*, pl. I, 6), and shared by Antigonos-Demetrios and the Ptolemies successively.

[3] Apollonia, Leteia, Artemisia, Britomartia, Aphrodisia, various 'vase' festivals, etc., Homolle, *B.C.H.* 14 (1890), 500ff. On the meaning of ῥυμός, ξύλα, and other accessories of the chorus, E. Schulhof–P. Huvelin, *B.C.H.* 31 (1907), 53–6, and K. Latte, *De saltationibus Graecorum*, pp. 67–8.

These artists could be musicians or actors or both. There is no direct reference to dramatic performances but we may well assume that they took place from some analogous cases: Dramas were produced at the Ptolemaia which succeeded the festivals of Antigonos and Demetrios (see below), at the 'Antigoneia and Demetrieia' which the Samians, apart from the federal festivals, decreed ἄγειν ἐπὶ τοῖς εὐαγγελίοις (sc. of Demetrios' victory at Salamis) in Samos (*S.E.G.* i 362), and which must have been less pretentious than the federal fêtes; and at the Demetrieia held at the cities of Euboea in honour of Poliorketes (*I.G.* xii.9 207$_{36ff.}$). One might also wonder whether the *skene*, i.e. the panel of scenery, that was carried from the theatre to the sanctuary of Apollo (*I.G.* xi 154 A 42–3 quoted above) had been used for performances at the Antigoneia. The sum paid for its transportation is recorded immediately after the expenses for the chorus of Antigoneia.

PTOLEMAIA

Tragic, and doubtless comic, performances were included in the programme of the Ptolemaia: ἀνακηρῦξαι| δὲ τὸν στέφανον Πτολεμαίων τῶι|¹⁵ ἀγῶνι τῶι πρώτωι, ὅταν οἱ τραγωιδοὶ ἀγωνί|ζωνται (*I.G.* xi 1043). This festival took the place of the Antigoneia and Demetrieia after the fall of Demetrios. Ptolemy gained command of the sea, and became the new master of the islands in 286 or early 285 B.C. The islanders offered him divine honours (*I.G.* xii.7 506$_{27-8, 48}$). A decree in honour of Sostratos of Knidos, the famous architect of the lighthouse of Alexandria, dated between 279 and 274 B.C. (*I.G.* xi 1038 = *Choix* 21), shows that the *panegyris* had been enlarged by then to include the cult of Ptolemy II. This festival has left no other traces in the inscriptions. But it must have been held annually[1] as long as the sea power of Ptolemy remained unchallenged, that is until the time of the naval battle of Kos,[2] in which

---

[1] If the Ptolemaia took the place of both Antigoneia and Demetrieia, it must have been annual. Therefore Tarn was probably wrong in thinking that it had been a *trieteris* like the earlier Antigoneia, *J.H.S.* 30 (1910), 224.

[2] Several dates have been assigned to this battle. The most probable ones are 258 (Tarn, *C.A.H.* vii 713, 862) and 262 B.C. (E. Bikerman, *R.É.A.* 40 [1938], 369ff.; A. Momigliano and P. Frazer, *C.Q.* 44 [1950], 107ff.) depending on whether

Antigonos Gonatas won a complete victory over Ptolemy
Philadelphos. Antigonos did not enjoy the command of the sea
for many years, and Ptolemy recovered Delos in 249 B.C., but
the Island League broke up about this time.[1] There is no
evidence that the islands offered their worship to Gonatas, and
in any case, it is doubtful whether he would have favoured it.[2]

DISTINCTION BETWEEN THE FOREGOING AND
HOMONYM 'VASE' FESTIVALS

The federal Antigoneia, Demetrieia, and Ptolemaia, must not
be confused with the so-called vase festivals under the same
names. The former were instituted by the islanders and held at
their expense, the deities worshipped being the kings. The
latter were founded by the kings Antigonos Gonatas, Demetrios
II of Macedonia, and the Ptolemies Philadelphos and Euergetes
who, at different times,[3] endowed the temple of Apollo with
various sums of money, from the interest on which a sacrifice
was performed, and a valuable vase was purchased and dedicated to the gods of Delos, Apollo, Artemis and Leto, every
year.[4] Some thirty festivals of this kind are mentioned in the
inscriptions of the *hieropoioi*, many of them being set up by, or in
the name of, well-known historical personalities (Philadelpheia
after Arsinoe II Philadelphos, Attaleia, Philetaireia, Philokleia,
Stratonikeia, etc.), others by otherwise unknown persons.[5]
Usually the chorus of Deliades participated in these festivals,
and it was they who dedicated the vase on behalf of the donor.

this naval battle belongs to the Second Syrian or to the Chremonidean War. Cf.
H. Volkmann, *R.E.* xxiii 1653, and Bengtson, *Griech. Geschichte*[2], p. 397, n. 1, who
finds the association of Kos with the Chremonidean War, and consequently the
earlier date, 'nicht sicher'.

[1] *C.A.H.* vii 715.

[2] Plut. *Mor.* 360 C, D; Tarn, *Antigonos Gonatas*, pp. 251, 453.

[3] Three series of Ptolemaia or Ptolemaieia were instituted by Philadelphos in
280 B.C. and 249 B.C., and Euergetes in 246 B.C. Gonatas founded three festivals,
one in 253 B.C., and two in 245 B.C. known also as Soteria and Paneia. Demetrios II
gave a similar token of his piety in 238 B.C. These are Tarn's dates which, however,
are not accepted by everyone, cf. n. 5.

[4] Tarn, *ibid.*, pp. 136, 380.

[5] About the vase festivals see Tarn, *ibid.*, *passim* (v. index), E. Schulhof, *B.C.H.* 32
(1908), 101–32, E. Ziebarth, *Hermes* 52 (1917), 425–41, F. Durrbach, *I.D.* no. 366,
pp. 169–70.

CHAPTER III

THE *TECHNITAI* OF DIONYSOS IN DELOS

THE ARCHONS' RECORDS

The great majority of Dionysiac artists known to have given performances in Delos are recorded in the so-called 'tabulae archontum' (*I.G.* xi 105–34). These inscriptions are a sort of official records in which the eponymous archons put down certain noteworthy events that had happened during the year of their office. The *choregoi* of the Apollonia and Dionysia, as well as a number of artists, are invariably enumerated in these records, and occupy a large part of them, so that the inscriptions were at first thought to be records of these festivals, and were published under the title 'Inscriptions choragiques'.[1] The lists of artists contained in these inscriptions are introduced by two typical headings: οἵδε ἐπεδείξαντο τῷ θεῷ, or οἵδε ἠγωνίσαντο τῷ θεῷ. The second type of introduction came into use between 259 and 236 B.C., and doubtless is absolutely equivalent to the earlier one. L. Robert pointed out in 1936 that the documents of Delos are not 'agonistic' inscriptions, that is to say catalogues of winners or participants in a certain festival or festivals, but lists of artists who offered free performances in honour of Apollo (τῷ θεῷ *par excellence*) throughout the year.[2] A similar terminology is used in Delphi for performances clearly given as offerings to Apollo (e.g. ἐπιδείξεις ἐποιήσαντο τῷ θεῷ, *S.I.G.*[3] 660, 703, ἐπέδωκε τῷ θεῷ ἁμέραν καὶ ἀγωνίξατο, *S.I.G.*[3] 659, cf. 738, 689).

The lists include actors and a few poets (see Table 1), flute-players,[3] kithara-players,[4] aulodes,[5] and kitharodes,[6] rhap-

---

[1] A. Hauvette-Besnault, *B.C.H.* 7 (1883), 102–25.
[2] *R.É.G.* 49 (1936), 244.
[3] *I.G.* xi 105–8, 110, 113, 133.
[4] *I.G.* xi 105, 120.   [5] *I.G.* xi 133.
[6] *I.G.* xi 105, 110, 112–13, 115, 120, 133.

sodes,[1] harpists,[2] marionette-show players,[3] θαυματοποιοί,[4] ῥωμαϊσταί,[5] an ὀρχηστής,[6] and a παρῳδός.[7] It seems reasonable to suppose that these artists made the sea trip to Delos in order to take part in a festival, and not only to pay tribute to the god. This appears to be confirmed again by Delphian parallels (see pp. 95ff., and p. 98, n. 1). The musicians would go to Delos for the Apollonia; actors and flute-players for the Dionysia. Before the inauguration of the festivals, or after the conclusion of the contests (*S.I.G.*³ 431; *B.C.H.* 73 [1949], 276), the time would be opportune for the artists to make their offerings. Harp-players, and popular entertainers—dancers, conjurors, and so on—who had no place in the official programmes of the Hellenistic festivals would probably take the opportunities offered to them by the numerous fêtes, including the great festivals, to appear in Delos.

Many of the actors are also found in the Soteria inscriptions of Delphi, where they are recorded first in their companies (see Table 3 B 19, E 42, 58, 72, F 50, G 53, 58, H 50, 60) except one recorded as *didaskalos* (E 71). Unless this is to be explained away as an extraordinary coincidence, which seems most unlikely, the implication is that only the protagonists were recorded in Delos.

ALL MAJOR GUILDS REPRESENTED

No local Dionysiac guild, or branch of a guild, existed in Delos, and we do not even know of any Delian actors. Of course, some of the artists recorded in the Delian documents by their first names only might be natives, but the omission of the place of origin is very frequent, and of no significance. We know that

---

[1] *I.G.* xi 105.   [2] *I.G.* xi 105, 120.   [3] *I.G.* xi 133.

[4] *I.G.* xi 110, 112–13, 115, 133; conjurors or trick-dancers? Cf. Athen. IV 129 d; P. Perdrizet, *Les terres cuites grecques d'Égypte de la Collection Fouquet* (1921), p. 157; Webster, *Miscellanea di studi alessandrini in memoria di A. Rostagni*, p. 539.

[5] *I.G.* xi 133; *rhomaistes*: 'qua voce inaudita quidem intellegendus sit histrio qui sermone latino scurrilitates pronuntiat' (Durrbach), cf. Appian, *Hannib.* 41; A. Wilhelm, *Jahresh.* 3 (1900), 49–50.

[6] *I.G.* xi 133.

[7] *I.G.* xi 120; on *parodoi* see Athen. XV 697 e; P. Maas, *R.E.* xviii 1684–6; and cf. *I.G.* xii.9 189₁₁.

many of the *technitai* whose origin is not recorded were not Delians, whereas the only instances of Delian artists known to me are the kitharode – – – mos, son of Nikon, who occurs in an inscription from Siphnos (*I.G.* xii.5 482, III/II s.) and the μουσικὸς καὶ μελῶν ποιητής Amphikles, son of Philoxenos, recorded in Delos (*Choix* 78=*I.D.* 1497, 165/4 B.C.) and at Oropos (*I.G.* vii 373), although the latter was probably not a *technites*, a member of a Dionysiac guild. Delos was, however, the great religious centre of the Aegean, and its festivals attracted many artists from all over the Greek world. Athens provided a large number of them. Others came from the islands (Rhodes, Samos, Paros, Euboea, Lesbos, etc.), the Greek mainland (Arkadia, Sikyon, Megara, Boeotia, Akarnania, Epeiros, Thrace, etc.), Asia Minor (Sinope, Chalkedon, Kyzikos, Soloi, etc.), and Italy (Taras, Rome).

This multitude of nationalities suggests that all the major Dionysiac associations took an interest in the island. The presence of Athenian artists and poets is many times attested by the archons' records, and it is to be taken for granted after 166 B.C. The Peloponnesians and Boeotians must have been members of the Isthmian and Nemean *koinon*, and a decree of this guild found in the island (*I.G.* xi 1059) proves that Delos was included in its sphere of activity. (Another decree, *I.G.* xi 1060, honouring a Delian for his goodwill toward the *technitai* was most likely issued by the same guild; the person charged to bring the decree to Delos, the flautist Hermaiondas, is known from a Delphic inscription to be a Boeotian, *S.G.D.I.* 2568.) Finally a decree of the Ionian and Hellespontian guild prescribes that delegates of the *koinon* should go to Delos and ask for a place to set up a statue of the flautist Kraton. This statue was to be crowned every year by the *technitai*, viz. the members of the guild who would visit Delos (*I.G.* xi 1061, cf. App. II, pp. 140ff.).

HONOURS BESTOWED UPON ARTISTS

Sometimes the performances offered by the *technitai* to Apollo gave occasion for certain ceremonies in which a chorus took

part: (1) ὅτ᾽ ἦν ὁ χορὸς 'Επικράτ[ει – –],[1] *I.G.* xi 159 A 34, 281
B.C. (2) χορῶι τῶι γε|νομένωι τοῖς κωμωιδοῖς καὶ τῶι τραγωιδῶι
Δράκοντι[2] τοῖς ἐπιδειξαμένοις τῶι θεῶι δᾶιδες παρὰ 'Εργο-
τέλους ΗΗ· ῥυμοὶ καὶ| ξύλα ΙΙΙΙ· [. . .] εἰς τὸν χορὸν τὸν γενό-
μενον Τιμοστράτωι[3] τῶι αὐλητῆι, ὅτε ἐπεδείξατο τῶι θεῶι,
δᾶιδες παρὰ 'Αρχικλέους ΗΗΙ· ῥυμὸς ΙΙ, *I.G.* xi 161 A 85–7, 100,
279 B.C. (3) ὅτε οἱ τεχνῖται ἐπεδείξαντο δᾶιδες τῶι χορῶι –, *I.G.* xi
219 A 16, c. 260 B.C.

E. Reisch[4] and A. Körte[5] argued that the chorus of the
second passage was dramatic but there can be no doubt that
these choruses, which were formed in honour of the *technitai*,
when they came to give performances in honour of the god,
consisted, like those which participated in ceremonies staged
on the arrival of foreign *theoroi*,[6] of Deliades, the young girls
who had a part in many festive occasions of Delos (see p. 16).

The Delians conferred the honours of *proxenia*, or crown of
laurel, or in some cases even statues, on a considerable number
of poets and artists. We have fifteen decrees in honour of
dramatic poets (*I.G.* xi 528, 638), lyric (or epic, cf. *I.D.* 1506)
poets who drew their inspiration from the legends of the island
(*I.G.* xi 544, 572, 573, 618), musicians (*I.G.* xi 575, 577, 646B,
705), etc. (the professions of the honoured artists have not been
preserved in *I.G.* xi 511, 652, 702, 744). About 200 B.C. a
statue of the famous flute player Satyros of Samos was erected

---

[1] Epikrates, son of Maiandrios, *kitharistes* from Myrina, performed in Delos in
284 B.C. (*I.G.* xi 105₂₆), and at Delphi in 260/59 B.C. (Dinsmoor) or 257/6 B.C.
(Daux), *S.I.G.*[3] 424₁₂. Another Epikrates, son of Asopon, Boeotian flautist, is
known (*S.G.D.I.* 256₅₈₂, 258/7 or 254/3 B.C.). The former seems more likely to be
the one who visited Delos in 281 B.C. The archon's record of that year is not preserved.

[2] Drakon, son of Lykon, tragic actor from Taras, is found among the artists of
279 B.C. (*I.G.* xi 108₁₈), and in *S.G.D.I.* 256₄₅₀ (Delphic Soteria, 259/8 or 255/4
B.C.).

[3] Timostratos of Kyzikos, the sole flute player of 280 and 279 B.C. (*I.G.* xi 107₁₇,
108₂₂).

[4] *R.E.* iii 2402, and in *Das griech. Theater* by W. Dörpfeld and E. Reisch, p. 259.

[5] *N. Jahrb.* 5 (1900), 84.

[6] τῶι χορῶι τῶι γενομένωι τοῖς Κώιων θεωροῖς λαμπάδες πα[ρὰ Λυσί]ου Η·
ῥυμοὶ ΙΙ · τῶι χορῶι τῶι γενομένωι τοῖς 'Ροδίων θεωροῖς λαμπάδες παρὰ Χαριδήμου Η·
ῥυμοὶ ΙΙ, *I.G.* xi 158 A 74–5. See also n. 159 A 35, etc., and cp. n. 161 B 72: φιάλη
λεία, Δηλιάδων ἀνάθημα, χορεία 'Ροδίων θεωρῶν ἐπιδόντων [ἐπὶ ἀρχ]εθεώρου
'Αγησιδάμου. Also n. 161 B 13, 162 B 10ff., 164 A 9, 55ff., etc.; K. Latte, *De saltationibus Graecorum*, pp. 83–4.

by the Delians (*I.G.* xi 1079; also Delphi set up a statue of the same man in 194 B.C., *S.I.G.*³ 648 B, see p. 96, cf. p. 56).

The Athenian cleruchs used to pay similar tributes to wandering artists. Two decrees honouring poets who had 'praised Apollo, the other gods who occupied the island, and the people of Athens' (*I.D.* 1497, 1506), and another in honour of a musician (*I.D.* 1502), are about all the inscriptional evidence we have for artists in Delos after 166 B.C.

'HOUSE OF MASKS'

A building, the so-called 'House of Masks', is supposed to have been a meeting place for theatrical companies.[1] Four of its main rooms are decorated with mosaic floors, three of which are set with subjects inspired from theatre productions (cf. p. 53): Dionysos in tragic costume riding a leopard, a comedy slave dancing before a flautist seated on a rock, and a series of comic masks bordering the geometrically patterned mosaic of the largest room, which might have been used for rehearsals. The house belongs to the 'insula' that is situated about a hundred metres south-east of the theatre. It may date back to the beginning of the second century B.C., and was used until 88 or 69 B.C.

[1] J. Chamonard, *Délos* xiv, pp. 8, 26; Webster, *M.N.C.*, p. 69.

CHAPTER IV

PLAYS AND POETS

KNOWN POETS

What plays did the Delians see? We should expect plays similar to those presented by the companies of Dionysiac *technitai* at other places. In fact we have no titles of plays, and the known number of dramatic poets who produced their plays in Delos is very limited. They are about a dozen throughout two centuries (early third to early first century). Poets do not figure frequently in the lists of artists. Out of fifteen inscriptions (some of them in a very bad state, it is true), only one includes tragic, comic, and dithyrambic poets (*I.G.* xi 120, cf. nos. ii, xii below); another contains three comic poets (*I.G.* xi 107, cf. no. iv), and two others contain one comic poet each (*I.G.* xi 113, 115, cf. nos. vi, xiii). No. x is known through a proxenic decree. Three more poets belong to the Athenian period (nos. iii, v, ix). With the exception of three names otherwise unknown (nos. ii, xii, xiii), the rest of them are connected with Athens. Most of them are Athenians, one or two others are known to have put on plays at Athens.

Competitions of dramatic poets took place at the Dionysia during the Athenian period (cf. no. v). It is also likely that the poets recorded among the artists who made ἐπιδείξεις in honour of Apollo at the time of Independence took part in the Dionysia as well. However, the number of poets found in the archons' records is so small compared with the number of actors (see Table 1) that I feel extremely uncertain whether competitions of poets were in fact a regular feature of the Dionysia at all.

There follows a list of the known dramatic poets in Delos:

(i) Ἀμεινίας, *comic poet*

He is registered together with Philemon and Nikostratos in the record of the archon Charmos, 280 B.C. (*I.G.* xi 107$_{25}$). Poets are rarely included in the archons' inscriptions, and this gathering of three comic poets might imply an extraordinary occasion. They could have taken part in the competition of either the Dionysia or the federal Ptolemaia. Ameinias made his début as a comic poet at the Athenian Dionysia in 312/11, when he was still an ephebe, and was placed third by his play Ἀπολείπουσα (*I.G.* ii² 2323 a 46–7). He gained a first prize at the Lenaia later (*I.G.* ii² 2325₁₆₇, Wilhelm, *Urkunden*, pp. 45, 123, 134).

(ii) Ἀριστείδης, comic poet (?)

It is not absolutely certain whether he was a comic poet. In the inscription of the archon Mennis, 236 B.C. (no. 120), tragic dithyrambic and comic poets are recorded in lines 50, 51, and 52 respectively. At the beginning of l. 50 we have τραγωιδιῶν ποητής, and of l. 51 διθυράμβων ποητής. Each line has about sixty letters, so in spite of the singular ποητὴς (cf. nos. 108₂₃, 115₂₅, 1337₁, 105₂₆?), more than one name must have been written in each line. In l. 52 we have κωμωιδ[ιῶν ποητής, followed by a long gap. Aristeides' name comes in l. 53, five letters from the beginning, succeeded by a gap. He is otherwise unknown.

(iii) Ἀσκληπιάδης Ἰκεσίου Ἀθηναῖος (Ἀλαιεύς), tragic poet

He was priest of Dionysos in 100/99 B.C. and, consequently, a resident of Delos (*I.G.* ii² 2336₁₂₂₋₃), where he must have produced some of his plays. A celebrated member of the Athenian guild of Dionysiac *technitai*, he served as hieromnemon of Athens (*S.I.G.*³ 826 B, II 2–3, 704 E 3 = *F.D.* iii. 269), and delegate of the guild to the Delphic Amphictyony (*S.I.G.*³ 704 E 24, 39) in 125(?) (archon in Delphi Eukleidas, son of Kalleidas, Daux, *Chronologie*, L 68). In the same document (Amphictyonic decree) he is called priest of Dionysos, priest of the *technitai*, and tragic poet (704 E 23, 39). In c. 85 B.C. he won a tragic victory at the Sarapieia of Tanagra, and the ἐπινίκιος (sc. στέφανος) of the same festival (*S.E.G.* xix 335). The inscription of Tanagra shows that he had been granted the citizenship of Thebes because he is registered as Theban (tragic victory, l. 12) as well as Athenian (*epinikios*, l. 18, cf. ll. 34, 41). He has also been identified as the second mint-magistrate of the

135/4 B.C. issue of Athenian New Style coinage. Hikesios and Asklepiades, supposed to be father and son, are the two magistrates whose names are struck on the coins of this issue (Margaret Thompson, *The New Style Silver Coinage of Athens*, New York, 1961, nos. 812–22, pp. 290–2, 557). The top date of our poet is thus removed one decade further, unless D. M. Lewis is right in arguing that M. Thompson's whole chronology of the New Style coinage is 30–35 years too high (*C.R.*, N.S. 12 [1962], 292, *Numism. Chronicle* 1962, 275–300; cf. Miss Thompson's answer in *Numism. Chronicle* 1962, 301–33).

(iv) Διόδωρος Σινωπεύς, *comic poet*

He participated as comic actor in two festivals of Delos, in 284 B.C. (*I.G.* xi 105$_{21}$) and 280 B.C. (no. 107$_{20}$). Though not recorded among the comic poets of 280 (Philemon, Nikostratos, Ameinias) he has been identified with the comic poet Diodoros, son of Dion, Athenian (deme of Semachidai), by E. Capps (*A.J.A.* 4 [1900], 83), and the identification has been accepted by Kirchner (*P.A.* 3959) and Durrbach (*I.G.* xi 105 com.). He was brother to Diphilos, the famous poet of New Comedy. On the grave-stone of the family, *I.G.* ii² 10321, Diphilos is called Sinopeus, but Diodoros Semachides. The Athenian citizenship was apparently conferred upon him after the death of Diphilos. Capps also conjectured that he must be the same person as the Athenian Diodoros, recorded just before Diodoros Sinopeus in *I.G.* xi 105$_{21}$. Durrbach did not agree, but cp. Asklepiades' double citizenship (p. 25). The double recording means he performed twice (δίς, ll. 20, 107$_{23}$, 108$_{18}$, and cp. no. 112$_{15ff.}$ in which many artists are recorded twice). Very few fragments are preserved, the longest consisting of 42 verses on the 'art' of παρασιτεῖν spoken by a parasite. The fragment comes from the play Ἐπίκληρος. Other titles are Αὐλητρίς, Μαινόμενος, Νεκρός, Πανηγυρισταί. Kock, ii, 420; Wilhelm, *Urkunden*, pp. 61, 245; Webster, *Studies in Gr. Com.*, p. 152.

(v) Διονύσιος Δημητρίου Ἀθηναῖος (Ἀναφλύστιος), *tragic and satyric poet*

On an inscribed marble base found in the theatre of Delos we are informed that he had won the contests of tragedy and satyr play at the Dionysia, and had been priest of Apollo (before 111/10 B.C.) and *epimeletes* of Delos (in 111/10 B.C., *I.D.* 1959). Dionysios was a very active political personality. Ferguson may not be right in identifying him with the Athenian archon Dionysios of 128/7 B.C. (*Klio* 7 [1907], 224, but cf. Roussel, *B.C.H.* 32 [1908], 325, no. 177, and stemma *ibid.* no. 176), nevertheless he served as *strategos* of *hoplitai* at Athens in 106/5 B.C. (year of Agathokles), and led the third Pythaid to Delphi (*F.D.* iii.2 5, *S.I.G.*³ 711 B 5, 12–13). He is not to be confused with the Middle Comedy poet Dionysios Sinopeus.

(vi) Νικόμαχος Ἱεροκλέους Ἀθηναῖος, *comic poet*

The only κωμῳδοποιός of 263 B.C. (no. 1132₆). He was awarded the *proxenia* of Delos about the same time (*I.G.* xi 638, letters of the mid-third century), and was also honoured by Samos (Chr. Habicht, *Ath. Mitt.* 72 [1957], 224–6, no. 58, cf. J.-L. Robert, *R.É.G.* 73 [1960], 183, no. 295a). Recorded at Delos as a comic actor in 259 B.C. (*I.G.* xi 115+Habicht, *loc. cit.*). Athenaeus (VII 290 e) has preserved 42 lines by Niko-machos, in which a proud cook informs the astounded person who has hired his services about the 'scientific' aspects of his profession. Three more small fragments in Kock, iii, 386. Titles of his plays are Εἰλείθυια, Ναυμαχία, and possibly Μετεκβαίνουσαι, cf. Meineke, *F.G.C.*, i, 496 and *I.G.* ii² 2363₂ and comment.

(vii) Νικόστρατος, *comic poet*

Ἐπεδείξατο τῷ θεῷ in 280 B.C. together with Ameinias and Philemon. He was second at the Athenian Dionysia in 312/11 B.C., when Ameinias was placed third, with his comedy .....οσκόπος (*I.G.* ii² 2323 a 43). He is also included in the list of poets who had won the contest of the Lenaia (*I.G.* ii² 2325₁₆₅). The title of a play, Ὀρνιθευτής, is given by Harpokration, and two verses of a comedy entitled Βασιλεῖς, spoken by a *miles gloriosus*, have been preserved (Athen. VI 230 d). Kock attributed these plays to Nikostratos of Middle Comedy (ii, 219ff.), but cf. Kirchner, *P.A.* 11038; Wilhelm, *Urkunden*, pp. 132–3; Edmonds, *The Fragments of Attic Comedy*, iii A, p. 182.

(viii) Ποσείδιππος Κασσανδρεύς, *comic poet*

Πο[λύ]κριτος Κασσ[ανδρεὺς] was included among the comic actors of 259 B.C. (A. Hauvette-Besnault, *B.C.H.* 7 [1883], p. 113, no. VIII). F. Studniczka (*Hermes* 28 [1893], p. 9, n. 1) suggested that we must read Πο[σείδιππ]ος, and understand the comic poet, a statue of whom was erected in Delos (*I.D.* 2486: Ποσείδιππον– Κασσανδρει–). Wilhelm (*Urkunden*, p. 153) thought that we should not attribute such a gross mistake to Hauvette-Besnault. But when Durrbach re-edited the same inscription (*I.G.* xi 115) he was not so sure about Polykritos as Hauvette had been. He read Πο[λύ]κριτος and put a mark of interrogation. He was sure, however, that the name ends in -*tos*. As far as the statue of Poseidippos is concerned, it seems that the lettering of the inscription points to a later date, but we must remember that if a poet was famous enough he could have a statue erected after his death. About the poet Poseidippos, Körte, *R.E.* xxii 426; Kock, iii, 335; Webster, *Studies in Gr. Com.*, pp. 71, 109, 146.

(ix) Ποσῆς ᾿Αρίστωνος ᾿Αθηναῖος (Φαληρεύς), *comic poet*

Another well-known personality of the late second/early first century like Asklepiades and Dionysios. He resided in Delos for some time at the beginning of the first century, where he held the office of gymnasiarch (*I.D.* 1928). As in the case of Asklepiades, one would be inclined to think that the Delian theatregoers saw some of his plays produced on their stage. In the year 88/7 B.C. he was *thesmothetes* at Athens (*I.G.* ii² 1714; for the date see S. Dow, *Hesperia* 3 [1934], 144–6). A few years later he won the prize for comic poets at the Sarapieia of Tanagra (*S.E.G.* xix 335). According to Kirchner (*P.A.* 12149, stemma 13824) he also served, together with his brother Timostratos, as mint-magistrate at Athens. The Timostratos-Poses issue of New Style coinage is placed in 134/3 B.C. by Margaret Thompson (*op. cit.*, 579) who believes that this date does not conform to Poses' first century activities. So she inserts another generation in the stemma of the family, and dissociates the mint-magistrate from the poet. But cf. Asklepiades (no. iii), also D. M. Lewis, *Numism. Chronicle* 1962, 292–3. Moreover, the symbol of magistrates on the coins of the

Timostratos-Poses issue is Dionysos holding a mask. About the same time when Poses participated in the Sarapieia his son Ariston contested at Oropos, and took the comic poets' prize (*I.G.* vii 416).

(x) Φανόστρατος Ἡρακλείδου Ἁλικαρνασσεύς, *tragic poet*

The Delians awarded him *proxenia, ateleia*, and all the other honours they used to confer upon '*proxenoi* and benefactors' (*I.G.* xi 528, beginning of the third century B.C.). Phanostratos is a known figure of the late fourth/early third century. In 307/6 B.C. he won a tragic victory at Athens (*I.G.* ii² 3073). His native city, Halikarnassos, honoured him by erecting his statue at Athens (*I.G.* ii² 2794).

(xi) Φιλήμων, *comic poet*

In 280 B.C. he produced plays in Delos (see Ameinias, Nikostratos). Durrbach took him for the illustrious poet of New Comedy (sc. son of Damon, Diomeieus, Kirchner, *P.A.* 14277; Körte, *R.E.* xix 2137ff.; Webster, *Studies in Gr. Com.*, pp. 125ff.). Philemon died in 263/2 B.C., but he was about eighty in 280 B.C. However, his age did not prevent him from accepting an invitation to visit Egypt, where he apparently was in 274 B.C. (Fr. 144K; Webster, *Studies in Gr. Com.*, p. 125). Therefore he could be identified with Philemon of Delos. On the other hand his son, Philemon II (*P.A.* 14278; Körte, *ibid.*, 2145), won his first victory before 279/8 B.C. (*I.G.* ii² 2325 com. on ll. 70, 74; Körte, *ibid.*), and is even more likely than his father to have gone to Delos in 280 B.C. Perhaps he is also to be recognized as the comic actor Philemon whose name is inscribed on the base of a statue of Comedy discovered at Thasos in a small building considered as a choregic monument at first, and later claimed to be a Stibadion (*I.G.* xii suppl. 400; G. Daux, *B.C.H.* 50 [1926], 234ff.; Ch. Picard, *Manuel d'archéologie grecque*, iv.2, pp. 1153ff. with bibliography). One title, Φωκεῖς, and two fragments of unknown plays have been preserved (Kock, ii, 540). The comedy Μιλησία, assigned to Philemon II by Kock, belongs in fact to Philemon III; Wilhelm, *Urkunden*, pp. 119, 121; *I.G.* ii² 2323₁₅₉ and com.

(xii) Φιλτέας, *tragic poet*(?)

He contested in Delos in 236 B.C. It is not certain that he was a tragic poet, but it is very probable:

I.G. xi 120₅₀₋₅₁:

> τραγωιδιῶν ποιητής [– c. 30 letters – Δ]ελφός? Φιλτέας
> διθυράμβων ποιητής – – – – – – – τρίς – – – – ΣΑ

If there were τραγωιδιῶν ποιηταὶ at the beginning of the line we should not doubt that Philteas was a tragic poet. Cf. Aristeides above. Philteas is otherwise unknown. The Delphian (?) whose name is missing must have been a tragic poet too.

(xiii) Χρύσιππος, *comic poet*

This is the only poet of comedies recorded in 259 B.C. (*I.G.* xi 115). He is mentioned nowhere else so far as I know.

OLD PLAYS, SATYR PLAYS

No evidence exists for old plays (but cf. App. I, p. 132). Nevertheless, considering how few poets are found in Delos, we may well suppose that old tragedies and comedies were staged by the actors who must have had the choice of plays, and who, together with the producers, had always been responsible for the revivals of old plays since 386 B.C. when παλαιὸν δρᾶμα πρῶτον παρεδίδαξαν οἱ τραγῳδοὶ at Athens (*I.G.* ii² 2318₂₀₂).

The base commemorating the poet Dionysios (no. v) attests to satyr play in the Athenian period. Compare the scanty archaeological evidence for the second century B.C. (p. 53). In view of the increased taste for satyr play in Hellenistic times, it seems likely that satyric performances were given during the third century as well, notwithstanding the silence of epigraphy.

CHAPTER V

FINANCIAL ASPECTS OF THEATRE PRODUCTION

CHOREGIA

The *choregoi* were regularly recorded in the accounts of the eponymous archons. At both Apollonia and Dionysia four citizens were appointed *choregoi* of boys. At the Dionysia the *choregoi* of tragedy and comedy were six in each case, four citizens and two metics, grouped in one of the following formulas: (*a*) 4 + 2 (*I.G.* xi 106, 108, 110, 111, 113, 114), (*b*) 2 + 1, 2 + 1 (*I.G.* xi 105, 107, 126, 128, 130, 132, 133), (*c*) citizens: comedy 4, tragedy 4; metics: comedy 2, tragedy 2 (*I.G.* xi 115, 116). The first type does not occur after 261 B.C. (no. 114), the third not after 255 B.C. (no. 116). The second type is not only the older one (no. 105, 284 B.C.) but also persists till the end of the Delian independence. The winning *choregoi* were not recorded separately before the middle of the third century. But since later on a whole triad of type 'b' is nominated victorious, it is legitimate to infer the existence of a kind of *synchoregia*. Two groups of *choregoi*, each consisting of two citizens and a metic, must have been in charge of tragedies, and two similar teams in charge of comedies. This is confirmed by the fact that the *choregia* of dithyramb was also a collective liturgy. The victory was won by two of the four *choregoi*, and we know that only two cyclic flautists took part in the contest of the Apollonia.[1]

What were the functions of *choregoi*? To answer this question we have to take into consideration a number of inscriptions mentioning different sums of money described as χορηγικόν.

---

[1] Each of them received 1500 dr. as regular reward, and 205 dr. as σιτηρέσιον, ξένιον, χορηγήματα. A total of 3470 dr., including the prize of 60 dr., was temporarily deposited in the δημοσία κιβωτὸς of the sanctuary by the public treasurers at the end of each year, and withdrawn by the new treasurers in Gamelion, the first month of the Delian year, in which the Apollonia was celebrated (*I.D.* 316$_{7-8}$, 3547.9-10, 368$_{19-20}$, etc., see particularly *I.D.* 399 A $_{49-52}$).

From the accounts of the *hieropoioi* it appears that the *choregikon* money came into the sanctuary at frequent intervals but was never paid out. The exact amount of *choregikon*, its origin and destination, the way it was raised and spent, are obscure.

In the first part of the third century the *choregikon* is numbered among other receipts of the temple such as rents of houses or land belonging to the sanctuary and put out on lease, interest of moneys lent to private citizens, repayment of instalments of debts owed by the State or citizens, etc. It seems therefore to be an item of Apollo's yearly revenue, albeit a very irregular one. In 279 B.C. it amounted to 2056 drachmai and 4 obols (see Table 2, passage no. I), in 258 B.C. only to 50 dr. (no. IV), while the accounts of 282, 278, and 250 B.C. (*I.G.* xi 158, 162, 287), show that no *choregikon* money was received by the *hieropoioi* in those years. Like the payment of the public debt (*I.G.* xi 161 A 25) the *choregikon* was paid into the sacred treasury by members of the *boule*, which means that regardless of its origin it was administered by executives of the government.

In the documents of the second half of the third century *choregikon* is never mentioned. Nor is it included in the completely preserved receipts of 192 B.C. (*I.D.* 399 A 15ff.).

About 200 B.C., or soon after the beginning of the second century, the *hieropoioi* acquired the custom of keeping the sums of money they received in jars.[1] An inscription on each jar recorded the origin of the money, the date it was deposited, and, of course, the exact amount. So during the second century the administrators of the sanctuary, instead of stating in their accounts the total amount of money handed over to them by their predecessors, made a detailed list of the jars laid in both the sacred and the public κιβωτός (treasury),[2] and went on registering the jars that were lodged during the year of their office. As long as a jar remained unopened in the treasury, it was included in the new lists of *hieropoioi* from year to year. Thanks to this rather primitive method of reckoning we can

---

[1] Jars are mentioned already in *I.G.* xi 287 A 43 (250 B.C.): στάμνοι ὥστε τῷ ἀργυρίῳ. But even if they were used, they are not enumerated in the inscriptions until much later. In 192 B.C. (*I.D.* 399) the practice had been fully established.

[2] For the distinction see Durrbach, *I.D.* com. on 399 A 1–73.

now see that the *choregikon* which was usually deposited in the last month of the Delian calendar, Posideon, was not spent in the next year but could be kept intact in the ἱερὰ κιβωτός for a whole decade or more. After many years it was still referred to as *choregikon* not because it was intended for 'choregic' purposes but only because the label of the jar was repeated in the accounts. The money now belonged to Apollo, and could be used by the managers of his property, independently of its origin, for sacrifices, wages, maintenance of buildings, new constructions, and other expenses described in the inscriptions of the *hieropoioi*.

From 180 B.C. onwards, or possibly a few years before, the *choregikon* was deposited by the public treasurers, who were then, as the *bouleutai* had been in the third century, also in charge of the payment of the public debt which the government apparently could not or did not want to be rid of. But some time between 192 B.C., when no *choregikon* is registered, and 180 B.C. a jar came into the temple bearing the following inscription: 'In the month Posideon Apollodoros, son of Mantitheos, and Philokles, son of Philokles, who had been elected by the popular assembly, separated this money to be used as *choregikon* from the sacred money according to the decree.' A second inscription corrected the sum: 'There is left 5 dr. 3¼ ob.' (see Table 2, no. V). Another jar lodged in the treasury about the same time bore the label: '*Choregikon* deposited by Phokaieus, son of Apollodoros, and Diadelos, son of Diadelos, 162 dr. 1¼ $\frac{2}{12}$ ob.' (VI). The last two depositors were not treasurers, and have been taken as elected commissaries like Apollodoros and Philokles.[1] The passages V and VI are revealing, for they lead to the following conclusions:

(i) Between 192 and 180 B.C. a measure was passed in the *ekklesia* concerning the *choregikon* money.
(ii) According to this decree the *choregikon*, or part of it, should originate from the treasury of Apollo.
(iii) Two elected commissaries should administer the money.
(iv) What remained after the expenditure which the *choregikon* was intended for had been met, was returned to the temple.

[1] *I.D.* 442, p. 174.

(v) The decree remained in force only for a short time because elected commissaries do not occur again, and there is no hint in any of the fully preserved documents that *choregikon* money was taken out of the temple.

In the second century the entries of *choregikon* present some regularity as compared with those of the third century. The maximum sum of 486 dr. 4 ob. occurs at least twice (VII, VIII, cf. XII). In all other instances, except V and XV which are special cases, the sum recorded amounts to either $\frac{1}{6}$ or $\frac{2}{6}$ of 486 (81: X, XIV; 162: VI, XIII). It is unfortunate that in the sole passage (IX) which associates the *choregikon* with tragic performances part of the sum is missing. I think, however, that one should restore $HHHH[F\Delta\Delta\Delta FI]$. 486 is the product of 81 multiplied by 6, and 6 was the number of *choregoi* of tragedy at the Delian Dionysia. If this is right then we are forced to accept that all the second-century references to *choregikon* relate to the *choregia* of tragedy.

It is time now to return to the *choregoi* whose names and victories were recorded by the archons, and ask where they come in as far as the *choregikon* question is concerned.[1] First we must consider it probable that they contributed money to the performances. And since the artists (musicians, actors, etc.) were paid by the government (cf. p. 38) we must again consider it probable that the *choregoi* provided money for choruses. We have seen elsewhere that the dramatic performances in Delos wholly depended on the travelling groups of Dionysiac artists. Such groups usually included choreuts (*S.I.G.*[3] 424; *I.G.* xii.9 207) and, of course, chorus trainers who sometimes might also produce the plays (*S.E.G.* xix 335).

We must at this point call to mind that the *choregia* was a liturgy, i.e. a taxation, and as such it could not depend on such an external and changeable factor as the participation of certain foreign artists in a local festival. The *choregoi* must have been appointed well before the festivals and independently of the

---

[1] V. von Schoeffer, 'De Deli insulae rebus', *Berliner Studien* 9 (1889), 143–4, misled by a wrongly edited inscription (*B.C.H.* 7 [1883], p. 109, no. V, ll. 17–18; cf. *I.G.* xi 110), proposed the theory that the *hieropoioi* maintained a sort of theatrical wardrobe for hiring to *choregoi* the costumes and other equipment they needed for their choruses. Cf. Th. Homolle's objections, *B.C.H.* 14 (1890), 444.

arrival of the *technitai*. In Athens, where the *choregoi* were allotted to the poets as soon as they were appointed, it was impossible to escape this duty; in Delos another system had to be devised to ensure that all the *choregoi* would be taxed every year.

Let us make the supposition that a fixed amount of money, called *choregikon*, was collected by the government from the citizens and metics who had been nominated *choregoi*. This money would be put at the disposal of the festival manager(s) together with the fund set apart for the salaries of artists (τὸ ἀποτεταγμένον τοῖς τεχνίταις, see pp. 38ff.). Anything that remained when the festival was over was bestowed in Apollo's sanctuary, which was also endowed with such income sources as harbour-dues, tax on fishing of purple, on fares to neighbouring islands, and so forth[1]; after all both the *choregikon* and τὸ τοῖς τεχνίταις were originally intended for expenses of religious festivals.[2] At the beginning of the second century, and only for a limited period, the *choregikon*, or part of it, for some unknown reason was not collected from *choregoi*. The *ekklesia* decreed that the amount required should come from the sacred treasury. In two other cases the *choregoi* Thrasymedes and Sosos were not punctual in settling their liabilities, and had to pay their choregic tax straight to the temple later (XIII, XV, cf. XI).[3]

The amount of 486 dr. 4 ob. is described as τὸ χορηγικόν, *the* choregic money, all of it, while for the smaller sums the genitive is used: ἔθεσαν ταμίαι τοῦ χορηγικοῦ, the treasurers deposited so much of the *choregikon*. If the restoration of the sum in passage IX is right, it follows then that only the money collected from the *choregoi* of tragedy came into the temple during the second century. This probably explains the big difference between the sums of the third century and those of the second. Yet it can

---

[1] V. v. Schoeffer, *ibid.*, 162; Homolle, *B.C.H.* 6 (1882), 66, *ibid.* 14 (1890), 454.

[2] Cf. Homolle, *B.C.H.* 14, 449.

[3] The delay in paying the choregic tax had no effect on the regular carrying out of the festival, since the manager was in co-operation with the public treasurers, and not with the *choregoi* as far as salaries of artists were concerned. Furthermore, the last choregic inscription (*I.G.* xi 133) does not include *choregoi* of tragedy, which means either that tragic *choregoi* were not appointed in 170 B.C., or that those nominated never paid the sum they were liable for. In spite of that, tragic performances most probably took place, as the actors recorded in the same inscription suggest.

hardly be understood why the huge amount of 2056 dr. 4 ob. remained unused in 279 B.C., when a large number of artists gave performances in the island (*I.G.* xi 108).[1]

The fact that the numbers 81 and 162 are sub-multiples of 486 has helped us so far, nevertheless it needs to be accounted for. It might be argued that the rewards of artists were in many cases defined by law, and were not stipulated every year. See for example the well-known law 'de technitis conducendis' of Euboea, *I.G.* xii.9 207$_{21-5}$. In Delos itself the rewards, rates, etc. of the cyclic flautists were the same from 231 B.C. (*I.D.* 316$_{7-8}$) down to 178 B.C. (*I.D.* 443$_{21-2}$). It seems therefore that the sum of 486 dr. 4 ob. was the fixed reward given to tragic choruses for a certain number of performances. Perhaps one could think of two choruses (corresponding to the two teams of *synchoregoi*) taking part in six plays. If for some reason less than six plays were put on the remainder of the *choregikon* would be the fixed amount of one, two, and so on, sixths of the total. And whenever the total amount was left it is to be concluded that no tragedies were played at the Dionysia, though we must also consider the possibility of occasional chorusless productions.

However, the most difficult thing to apprehend is the criterion by which the winners would be selected, if all the *choregoi* contributed an equal amount of money. We have already seen that winners first appear about 250 B.C. Can this fact be related to the absence of *choregikon* from the temple accounts of the second part of the third century? Or is that absence from the half-dozen or so complete documents in question purely accidental? Whatever the case might be in the third century, the *choregoi* of the second century, at least those of tragedy, would have pursued victory through some other means than squandering their fortunes. It should be borne in mind that in Athens the *choregoi* not only provided for equipment and maintenance of the choreuts but acted as managers of their choruses as well.

---

[1] Homolle expressed the opinion that the *choregikon* was intended for theatrical expenses in general (*ibid.* 449), and such large remainders as 2056 or 1482 dr. could be ascribed to 'la générosité d'un citoyen ou d'un étranger, le désintéressement d'un artiste faisant abandon au profit du dieu de son salaire ou de ses récompenses··· (*ibid.* 448) on peut aussi supposer ... que la caisse du temple avait fait une avance dont on la couvrait, aussitôt les recettes opérées' (*ibid.* 449).

By so getting personally involved they invigorated the competitive spirit, and deservedly laid claim to the victory.[1] We could assume that similarly in Delos the choregic liturgy was not confined to a cash contribution only, but also implied a certain amount of personal work. The *choregoi* might be assigned to groups of artists with whom they would co-operate as administrative managers; that attachment to a particular group would subsequently become the decisive factor in their own win. However odd this situation may appear it is supported by a close parallel from Euboea. The law referred to before (*I.G.* xii.9 207) requires that choruses were to be hired together with the other *technitai*, at Chalkis, by special deputies of the major cities. In another section below the task of *choregoi* is described: 'The *choregoi* who have been appointed in the cities must receive the artists ...according to the laws.'[2] They are also mentioned in the section 'about the judgment', ll. 35–6: '[The herald?] will announce the names of the *choregoi* attached to the artists, and the archon those who have been judged ...'[3]

What kind of prize the victorious *choregoi* received, if any, is not known. We have already described (p. 8) the choregic monument of Karystios set up c. 300 B.C., and assumed with Vallois that some fragments of phalli found near the Dionysiac Stibadion come from similar monuments. Altogether two dedicatory inscriptions of *choregoi*, that of Karystios and another one of Kritodemos, are preserved. Neither of them mentions the *synchoregia*, and both boast that the dedicator performed all the *choregiai* (presumably in the course of several years), and won in all of them.[4]

It was only natural that the Athenians who took over the island in 166 B.C. would abolish the *choregia* which had ceased to exist as a liturgy in Athens since the time of Demetrios of

[1] On the personal involvement of *choregoi* cp. Arist. *Oecon.* II 1351 b.

[2] Ll. 32–3: τοὺς δὲ χορηγοὺς τοὺς ἀποδεδειγμένους ἐν ταῖς πόλεσι δέχε[σ]θαί τε τοὺς τ[εχνίτας — — — — —] κατὰ τοὺς νόμους.

[3] The whole section (ll. 33–6) runs as follows: [ὑ]πὲρ τῆς κρίσεως· ἐπειδὰν δὲ ὁ ἀγὼν γένηται, κρινόντων [οἱ κ]ριταὶ| — — — —ους γράψαντες εἰς γρ[αμμ]ατεῖον καὶ θέντες εἰς τὸ φανερὸν πρ[ὸ]s τὸν αρ......α.γο.| — — — —κηρ[υσσέ]τω [τὰ ὀ]νόματα τῶν χορηγῶν ἐπὶ τοὺς τεχνίτας, ὁ δὲ [ἄ]ρχων [τοὺς] κεκριμένους| — — — —ατος νικάτω.

[4] *I.G.* xi 1148: Πᾶσι χορηγήσας καὶ νικήσας, Διονύσωι| εὐξάμενός με ἀνέθηκε Καρύστιος ᾿Ασβήλου παῖς. *Ibid.* 1149: Πάντα χορηγήσας Πρεπεφύ[λ]ου π[α]ῖς Κριτόδημ[ος]| π[ά]ν[τ]α δὲ ν[ικ]ήσας Δι[ο]ν[ύσωι] τό[νδ]ε ἀ[νέ]θ[η]κ[εν].

Phaleron.[1] Two marble tripods with comic masks (p. 54) probably belong to this period, and might have been set up by *agonothetai*[2] of the Dionysia (cf. *I.G.* ii[2] 3073ff.).

STATE EXPENSES

The Delians displayed a high degree of generosity in dealing with the *technitai*. The normal reward granted to each of the two cyclic flautists who performed at the Apollonia totalled about 1700 drachmai (see p. 31, n. 1). We need to recall the vast sums received today by stars of the opera or moving pictures in order to understand how such an enormous amount of money could be given to an artist for a few performances, in a place where a skilled artisan earned 2 dr. a day when employed (his annual income being something between 100 and 240 dr.), and unskilled men had to content themselves with a wage of 3 or 2 obols, sometimes even less.[3] However, the Apollonia had succeeded the old Delia, the greatest festival of the Aegean, and the Delians apparently meant to invest it with splendour.

We do not know about the rewards of dramatic artists but, presumably, they earned smaller sums.[4] A certain amount of

---

[1] Pickard-Cambridge, *The Dramatic Festivals of Athens*, p. 92.

[2] The dedicatory inscription of an *agonothetes* is preserved on a base of unusual shape (*I.G.* xi 1150). A contest of choruses founded by some city is mentioned. P. Roussel (*I.G.*, *loc. cit.*) understood 'Deliacam civitatem ipsam'. W. Peek, who re-edited the inscription—two elegiac couplets—claimed that he read 29 more letters, or traces of letters, in the first line than anybody else had been able to read before (*Wissenschaftl. Zeitschrift d. Martin-Luther-Universität*, Halle-Wittenberg, vi [1956–7], Heft 4, p. 565). According to his reading this was a contest in honour of both Apollo and Dionysos, which was decreed and held for the first time: ξυνὸν ἐπεὶ τὰ πρῶτα πόλις Φοί[β]ωι Βρομίωι τε| θῆκεν ἀγῶνα χορῶν δόγματι κοινο-τελεῖ. The inscription is dated by the form of the letters to the second century B.C.

[3] W. W. Tarn in *The Hellenistic Age*, Cambridge, 1923, 121–4; F. Heichelheim, *Wirtschaftliche Schwankungen der Zeit von Alexander bis Augustus*, Jena, 1930, pp. 97ff., 125. The price of wheat fluctuated between 5 and 10 dr. a bushel in the third century, Tarn, *ibid.*, p. 117; idem., *Hellenistic Civilization*[3], p. 106; Heichelheim, *op. cit.*, pp. 50, 128. The average annual rent of houses was 38 dr. in 282 B.C., 61 dr. in 279, 73 dr. in 250, 125 in 246, 73 in 219, and over 100 dr. again in the early second century, Tarn, *Hell. Age*, p. 119. Bibliography of the economic history of the Aegean, which is largely based on Delian documents, in Rostovtzeff's *S.E.H.*, ch. iv, note 2.

[4] The Apollonia rewards were exceptional. In Corfu the sum of 50 minai (Corinthian) was considered enough for hiring the services of 3 flautists, 3 tragedians, and 3 comedians, excluding rates, *I.G.* ix.1 69425.91 (second cent.). In

public money was set aside every year for the *technitai* during and very probably before, the second century. At the end of the year the amount that might have been left unused was granted to the sanctuary like the *choregikon*. In the accounts of the *hieropoioi* the entries of these remainders are described as follows:

A. (1) τὸ περιγενόμενον ἀπὸ τῶν τεχνιτῶν, *I.D.* 442 A 21 = 453 A 17; *I.D.* 455 Aa 21 (= τὸ περιόν, *I.D.* 442 A 53, etc.), *I.D.* 453 A 12 = 455 Aa 9 (cf. A 3 below).

(2) τὸ περιὸν ἀπὸ τῶν τεχνιτῶν, *I.D.* 442 A 53 = 460 c 4 = 461 Aa 72; *I.D.* 442 A 98 (the sole entry to the *public* treasury, 180 B.C.); *I.D.* 460 b 4.

(3) ὃ ἔφασαν (ταμίαι) περιεῖναι ἀπὸ τῶν τεχνιτῶν, *I.D.* 442 A 13 = 461 Aa 40 (= τὸ περιγενόμενον, *I.D.* 453 A 12, etc.)

(4) τὸ περιὸν ἀπὸ τῶν τεχνιτῶν καὶ τὸ χορηγικὸν τὸ παρὰ Σώσου, *I.D.* 461 Aa 31.

B. (1) τὸ περιγενόμενον τοῦ διαταχθέντος τοῖς τεχνίταις, *I.D.* 461 Aa 29.

(2) τὸ περιὸν τοῦ διαταχθέντος τοῖς τεχνίταις, *I.D.* 453 A 30.

(3) τὸ περιγενόμενον ἀπὸ τοῦ ἀποταγέντος τοῖς τεχνίταις, *I.D.* 453 A 22 = 461 Aa 53.

(4) τὸ περιὸν ἀπὸ τοῦ ἀποταγέντος τοῖς τεχνίταις, *I.D.* 455 Aa 17.

(5) τὸ περιγενόμενον ἀπὸ τοῦ τοῖς τεχνίταις, *I.D.* 453 A 22 = 461 Aa 53.

C. ὃ ἔφασαν (ταμίαι) περιγενέσθαι ἀπὸ τοῦ διαταχθέντος εἰς τὰ ξένια τοῖς τεχνίταις, *I.D.* 442 A 16–18 = 453 A 15 = 455 Aa 12 (τοῦ διαταχθέντος τοῖς τεχνίταις ξενίου) = 461 A 37 (τὸ περιγενόμενον ἀπὸ τοῦ ξενίου τοῖς τεχνίταις).

D. [τὸ ἀποτετ]αγμένον τοῖς τεχνίταις, *I.D.* 399 A 6.

E. (1) τὸ περιὸν ἀπὸ τῶν τεχνιτῶν εἰς τὸ θέατρον, *I.D.* 461 Aa 66.

(2) ἀπὸ τοῦ εἰς τὸ θέατρον, *I.D.* 461 Aa 48.

The remainders of the amounts of money appropriated to the artists ranged from small sums like 9 dr. to 4 ob. (181 B.C.,

Euboea a flautist was paid 600 dr. (of Demetrios), a comic actor 400 dr., *I.G.* xii.9 207₂₁₋₂ (294–87 B.C.). Cp. *S.E.G.* xix 335 for the first century, and *C.I.G.* 2758, 2759 = *M.A.M.A.* viii 420 for imperial times.

I.D. 442 A 21–2), or 15 dr. 1 ob. (179 B.C., *I.D.* 442 A 52–3)
up to 313 dr. (before 171 B.C., *I.D.* 460 b 4), or even 685 dr.
(before 169 B.C., *I.D.* 461 Aa 29). An amount of 27 dr. that
was deposited by the treasurers of 183 B.C. (*I.D.* 442 A 16–8,
etc.) is described as the remainder of the lodging allowance
(ξένια) of the previous year (C). But this sole instance by no
means suggests that the money which was set apart for the
technitai (τὸ ἀποταγὲν/διαταχθὲν τοῖς τεχνίταις) every year
represented only the cost of their accommodation. On the contrary the passages E 1–2 imply that τὸ τοῖς τεχνίταις was
intended for defraying the whole cost of hiring theatrical artists:
salaries, accommodation, food allowance, and prizes.

ARCHONS' EXPENSES

It is likely that a part of the expenditure on the performances of
Dionysia, namely the hire of costumes (cf. pp. 81f.), was sus-
tained by the archon himself. This is suggested by two inscriptions, and endorsed by such authorities on epigraphy as Hiller,
Durrbach and Wilhelm.

The two passages are as follows:

(i) *I.G.* xi 110 17–18:
> Καὶ τῶν ἱματίων τοὺς μισθοὺς οὐ κατεθέμην
> τῶν εἰς τὰ Διονύσια. vac.

l. 17 οὐκ ἀπ[έδο]ν[το] Hauvette-Besnault, *B.C.H.* 7 (1883), 109,
n. V; οὐ κατέγρ[αψα] Hiller: 'ita archontis laus evadit; haec
ἐκ τῶν ἰδίων dederat', *apud* Durrbach, *I.G.* com.; οὐ κατε-
θέμην Durrbach: 'ectypo iterum adhibito de litteris κατεθ
minime dubito; ceterum κατατίθεσθαι eodem sensu quo
καταγράφειν intellegendum: cf. Ps. Dem. LXI 2', *I.G.* com.

(ii) *I.G.* xi 118 25–28:
> Τάσδε ἐ[– – – – – – – τοὺς μισ]-
> θοὺς τῶ[ν ἱματίων? – – – – – – – –]
> κατεθυμ – – – – – – – – – –
> κατὰ τὸν [νόμον? – – – – – – – –]

l.27 'lectio liquida, nisi quod τ etiam ι esse potest; non ex-
pedio', Durrbach, *I.G.* com.; 'immerhin liegt es nahe οὐ]

κατεθ⟨έ⟩μ[ην] zu vermuten ... Über die Bedeutung des κατατίθεσθαι ... bleibt kein Zweifel (das Aktivum von einer Handlung, bei welcher die Rücksicht auf den eigenen Vorteil nicht in Betracht kommt)', A. Wilhelm, *Griechische Inschriften rechtliche.ι Inhalts*, Πραγματεῖαι τῆς 'Ακαδημίας 'Αθηνῶν, vol. 17, no. 1, Athens , 1951, p. 79.

But were the archons' contributions optional or regular and κατὰ τὸν [νόμον]? It seems absurd that the first magistrate of the State should be obliged to share in the cost of a festival. Moreover, why did only two of the archons think their generosity worthy of being put on record? I would rather be inclined to think that the passages quoted above reflect occasional displays of munificence on the part of some theatre-loving archons.

CHAPTER VI

THEATRE BUILDING

The theatre of Delos rests on the western slope of a hill situated in the southern part of the city. One of the most remarkable edifices of the Independence, it was used for many performances at the numerous Delian festivals, and mainly for the musical contests of the Apollonia, and the dramatic ones of the Dionysia.[1]

The theatre had originally been constructed in wood, and was gradually converted into stone during the third century.[2] The wooden structure could have been set up well before Delos broke off from the hegemony of Athens. The expenses for the works done at the theatre were met with money from the sacred treasury of Apollo, and are recorded in the accounts of the sanctuary.[3] This unique documentation has attracted the attention of many students of the ancient stage,[4] but the theatre of Delos has not yet been the subject of a full architectural study. Vallois devoted about twenty pages of his *Architecture hellénique et hellénistique à Délos* (220–37, 259–61) to the theatre, in which he attempted a reconstruction of the stage building based on archaeological as well as inscriptional evidence. But his study was not apparently meant to be exhaustive, for he left a considerable number of architectural members which lie in the theatre unaccounted for (for instance five or six very interesting blocks of stone bearing cuttings and sockets, which probably belonged to the mechanical equipment of the theatre), and never[5] gave pictures either of the material he

[1] Another, very small, theatre without a 'stage' building survives among the ruins of the Syrian sanctuary in Delos. It was dedicated to Hagne Aphrodite in 108/7 B.C. (*I.D.* 2628), and must have been used for religious ceremonies. E. Will, 'Le sanctuaire syrien de Délos', *Les Annales Archéologiques de Syrie*, 1 (1951), 59–79.

[2] Valloix, *Architecture*, pp. 230–8.

[3] The texts were collected by Homolle in *B.C.H.* 18 (1894), 162–5, and H. Bulle, *Untersuchungen an griech. Theatern*, München, 1928, pp. 174–80.

[4] The references in Vallois, *Architecture*, p. 220, n. 2.

[5] The illustrations of his book appeared nine years later under the title *Les constructions de Délos: Documents*, Paris, 1953.

made use of, or of his conception of the building. However, it is to be hoped that the French School will in time devote a detailed study to the theatre, which will bring order to the muddle of ruins with which the visitor to the site is now faced, and cast new light on Hellenistic theatre building.

In the following pages some of the inscriptions mentioning the theatre are reconsidered. An attempt at a reconstruction of the stage building comes as a result: I am fully aware that this may be of little archaeological value but, being primarily concerned with the functional aspects of the stage building, I have only aimed at a reasonable interpretation of the inscriptions.

A RECONSTRUCTION OF THE STAGE BUILDING

The main difficulty in reconstructing the stage building is due to the fact that the inscriptional information does not appear to be in accordance with the actual remains. This difficulty is easily surmounted if we accept with Dörpfeld and others that the inscriptions and the building to which they refer on the one hand, and the remains of the stone building unearthed at Delos on the other, belong to different periods.[1] But this assumption is unacceptable because the stone building actually goes back to the third century, and is, therefore, contemporary with the inscriptions of the *hieropoioi* (cf. p. 44, n. 1, p. 45, n. 1, and the inscriptional passages quoted on pp. 45–6).

The plan of the *skene* is a rectangle c. 15·35 m long and 6·68 m wide with its long axis running towards the north. The eastern wall, which was a tangent of the orchestra circle, had three doors, and the back (western) wall had one. It seems that the building had no internal walls. According to Vallois there were six supports put on the long axis. A *proskenion* of fourteen Doric half-column-pilasters was attached to the front, and continued along the three other sides thus forming a *stoa* around the scene building. This *stoa* supported by rectangular piers had six intercolumniations at the narrow sides and ten at the back (see ground plan on p. 147).

---

[1] Dörpfeld-Reisch, *Das griechische Theater*, p. 147; Flickinger, *The Greek Theater and Its Drama*[4], pp. 107–8.

The archaeological evidence is clear so far. But when we come to consider what the inscriptions of the *hieropoioi* can yield we find that although the administrators of Apollo's treasure took the greatest care to put down in their accounts even the smallest amount they spent, say, for nails, they do not try at all to be descriptive. In a fairly large number of passages materials purchased or wages paid to workmen and contractors for the construction of certain parts of the theatre are recorded. But the flexible terminology employed has led to entirely different interpretations and, consequently, different conceptions of the scene building.

However it is certain that the first wooden *skene* goes back to the late fourth century, probably up to the beginning of the Delian independence (*I.G.* xi 142₄₃₋₄₄, 314–300 B.C.). In 274 B.C. the main *skene* had been constructed in stone.[1] The *proskenion* is recorded for the first time in *I.G.* xi 153₁₄, which is dated between 297 and 279 B.C. It is stated that the contractors of the *skene* and *proskenion* were paid 410 dr. This comparatively small sum as well as the association with the *skene* do not suggest a construction of the *proskenion* but rather some additional work on the stage building, which consisted already of a main two-storeyed *skene* and a *proskenion* attached to the front of it. The date of that inscription can be confined within narrower limits, since in 282 B.C. several *pinakes* of the *proskenion* were made for 30 dr. (excluding the value of timber) and painted for 100 dr. each (*I.G.* xi 158 A 67–9). The *proskenion* was undoubtedly a high stage, or more accurately the front below a high stage, the roof of which appears in 279 B.C., when an eleven-ell beam was used εἰς τὸ λο[γ]εῖον τῆς σκηνῆς (*I.G.* xi 161 D 125–7). *Logeion* should refer to the high stage because in later inscriptions *logeion* stands for the structure as a whole: τοῦ] λογείου πίνακες ΔΙΙΙ occurs in an inventory of 233 or 232 B.C. (*I.D.* 314 B 167), and in 179 new *pinakes* were made ἐπὶ τὸ λογεῖον (*I.D.* 442 A 232). Panels, therefore, reconditioned or renewed from time to time,

---

[1] Τῶι ἐγλαβόντι ἀπαγαγεῖν τὴν γῆν ἐκ Πανόρμου τ(ῆς) Μυ[κόνου δραχμ]ῶν ΗΓϜΗ καὶ καταχρίσαντι τὸ τεῖχος τῆς σκηνῆς, *I.G.* xi 199 A 101–2; Vallois, *ibid.*, p. 234. Some parts of the *skene* remained wooden, and were covered with pitch, apparently to make them waterproof, several times after 274; see *I.G.* xi 204₅₉ (268 B.C.), 219 A 46 (c. 260 B.C.). Cf. also 158 A 77–9 (282 B.C.), 161 A 114–15 (roof 279 B.C.), 199 A 37–8 (doors 274 B.C.).

were always used for covering the spaces between the wooden pillars at first and the marble half-columns later. The *pro-skenion* had been turned into stone in 250 B.C. when a dedicatory inscription was cut on its architrave.[1]

The main difficulty comes from the obscure meaning of the terms *paraskenion*, *paraskenia*, of which no trace can be seen in the plan of the building. We come across the word π]αρασκη-νίου for the first time in *I.G.* xi 175 Ab 4, dated between 300 and 275 B.C., but it is preceded and followed by gaps. In 274 B.C. *paraskenia* were involved in large works done at the theatre. Before any discussion we must quote here the relevant passages of *I.G.* xi 199 A:

51–2

εἰς] τὸ θέατρον ἀπὸ τοῦ νεωκορίου τοὺς λίθους οὓς ἠργάσατο
Βάκχιος εἰς τὰ παρασκήνια – – – – – – – – – – ὅμωι ἐργασαμένωι
.ΕΠ....|[..σ]υστήσαντι τὸ παρασκήνιον [ἡμερῶν] δέκα μισθὸς
ΔϜ.

62–3

ΤΩΓ..αντι ξύ[λα]|ταῖς σκηναῖς καὶ τοῖς παρασκηνίοι[ς.

91–9

Κτήσονι τῶι τοὺς ἥλους ἐγλαβό[ντι εἰς τὰς σκ]ηνὰς καὶ τὰ παρα-
σκήνια ποιῆσαι τὴ[μ]| μνᾶν Η, ἀπεστησάμεθα κατὰ τὴν συγγραφὴν
μνᾶς τριάκοντα ἑπτὰ κ.τ.λ. Δεξίωι ἐγλαβόντι κατὰ τὴ[ν αὐτὴ]ν
συγγραφὴν ποιῆσαι ἥλους εἰς τὰ παρασκή|νια τὴμ μνᾶν δραχμῶν Η
ἀπεστησάμεθα κ.τ.λ. μνᾶς ὀκτώ. Θεοδήμωι τῶι ἐγλαβόντι ἐργά-
σασθαι τὴν [σκηνή]ν τὴν μέσην καὶ τὰ παρασκήνια τὰ κάτω
δραχμῶ[ν]| ΗΗΗΗϜᴵᴵΔΔΔΔϜΗΗΗ (499) κ.τ.λ. Ἐπικράτηι τῶι

---

[1] The dedication concerns the whole theatre: [Δ]ήλιοι τὸ θέ[ατρον καὶ ....]ν κατεσκεύ[ασαν....], *I.G.* xi 1070. Cf. *ibid.* 287 A 80: Νεογένει ἐπιγράψαντι ἐπὶ τὸ προσκήνιονϜ. According to Dinsmoor (*The Architecture of Ancient Greece*, p. 299, n. 2), 'the inscription on the proscenium for which payment was made in 250 B.C. was undoubtedly on wood; the total cost of 5 drachmas was insufficient for carving in stone, and it is quite impossible that the fragmentary inscription on the architrave of the stone proscenium, *I.G.* xi.4 1070, should have been the one mentioned in 250 B.C. as has been suggested'. But Dinsmoor is wrong because in the same line 80 of n. 287 A it is stated that the same man, Neogenes, who was a stone cutter, inscribed on a stele an Aitolian decree for 2½ dr.; he also carved the whole n. 287 for 120 dr., that is about 390 letters per drachma (line A 197).

ἐγλα[β]όντι τὰς σκηνὰς τὰς παλαιὰς ξῦσαι καὶ ἐπισκευάσαι|⁹⁵ καὶ
τὰς ἐπάνω σκηνὰς καινὰς ποιῆσαι δύο καὶ τὰ παρασκήνια τὰ ἄνω
καινὰ ποιῆσαι δύο καὶ τοῖς παλαιοῖς πίναξι τῶν παρασκηνίων
κύκλωι περιφ[ρά]ξαι καὶ τὰ ἔξωστρα καὶ τὴν κλίμακα καὶ τοὺς
βω|μοὺς ἐπισκευάσαι ⊢ΔΔΔ⊢Η (537) κ.τ.λ. Γονεῖ καὶ
᾿Ασκληπι|[ά]δηι τοῖς ἐγλαβοῦσι γράψαι τὰς σκηνὰς καὶ τὰ
παρασκήνια τά τε ἐπάνω καὶ τὰ ὑποκάτω δραχμῶν ΧΧ⊢
(2500) κ.τ.λ.| τῶι ἐγλαβόν[τι] ποιῆσαι τὸ παρασκήνιον τὸ ἐν
τῶι θεάτρωι δραχμῶν ΗΗΗ⊢ΔΔΔΔ (390) ἔδομεν κ.τ.λ.

We find the *paraskenion* again in 269 B.C., *I.G.* xi 203 A:

88–9

᾿Αριστοκλεῖ καὶ Καλλιγένει τῆς λιθείας τῆς εἰς τὸ παρασκήνιον
ἐκ ποδῶν [πε]ντακοσίων ἔδομεν τὴν πρώτην| δόσιν κατὰ τὴν
συγγραφὴν δραχμὰς ΧΗ⊢ΔΓ·ΗΙΙΙ (1166 + 3 ob., total paid
2333 dr. + 2 ob.).

R. Vallois gives the *paraskenia* three different meanings:
(1) Projecting wings of the two upper storeys (*logeion, theo-logeion*),[1]
(2) *Parodos* gates (*I.G.* xi 199 A 51–2, 99),
(3) The *stoa* that embraces the main building (*I.G.* xi 203 A
88).[2]

According to H. Bulle they are parts of the *scenae frons*, and
sometimes either the singular or the plural means the side and
back walls or only one side wall (199 A 51–2, 99; 203 A 88).[3]

There is no doubt that the *paraskenia* have more than one
meaning. Nevertheless it would be reasonable to think that
those meanings ought to be somehow connected. How could
the same term mean two such different things, *parodos* gates and
projecting wings above the *proskenion*, in the same inscription?

[1] Chamonard, too, had suggested in his first publication of the theatre, *B.C.H.*
20 (1896), 287–8, that the *paraskenia* must be understood to be on the upper floor.
According to him the *paraskenia* were not needed on the orchestra level as a frame
of any action because the chorus had disappeared in the third century.

[2] *Loc. cit.*, pp. 227–30, 235–7; *R.É.A.* 28 (1926), 177.

[3] *Untersuchungen an griechischen Theatern*, pp. 182–6. Also Pickard-Cambridge,
Theatre of Dionysus, p. 208, calls the *paraskenia* 'portions of the *scaenae frons*', and
Frickenhaus, *Die altgriechische Bühne*, p. 50, feels certain that *skene* and *paraskenia*
are three large *thyromata* of the upper floor (he adduces Suda *s.v.* σκηνή as evidence
for this assumption).

The usage of the words *skene-skenai* offers an instructive analogy. The singular usually means the scene building[1] while the plural means decorative panels, a set of scenery, which could be attached to the front of the scene building.[2] When we hear of money paid for the construction in wood or painting of '*skenai* and *paraskenia*', it is clear that the *paraskenia* are a kind of wooden panels, also intended to be attached to some part or parts of the stage building. But what parts? Vallois' theory of projecting wings on the *logeion* floor is not convincing, for he puts the façade of the main (*logeion*) storey above the long axis of the *skene* (supported by internal props), and the *paraskenia* projecting up to the front wall, thus allowing the *logeion* a width of about 6·5 m which is unacceptable as too wide. However, passages like 199 A 51–2, 99 and 203 A 88ff. suggest an architectural member of the building.

When one goes through the inscriptions relating to the theatre of Delos, one is surprised not to find mentioned at all the most unusual of its features, the *stoa*. This might be explained on the grounds that the *stoa* was not constructed before 166 B.C., when Delos ceased to be independent and became again a colony of Athens. But it does not seem very likely that the Athenians altered the theatre of Delos, which was already fully constructed in stone.[3] Moreover the *proskenion*, which originally had only 12 columns instead of 14,[4] had been elongated in 233 or 232 B.C., since 13 panels of the *logeion* were found among other stored objects (*I.D.* 314 B, cf. p. 44 above). And the elongation of the *proskenion* must have taken place at the time when the *stoa* was erected.[5] So it would not be unreasonable to think that the *stoa* is to be understood under the term *paraskenion*. This *stoa* is a part of the stage building closely connected with the main *skene*; it is literally a *para-skenion*. Passages like *I.G.* 199 A 52, 99 and 203 A 88ff. strongly suggest this interpretation. *The paraskenion* τὸ ἐν τῷ θεάτρῳ seems to be rather a single structure than one of a pair. Vallois following

---

[1] *I.G.* xi 142.43; 158 A 77–9; 161 A 115; 199 A 37, 102; 204.59, etc.
[2] Cf. the passages of n. 199 quoted above, pp. 45–6.
[3] See Vallois, *Architecture*, pp. 230ff.
[4] Vallois, *ibid.*, p. 223.
[5] Vallois believes it was erected a little later, *ibid.*, p. 235.

O. Puchstein[1] accepted that the *stoa* was to be understood in
I.G. 203 A 88, and on the grounds of that passage dated it in
269–268 B.C.[2] But if we are right in believing that the *paraskenion* of *I.G.* 199 is the *stoa*, then it is pushed back to 274
or 275 (cf. *I.G.* 175 Ab). In 269 B.C. it acquired its stone
piers.

As the front part of the square colonnade is called *proskenion*,
the rest of it is called *paraskenion*. But anyone wanting to point
out the two side parts of the *stoa* should name them *paraskenia*.
These are of course the lower ones. And since the lower *paraskenia* were not projecting wings of the *scenae frons* but narrow
side rooms or corridors, the upper ones must have been side
corridors as well, not sticking out from the line of the middle
skene. Openings at the fronts of them would be used as upper
parodoi leading to the *logeion* (see fig. 2, p. 147). Both lower and
upper *paraskenia* partly consisted of painted wooden panels.
The panels would have covered the spaces between the piers of
the lower *paraskenia*.[3] There is no evidence for the upper ones,
but the case of a second row of pilasters above the lower one
must not be ruled out, especially if the front of the *skene* had a
row of half-column-pilasters as Vallois suggested,[4] and as it has
been assumed for the Lycurgean *skene* of the theatre of Dionysus
in Athens, and the theatres of Segesta and Tyndaris.[5]

The objection that may be raised against this conception of
paraskenia is that such painted flanks would be without any
parallel as far as we know, and would have been unnecessary
with regard to the production of plays. But we can reply that,
firstly, the *stoa* is in fact unique, secondly, the flanks of the
original shorter *proskenion* were boarded with wooden panels as
has been adequately shown,[6] and thirdly, we need not imagine
that the *paraskenia* were elaborately decorated; if they were not
painted in plain colours they presumably bore very simple
designs.

---

[1] *Die griechische Bühne*, Berlin, 1901, pp. 56–7.
[2] *Op. cit.*, p. 237.
[3] 'Dans l'intervalle des piliers du portique on pouvait glisser les panneaux de
decoration,' T. Homolle, *B.C.H.* 18 (1894), 167.
[4] *Ibid.*, pp. 225ff.
[5] Bulle, *ibid.*, p. 110–31, 131–52, pls. 23, 25, 37.
[6] Vallois, *ibid.*, p. 224.

SCENERY

The panels of the façade constituted the scenery. The *skenai* were attached to the stage front with pegs (*I.G.* 199 A 64) and were removable.[1] Thus the tragic scenery could give way to the comic and so on. Change of scenery between similar plays, though not technically impossible, is not probable, because the scenery was commissioned by the *hieropoioi* together with much other work in the theatre without regard to particular plays. Nevertheless an ambitious producer could provide a special set for a particular play. (See App. I, p. 132, and, on the use of the *periaktoi*, p. 135.)

The word *skene* with the meaning of scenery occurs for the first time in 296 B.C. (*I.G.* xi 154 A 43). In 274 B.C. new *skenai* were made and some old ones repaired. The whole lot and the panels of the *paraskenia* were painted for 2500 drachmai, a vast amount indeed. But the painted area was also very big. A workman sawed 1110 ells of wood for the *skenai* and was paid 8 *chalkoi* ($\frac{1}{12}$th of an obol) for each ell. That is to say he sawed logs or lumber into boards fit for panel-making, and the total length of the boards sawn was found to be 1110 ells:
Ἀριστογείτωι Κορινθίωι ἐγλαβόντι τὴν πρισμὴν τῶν ξ[ύλ]ων τῶν εἰς τὰς σκηνὰς τὸμ πῆχυ[ν......]δα χαλκῶν [ὀκτ]ὼ ἀπε-[λογισά]μεθα μετὰ τοῦ ἀρχιτέκτονος| [κ]αὶ τῶν ἐπιμελητῶν Ἀρησιμβρότου καὶ Ἀνδρομένους πή[χεις] χιλίους ἑκατὸν δέκα (*I.G.* xi 199 A 89–90).

The figure 1110 represents only one 'dimension' of the sawing. However, for an accurate calculation of the amount of work done by the carpenter Aristogeitos the second dimension of the sawing, or the (average) width of the boards, would be necessary, and was actually stated. A new examination of the stone which I made at the Museum of Delos with the help of Dr. Jan Pečírka of Prague enabled me to distinguish traces of some more letters than Durrbach had seen. The part of l. 89 in question can be restored as followed: ἐγλαβόντι τὴν πρισμὴν τῶν ξ[ύλ]ων τῶν εἰς τὰς σκηνὰς τὸμ πῆχυν [ἐπ]ι̣[2] τὸν πόδα

---

[1] See *I.G.* xi 154 A 43; *I.D.* 403.45.

[2] In the place of the two bracketed letters there are some deep scratches which would suggest a Γ or Σ, and a Δ. Of these the latter does not make any sense and in view of the whole passage I am inclined to take it as an odd combination of

χαλκῶν [ὀκτ]ώ, etc. So the total area of the boards, which our carpenter produced for the construction of *skenai*, was 1110 ells by 1 foot, or 455 m by 0·31 m, that is about 141 square metres. Even if the two painters who received the 2500 dr. were to paint this area only, which at any rate was enough to cover the two-storeyed *scenae frons* above the *proskenion* and the flanks of the building, their fees would have been much more reasonable than those paid in 282 B.C. for the *pinakes* of the *proskenion*.[1] In addition they were to paint the repaired *skenai* and the *paraskenia*.[2] About the men who did the job, Goneus and Asklepiades, we know nothing. Were they fashionable and expensive painters? It cannot be ruled out, though it does not appear to be very likely, to judge from the equally expensive painters of 282, Antidotos and Herakleides, who used to do other jobs of much less artistic prestige. The former painted white the lilies of the ceiling and gilded the rosettes of the capitals of Asklepios' temple in 279 for 44 dr. (*I.G.* xi 161 A 72–3). The latter painted the '*agalma*' of Dionysus, i.e. the phallus carried at the procession of Dionysia, in 282 for 3 dr. (*I.G.* xi 158 A 71). Therefore such expensive *skenai* must have been very elaborately decorated, perhaps with realistic pictures drawn in perspective of columns, pediments, statues, and other objects befitting a king's palace, or private houses with balconies and windows, or landscapes with trees, caves, mountains and other rustic things (Vitr. V 6, 9).[3] The valuable panels

scratches. The last letter of the following word, τόν, is rather a ν than a μ which one would normally expect. However, the stone cutter does not observe his phonetic conventions very strictly: cp. τῶμ πρός (l. A 9), τῶν πρός (l. A 8); τὴμ παλαίστραν (ll. A 29, 30, 34, 40, 41, 60, 64, 65), τὴν παλαίστραν (ll. A 53, 54, 58, 60); τὴμ πρώτην (l. A 97), τὴν πρώτην (ll. A 99, 105, 114), etc.

[1] 100 dr. for the painting of an area less than 3·5 m², a total of 1100 dr. for less than 40 m².

[2] But we might suppose that the panels of the *paraskenia* were made of the newly sawn boards.

[3] I am aware that this description of scene-painting by Vitruvius has been connected with the *thyromata* of the late Hellenistic (c. 150 B.C.) *scenae frons* (Oropos, Priene, Ephesos), and with the development of landscape-painting dated to the second quarter of the second century B.C. by A. Rumpf, *J.H.S.* 67 (1947), 17–19. The originals of the wall-paintings from the cubiculum of the Villa Boscoreale in New York, which are usually taken as illustrations of Vitruvius' description (the case made by P. W. Lehmann, *Roman Wall Paintings from Boscoreale in the Metropolitan Museum of Art*, Cambridge, Mass., 1953, pp. 90ff., against the theatrical character of the frescoes is not very strong), are dated by Rumpf to the same period

were removed and stored after the performances. In the second century a special warehouse, a *skenotheke*,[1] was erected for this purpose.

MECHANICAL EQUIPMENT

The big account of 274 B.C. (*I.G.* xi 199) yields some information about the stage properties too. The same carpenter who repaired the old *skenai*, repaired τὰ ἔξωστρα καὶ τὴν κλίμακα καὶ τοὺς βωμοὺς as well (ll. A 95–6). We need hardly say that this passage does not concern any permanent altar in the orchestra but some wooden and, most probably, movable altars which would be placed on the *logeion* according to the requirements of the plays. It also implies more than one *ekkyklema*.[2] The staircase might of course be inside the building. But there are some good reasons to believe it was a visible feature of the theatre, and it led in fact from the orchestra to the high stage (see App. I, p. 132).

One more thing needs our attention, and that is the *torniskos* or *tornos*, which was constructed in 279 B.C. by a carpenter for .ΔΔ, i.e. 30 or 70 or 120 dr., excluding the value of timber (*I.G.* xi 161 A 65, 162 A 53). This object had obviously something to do with revolving, and according to Homolle it was a part of the decoration or the machinery of the theatre.[3] Bulle understood it as 'Schwebekrahn'[4] but his opinion is not very plausible because it is not certain whether the crane was used

because 'pictures of such size could not have been painted on the small *pinakes* between the half-columns of the proscenium-front. They must have been wooden panels set as *thyromata* in the large openings of the scene itself which was over the roof of the proscenium' (*loc. cit.*, p. 18). Rumpf appears to think that before the introduction of the *thyromata* the plays were performed on the ground level with the *pinakes* of the *proskenion* as a background (on the question of *proskenion* see App. I). In Delos, however, we have a clear distinction between *pinakes* and *skenai* of the *logeion* level already in the third century. The latter were certainly much larger panels than the former. And although landscape-painting may have been a later development, perspective painting was used in theatrical decoration already in the second part of the fifth century (Agatharchos; Rumpf, *loc. cit.*, p. 13).

[1] *I.D.* 444 B 104 (177 B.C.).

[2] Pollux, IV 129, gives the feminine form, ἡ ἐξώστρα: τὴν δ'ἐξώστραν ταὐτὸν τῷ ἐκκυκλήματι νομίζουσιν. He also states that each door had an *ekkyklema*, ἵν' ᾗ καθ'ἑκάστην οἰκίαν (IV 128).

[3] *B.C.H.* 14 (1890), 472.

[4] *Op. cit.*, pp. 181–2. Cf. Webster, *Gr. Bühnenalt.*, p. 41 ('vielleicht mechane').

at the Hellenistic theatre at all, and the name *tornos* hardly applies to a machine that may turn partially round but does not revolve. The *ekkyklema* should be eliminated as well. The name *exostron* used in Delos implies a platform pushed outwards. So we might perhaps take it as one of the μηχαναὶ πρὸς αἷς αἱ περίακτοι συμπεπήγασιν (Pollux IV 126).

CHAPTER VII

DRAMATIC MONUMENTS

A large number of dramatic antiquities have been discovered in Delos. I do not propose to make a detailed study of these monuments here, because most of them have been published, discussed, and interpreted, in excellent modern works which are easily available. The list that follows below aims at bringing together all the objects in question.[1] Comic mosaics and terracottas which were recently classified and identified with Pollux' mask types by Professor Webster in his *Monuments Illustrating New Comedy* (1961) are not described here again.

Satyric:

(i) Bronze relief showing two young satyrs in loincloths making sacrifice to Artemis, F. Courby, *Mon. Piot*, 18 (1910), 21ff., pl. VI; R. Vallois, *B.C.H.* 45 (1921), 242ff., fig. 2; Webster, *M.T.S.* DB 1; Bieber, *Hellenistic Sculpture*, fig. 651; Ph. Bruneau—J. Ducat, *Guide de Délos*, Paris 1965, pl. 8/2.

(ii) Two marble statues of *papposilenoi* in theatrical costume, *B.C.H.* 58–9 (1944–5), 259–50, figs. 10–11.

Tragic:

(i) Mosaic representing Dionysos in tragic costume riding a leopard, *Délos* xiv, pp. 11ff., p. 3; Rumpf, *Malerei und Zeichnung*, pl. 56/7; Webster, *M.T.S.* DM 1, *Griech. Bühnenalt.*, pp. 42, 49, 62; Bruneau—Ducat, *ibid.*, pl. 14/2; C. M. Robertson, *J.H.S.* 85 (1965), 88–9, suggests that the figure on the leopard is female.

(ii) Grave stele with a draped man (head wanting) and a mask of a woman (?) with low *onkos* lying on the ground by his right foot, *Délos* ii, p. 62, n. 6, fig. 88.

(iii) Little bronze mask, ornamental addition to a vase, *Délos* xviii, p. 323, n. 13.

(iv) Plastic vase in form of a tragic mask, *Délos* xviii, p. 323, n. 12.

(v) Fragment of a tragic terracotta mask (?), *Délos* xxiii, no. 1243, cf. *M.N.C.* DT 24.

[1] But see Addendum to ch. VII, p. 56.

Comic:

(i) Mosaics: 10 masks, and a slave dancing before a flautist, *Délos* xiv, pp. 26ff., pl. 4–7, Webster, *M.N.C.* DM 1–2, *Griech. Bühnenalt.*, pp. 42, 63.

(ii) Three masks of old men and one of a slave preserved on two fragmentary marble tripods (p. 38) lying in the theatre, *Délos* xviii, p. 71, pl. 30/217–18 (masks not mentioned, and indistinguishable in the photographs). For similar structures see *Délos* xviii, p. 70, pl. 30/216, *Milet* i.2, pp. 90–4, pl. 19–20, *Milet* i.6, pp. 70–2, pl. 22, *Ath. Mitt.* 27 (1902), 91. For comparable monuments of *agonothetai* at Athens see E. G. Stikas, *Arch. Ephemeris*, 1961, pp. 163–6, figs. 9–13.

(iii) Plastic vase in form of a *panchrestos* mask (Webster) published as tragic in *B.C.H.* 30 (1906), 605, fig. 49.

(iv) Terracottas: 17 masks, 6 statuettes plus 3 heads of statuettes, 4 heads, and 4 lamp lids, *Délos* xxiii, nos. 1216–49, 1285–9; Webster, *M.N.C.* DT 1–29, *Gr. Bühnenalt.*, pp. 42, 56, 63. Three more masks were published in 1961 by G. Daux, *B.C.H.* 85 (1961) 915–17, figs. 7, 8, 9, as διάχρυσος ἑταίρα, κάτω τριχίας and λυκαίνιον respectively (Pollux IV 143ff.). Fig. 9 is very much like *M.N.C.* AV 25, and is therefore an οἰκουρὸν γράδιον. I think that fig. 8 is an ἐπίσειστος ἡγεμὼν comparable to *M.N.C.* AT 29, DT 23, IS 17, IT 64. Fig. 7 looks very young for the διάχρυσος and Professor Webster supposes that she is the ἑταιρίδιον.

In addition to the above monuments some wall-paintings were recently discovered in the main room of a house excavated for the first time in 1951 at the bay of Skardhana. Seven panels 20 cm high and of variable length showing tragic and comic scenes run continuous to each other. They are distinguished only by the alternating black and red-brown colours of the background, but do not seem interrelated. Of these only a tragic scene (Oedipus and Antigone?), and a picture of a comic leading slave have been published (Daux, *B.C.H.* 87 [1963], 870, fig. 15, 872, fig. 19). The 'Maison des Comédiens', as it has been named, dates from the second part of the second century B.C.

We must not fail to mention here a number of masks on terracotta braziers found in Delos. There are eight comic masks (*M.N.C.* AV 25 = *B.C.H.* 85 [1961], 495–8, figs. 26–8; *M.N.C.* AV 27; *M.N.C.* AV 31 = *B.C.H. ibid.* 490, fig. 18;

M.N.C. AV 33 = *B.C.H. ibid.* 494, fig. 23; *B.C.H. ibid.* 494–5, figs. 24–5), and a tragic Herakles (published as μέλας νεανίσκος, *B.C.H. ibid.* 493, fig. 22). Similar braziers have been found in other islands, the Greek mainland, and Asia Minor. Conze[1] had suggested Athens as their place of manufacture, but Chr. Le Roy[2] recently argued that the centre of their distribution was Alexandria.

Nearly all the dramatic monuments found in Delos date from the second and early first centuries (Athenian period), and so counterbalance the inscriptions of the third century.[3] As far as the terracottas are concerned, it is not accidental that we have almost no pieces inspired by the theatre production of early Hellenistic times. The art of coroplasts flourished in Delos after the middle of the second century, and, except for the archaic terracottas, finds of this kind that can be dated before 150 B.C. are very scarce indeed.

Comedy, as usual, is much better represented. The people of the New Comedy stage, old men and youths, slaves, braggard soldiers, procurers and hetairai, inspired the mosaicists and coroplasts to a much greater extent than the tragic heroes. It is likely that the magic qualities attributed to comic terracottas would have affected the taste for them but, in spite of that, all the above works of decorative art, comic and tragic, reflect an image of the popularity of drama.

Unfortunately, we cannot also say that they illustrate a particular, local style of play production. Except for two mosaic masks showing Pan as an old man of New Comedy with long beard and horns (one is reminded of the initial scene of the *Dyskolos*), and a satyr more or less like a bearded slave, almost all the rest belong to types known by hundreds of similar monuments discovered around the Mediterranean. The masks were the most personal articles of actors' equipment, and were probably made to fit a particular face, or rather head.[4] In consequence they must have been the personal property of

---

[1] *J.d.I.* 5 (1890), 141.

[2] 'Réchauds Déliens', *B.C.H.* 85 (1961), 474–500.

[3] A fragmentary terracotta mask dates from the second century A.D., *Délos* xxiii, no. 1387, *M.T.S.* DT 29. A statuette and a mask are considered by Professor Webster as 'perhaps early Hellenistic', *M.T.S.*, DT 20, 25.

[4] I owe this suggestion to Professor Webster.

each actor, and not of σκευοποιός or ἱματιομίσθης. We know actually two cases of actors who dedicated their masks in the temples of Apollo in Delos (*I.D.* 1421 Bb 19–20), and of Dionysos in Teos (Le Bas—Wad. 92) in token of reverence, as the flute-player Satyros (see pp. 22, 96) offered his instrument to Apollo (*I.D.* 442 B 62). And to the evidence of inscriptions testifying to dedications of masks by actors we must add Callimachus' epigram on Agoranax of Rhodes (49 Pf.), and a well-known painting from Herculaneum representing an actor, who has just taken off his mask, and a kneeling figure writing an inscription beneath the mask, which is placed in its receptacle upon a low pillar on the left of the seated actor.[1] Taking into account the widely separated places in which actors performed, it will appear not surprising that the masks should soon have become standardized. Besides, the characters of New Comedy, and to some extent those of tragedy— owing to repetition of the same legends—had become types already before the end of the fourth century; and this certainly helped the standardization of masks.

In any event, although the finds of Delos throw no light upon aspects of production which may have been peculiar to Delos, viz. stage arrangement and scenery, they nevertheless represent the dramatic characters seen on the Delian stage, and contribute a good deal towards our visualizing the ὄψις of late Hellenistic comedy.

ADDENDUM

The known number of dramatic monuments found in Delos has now been considerably increased by the publication of *Délos* xxvi: *Les lampes* (Paris, 1965) by Philippe Bruneau. About 260 terracotta lamps and a bronze one—out of a total number of 4786—are decorated with theatrical masks (see Index under 'masque de théâtre'). Almost all the lamps with dramatic subjects are dated in the latter half of the second and the first quarter of the first century B.C. Most of them (about 190) belong to the so-called 'Ephesos type', others belong to types associated

[1] M. Bieber, *The History of the Greek and Roman Theater*,[2] fig. 302; Pickard-Cambridge, *Festivals*, fig. 43; *M.T.S.* NP 33.

with Knidos or Pergamon, but none to the 'Delos type'. The masks of leading slaves (nos. 1828ff., 1981ff., 2235ff., 2344ff., 2423f., 2466ff., 2735ff., 4258ff., 4409ff.) and old men (nos. 2252ff., 2332ff., 4184ff., 4202ff.) predominate. Dramatic silens also occur frequently (nos. 2437, 2502ff., 2601ff., 2609, 2903ff., 3178f.), and sometimes it is very difficult to distinguish a *papposilenos* from a *pornoboskos* (e.g. nos. 2499, 2616, 2658, 2718ff., 2833, 4202ff., etc.); no. 4602 (late Roman) is the only satyr mask. No. 2716 has a perfectly circular mouth and may be a slave (or the *agroikos*?). No. 2732 is probably the *maison*. No. 2914 has an uncommon, wide-faced mask with massive beard and hair—but no *onkos*—, and swinging brows (could it be tragic?). No. 3035 is a finely modelled *leno*, bald, with swinging brows, hooked nose, trumpet-mouth, long flowing beard, described as 'portant sur chaque tempe deux baies de lierre' (but they may be tufts of curly hair, cf. no. 2915). No. 3187 is not published but is described as having a 'masque de vieille femme'; if so, it seems to be the only one with a female mask because no. 4280, although it looks like a round-faced woman, has a big mouth—almost a trumpet—, and may be a parasite. No. 3211 is decorated with three masks of *agroikoi*. No. 4219 has an uncommon, wide-faced mask, very finely modelled, with rich flowing beard—not very long—, wide twisted mouth—but no trumpet—, raised brows, marked pupils, hooked nose, large ears, a band or perhaps an ivy wreath round the forehead, and a fierce expression. No. 4402 has rough hair and beard united in a circle, and a semi-circular mouth (?comic; poorly modelled). Nos. 4764–7 are plastic lamps in form of a mask; no. 4765 is a wavy-haired leading slave; no. 4766 is a late Roman leading slave with striated hair and trumpet, and highly stylized forehead wrinkles and raised brows; no. 4767 (fragmentary) is a leading slave; no. 4764 (fragmentary) has an almost closed mouth, and may not be dramatic. The bronze lamp no. 4781 has a late Hellenistic leading slave on its lid.

PART II
Delphi

CHAPTER VIII

EARLIEST EVIDENCE FOR DRAMA
IN DELPHI

No other god except Apollo was so closely connected with, and worshipped at, Delphi as Dionysos,[1] yet drama had no share in the festivities of his cult. Drama was a development of Dionysiac rites in Attica, but at the time of its great expansion the Dionysiac character had become merely nominal. This is probably the reason why dramatic performances were not introduced into the orgiastic cult of Dionysos which was deeply rooted in a very old and highly respected Delphian tradition. Our evidence shows that drama at Delphi was associated with Apollo. But when plays were mounted on the Delphian stage for the first time we do not know. Three comic terracotta figurines found in Delphi and dated to the second quarter of the fourth century B.C. can hardly be considered as evidence for local performances. Two of them belong to well-known Attic types, copies of which have been discovered at places as far away from each other as the Crimea and South Italy, and all three were in all likelihood made in Athens (see p. 108). Nor has the generous subscription of the famous tragic actor Theodoros of Athens to the fund for the reconstruction of Apollo's temple (*F.D.* iii.5 3.67 = *S.I.G.*³ 239 B 67, 363/2–361/0 B.C.) an immediate bearing on the theatrical history of Delphi. However, the terracottas as well as Theodoros' 'interest in Delphi'[2] suggest that drama was

---

[1] L. R. Farnell, *The Cults of the Greek States*, v, pp. 112ff., 153, 173, 177ff., 186f., 193, 196; U. v. Wilamowitz, *Der Glaube der Hellenen*, ii, pp. 60, 66, 74; W. F. Otto, *Dionysos* (1933), pp. 187ff.; O. Kern, *Die Religion der Griechen*, ii, pp. 116ff.; E. Rohde, *Psyche* (transl. by W. B. Hillis, 1925), pp. 287 ff.; H. Jeanmaire, *Dionysos* (1951), pp. 187–98, 492–3; M. Nilsson, *Gr. Feste*, pp. 283–5, *Gesch. d. gr. Rel.*, i, pp. 536ff., *The Dionysiac Mysteries of the Hellenistic and Roman Age*, pp. 4ff., 38ff.; W. Fauth, *R.E.* xxiv 538f.

[2] Webster, *Gr. Bühnenalt.*, p. 39. A. Nikitsky identified two more subscribers listed before and after Theodoros as Athenian artists with a certain amount of plausibility, cf. *S.I.G.*³ 239 B, n. 11. On Theodoros see *S.I.G.*,³ *loc. cit.*, Wilhelm, *Urkunden*, pp. 250–1, O'Connor, *Chapters in the Hist. of Actors and Acting*, p. 100, no. 230.

not unknown to the Delphians of the first part of the fourth century. The construction of the theatre in stone is now firmly dated to the late fourth century, but it is likely that a theatre of wood occupied the same place in the sanctuary of Apollo even earlier.[1] One might suppose that the theatre was used for the musical performances of the Pythia but this is not the case, for the contests of music took place in the Pythian stadium as late as the second half of the third century, long after the theatre had been built. A kind of stage called *skene*[2] in the fourth century and *proskanion*[3] in the third century was constructed for that purpose in the stadium every time the Pythian Games were to be held, and dismantled when the festival was over. At all events, the earliest concrete evidence for dramatic performances is a group of third century inscriptions pertaining to the festival of Soteria.

---

[1] F. Schober, *R.E.* Suppl. v.138.

[2] τὴν|¹⁹ σκην[ὴν τὴν τ]οῦ πυθικοῦ σ[ταδίου, *F.D.* iii.5 75, col. II 19, late fourth century B.C. On the use of the Ionic-Attic *koine* see E. Bourguet, *F.D.*, *loc. cit.*, p. 24.

[3] τοῦ προσκανίου τὴν πᾶξιν ἐν τ[ῶι]|²⁹ πυθικῶι σταδίωι Νίκων· ΠΣ·, *B.C.H.* 23 (1899), 566–7, 247/6? B.C. (archon Dion, Daux, *Chronologie*, K 1). A similar '*proskanion*' was set up every year for the festival of Herakleia, *S.I.G.*³ 481 B. On this inscription see A. Wilhelm, *Anzeiger der phil.-hist. Kl. d. Akad. d. Wiss. in Wien*, 1922, No. vii, p. 8, and G. Daux, *Rev. Phil.* 8 (1934), 361–6.

CHAPTER IX

SOTERIA

THE HISTORICAL PROBLEM

The Soteria was a festival instituted at Delphi to commemorate the salvation of the Oracle, and indeed of Greece, from the Gauls (279/8 B.C.). Twenty or so records of contestants or winners at the musical and dramatic events of the festival have been preserved on stone. We also possess decrees of six cities answering an invitation of the Aitolians to recognize the Soteria.[1] These documents constitute an important source for the history of the third century, and particularly for the chronology of Delphi, as well as that of Athens. They have therefore been extensively discussed, though little advance has been made in about forty years towards a general agreement on their interpretation and dating. It would be outside the compass of the present study to give here an account of the dispute over the foundation of the Soteria and the chronological problems raised by the inscriptions. This dispute, which still goes on, started when the Athenian archon Polyeuktos, and consequently the Athenian acceptance of the Soteria, was shown by a Salaminian inscription published in 1923 (*S.E.G.* ii 9) to date more than twenty years after the Gallic invasion. It will suffice for my purpose to repeat the points which are more or less commonly agreed upon, or seem to turn the scale of probability.

The Soteria was founded by the city of Delphi and the Amphictyony soon after the Gauls had been repulsed. It comprised musical and dramatic contests, and was held in honour of 'the god', namely Apollo, sometime between midsummer

---

[1] These decrees are: *I.G.* ii² 680 = *S.I.G.*³ 408, Athens; *S.I.G.*³ 402, Chios; *F.D.* iii.1 482, Tenos; *F.D.* iii.1 481, another island of the Cyclades possibly Ios or Andros, L. Robert, *B.C.H.* 54 (1930), 322–6; *F.D.* iii.1 483, Smyrna, Robert, *loc. cit.*, 327ff., M. Segre, *Historia* 5 (1931), 241ff.; and *B.C.H.* 64–5 (1940–1), 100ff., Abdera. For the lists of contestants and victors see pp. 73–4, 83.

and the autumn equinox every year.[1] The agonistic inscriptions relating to this festival contain all the participants in the contests, and are dated by the names of the Delphian archon, the delegates to the Amphictyonic Council (hieromnemons), and a priest of the Dionysiac artists.

Around the middle of the third century the Aitolians, who had occupied Delphi since the beginning of the century, reorganized the Soteria, and placed it under the auspices of their confederation and the management of an Aitolian *agonothetes*. At that time they probably changed the periodicity of the festival from annual to quadrennial, enlarged it to include athletic contests, and asked the Greek cities to recognize its musical contests as isopythian, and the gymnic and hippic ones as isonemean, which means that the Soteria became an ἀγὼν στεφανίτης, like all the great panhellenic games, being presumably an ἀγὼν χρηματίτης before the reformation.[2] Finally, besides Apollo, Zeus Soter would also be honoured by the new festival. So the only thing that remained unaltered was actually the *raison d'être* of the festival which was established and held 'in memory of the battle against the barbarians who marched against the Greeks, and Apollo's common sanctuary of the Greeks' (*I.G.* ix.1 [2] 194 a). After all, that battle had been fought chiefly by Aitolian forces. In addition to the surviving six acceptances, eleven records including only the victors and dated by the Aitolian *agonothetes* and the hieromnemons pertain to this festival.[3]

The motive of the reformation was merely political. The Aitolians themselves had encroached on Delphi and 'Apollo's common sanctuary of the Greeks' long before the Gallic invasion,[4] something which the other Greeks, with few excep-

---

[1] Beloch, *Griech. Gesch.*,[2] iv.2, p. 492.

[2] P. Roussel, *R.É.A.* 26 (1924), 107; R. Flacelière, *Aitoliens*, p. 140.

[3] Roussel in his fundamental article 'La fondation des Sôtéria de Delphes', *R.É.A.* 26 (1924), 97–110, was the first to perceive that the assumption of the reorganization was imposed by the evidence after the discovery of Polyeuktos' approximate date. Several scholars (Beloch, De Sanctis, Kirchner, Kolbe) objected to this theory then, but the progress which has been made in the study of the Athenian, and the Delphian, chronology in the last twenty-five years or so has corroborated Roussel's thesis.

[4] Between 301 and 298, Flacelière, *Aitoliens*, p. 57.

tions,[1] did not condone though they could do nothing about it. In 290 B.C. Demetrios Poliorketes celebrated the Pythia in Athens, his action being 'a protest against the Aitolian occupation of Delphi in the eyes of the whole Greek world' (Beloch),[2] but failed to drive them out of the holy city. The Gallic war and the prime part the Aitolians played in it reinforced their position in Delphi. Immediately after the war they got two votes in the Amphictyonic Council for the first time, in the subsequent year they were represented by three hieromnemons, and not later than c. 262 they came to dominate the Amphictyony by an absolute majority.[3] Having reached the peak of their power round the middle of the century the Aitolians decided to elicit some kind of formal recognition of the Delphian *status quo*. The reformation of the Soteria was aimed at obtaining this recognition. In the first place they tried to pose as founders of a new panhellenic festival. To achieve this they transformed the Soteria as far as possible, whereas in the wording of the invitation which they launched into the Greek world any correlation or reference to the older Soteria was carefully avoided. The Greek cities were asked to accept the festival which 'the confederation of the Aitolians manifesting its piety to the gods had decreed to set up ($\tau\iota\theta\acute{\epsilon}\nu\alpha\iota$)... in honour of Zeus Soter and Apollo Pythios' (*S.I.G.*[3] 408, *I.G.* ix.1[2] 194). And acceptance of an Aitolian festival to be held at Delphi would ultimately mean recognition of the Aitolian domination of the Delphian territory by the other Greeks.

The date of the re-foundation of the Soteria has been keenly disputed. The crucial point is whether all the acceptances are of the same date or not. The year 246 B.C. has been shown by L. Robert[4] as the *terminus post quem* of the Smyrnian decree, and consequently, according to him, of the other acceptances as well as of the foundation of the Aitolian Soteria. But Ferguson[5] was of opinion that the various acceptances of the invitation

---

[1] The Boeotians and a part of the Phocians were allies of the Aitolians, Flacelière, *op. cit.*, pp. 57ff.

[2] *Griech. Gesch.*,[2] iv.1, p. 227.

[3] Flacelière, *op. cit.*, p. 367.

[4] *B.C.H.* 54 (1930), 331–2, *R.É.A.* 38 (1936), 9–10.

[5] *Athenian Tribal Cycles*, pp. 128–31, *A.J.P.* 55 (1934), 322. Ferguson changed his mind later about Polyeuktos whom he placed in 243/2, *Hesperia* 8 (1938), 69.

were not necessarily synchronous, and argued that his date of
Polyeuktos, 255/4 B.C., could be reconciled with an answer by
Smyrna even as late as 243/2. Dinsmoor would not be in full
agreement with this theory, though he considered it right in
principle, and felt that a few years' difference between decrees
was quite possible. So the top date of the Smyrnian decree did
not prevent him from placing Polyeuktos and the Aitolian
foundation in 248/7.[1] More recently[2] he returned to the date
he had originally[3] proposed for Polyeuktos, 249/8. The same
year was assigned to Polyeuktos by W. K. Pritchett and
B. D. Meritt,[4] and was retained in the list of Athenian archons
included in Meritt's *Athenian Year*, p. 234. However, the latest
contributor to this question, Chr. Pelekidis,[5] shifted Polyeuktos
to 247/6 and the first celebration of the Soteria to the next
year, 246/5, which is a Pythian year, on the ground of the
Smyrnian acceptance, and the assumption that the Aitolian
Soteria was a quadrennial festival held in the same years
as the Pythia. But Pelekidis has not succeeded in settling
the question because the assumption that the Pythia and the
Soteria concurred in the same years is debatable, as we shall
see.

The quadrennial periodicity is suggested by the answer of
Chios stating that the Chian *theoroi* for the Soteria were to be
elected every fifth year at the same time when the *theoroi* for
some other festival were chosen: γίνεσ[θαι δὲ εἰς τὸ λοιπὸν] τὴν
ἀπόδειξιν τῶν θεωρῶν καθ' ἑκάστην πενταετηρίδα ὅταν καὶ—c. 18
letters—ωνται (*S.I.G.*[3] 402₂₈₋₃₀). The restoration of the missing
festival depends upon deciding whether the Soteria was celebrated in Pythian or Olympic years.[6] The clue for this decision
is supposed to be provided by an inscribed sepulchral urn containing the ashes of Sotion, a Delphian *theoros*, who died and

---

[1] *Athenian Archon List*, p. 118.

[2] *Hesperia* 23 (1954), 315.

[3] *Archons of Athens* (1931), pp. 112ff.

[4] *The Chronology of Hellenistic Athens* (1940), p. xxi.

[5] 'L'archonte athénien Polyeuktos (247/6)', *B.C.H.* 85 (1961), 53–68.

[6] Pomtow restored at first ὅταν καὶ [οἱ εἰς τὰ Πύθια καθιστ]ῶνται, *S.I.G.*[2] 206, and
later ὅταν καὶ [οἱ εἰς τὰ Ὀλύμπια αἱρέ]ωνται, *S.I.G.*[3] 402. G. De Sanctis, *Riv. Fil.*
N.s. 7 (1929), 571–2, proposed the restoration ὅταν καὶ [οἱ λοιποὶ θεωροὶ καθι-
στ]ῶνται supposing that the cities elected their *theoroi* for all festivals at the same
time, but he was refuted by L. Robert, *R.É.A.* 38 (1936), 10, n. 8.

43208

was buried at the Hadra necropolis, east of Alexandria, by Theodotos *agorastes*,[1] a Ptolemaic official, while proclaiming the Soteria in the ninth year of one of the Ptolemies.[2] Would that year be Olympic or Pythian? The ninth year and Theodotos figure again in the inscriptions of two similar sepulchral vases, one of which bears in addition to the regnal year a Macedonian and an Egyptian month and day: Hyperberetaios 30, Pharmouthi 7.[3] This equation confined to the ninth year of a Ptolemy of the third century has furnished the clue to dating the vases in question to the reign of Ptolemy IV Philopator. In terms of absolute chronology the date was fixed as May 19, 212 B.C. by Beloch[4] and Dinsmoor.[5] 212 is an Olympic year, and this was for Dinsmoor as good as proof that the Soteria were celebrated in Olympic years.[6] He therefore distributed the eleven lists of winners, the relative order of which is fairly certain, in the years of the Olympic Games beginning from 248/7 and ending in 208/7.[7] This arrangement conforms to the date the American specialists on Athenian chronology have given to Polyeuktos, 249/8, though it presupposes that the acceptance of Smyrna post-dates the first celebration of the festival. Daux concurred with Dinsmoor as regards the Olympic years. But he thought that the latter's scheme might be one Olympiad too high and dated the archons Praochos II, Herys, and Kallias, in 240/39? or 244/3?, 228/7? or 232/1?, and 220/19? or 224/3? respectively.[8] These are the only Delphian archons in whose

---

[1] About this office see P. M. Fraser, *J.E.A.* 39 (1953), 87, n. 7.

[2] *O.G.I.S.* 36; Breccia, *Catal. gener. du Musée d'Alexandrie, Iscrizioni greche e latine*, p. xvii, no. 14; Pagenstecher, *A.J.A.* 13 (1909), 408, no. 23; Braunert, *J.d.I.* 65/6 (1950/1), 237, no. 26.

[3] *S.B.* 1642; Breccia, *loc. cit.*, p. xvi, no. 13; Pagenstecher, *loc. cit.*, 408, no. 22; Braunert, *loc. cit.*, 237, no. 25.

[4] *Gr. Gesch.*,[2] iv.2, pp. 42, 494–6.

[5] *Archons of Athens*, pp. 124–5, 136, 471, 491, *Athenian Archon List*, pp. 123–6.

[6] Another inscription of 157/6 (arch. Patreas) seems to support the occurrence of the Soteria in Olympic years. It is a Delphian decree honouring an Alexandrian because of his hospitality toward two Delphian *theoroi*. The publication of the decree was to be taken care of by the *epimeletai* of the Soteria. It has been suggested that the two *theoroi* were in charge of proclaiming the Soteria of 156; L. Couve, *B.C.H.* 18 (1894), 248–54; *S.G.D.I.* 2737; *O.G.I.S.* 150, Daux, *Delphes*, p. 516; Dinsmoor, *List*, p. 126.

[7] *List*, pp. 128ff.

[8] *Chronologie delphique*, K 5, K 7, K 9.

years Soteria were certainly celebrated, and had been ascribed
by Dinsmoor to the higher of the above dates.

However, recent studies in Egyptian chronology have shown
that Dinsmoor's calculations of Sotion's date were inaccurate.
According to T. C. Skeat's[1] tables Pharmouthi 7 is equated with
May 19, 213. But the double-dated vase is not that of Sotion
but of a Rhodian called Timasitheos. Sotion's urn bears only
the regnal year. The accession of Ptolemy IV was fixed by
Skeat between 5 and 16 February 221. Accordingly his ninth
year falls between February 213 and February 212. But in the
latest work on the subject A. E. Samuel[2] shifted the accession
date a few months earlier, between October 18 and December
21, 222. Moreover, Samuel argued that 'the date used during
this (Philopator's) reign for the beginning of the Macedonian
regnal year was in (the Macedonian month) Dystros. This date
was not the anniversary of the accession but rather due to a
continuation of the practice of the reign of Philadelphus, which
continued through the reign of Euergetes.'[3] In other words, the
ninth year of Philopator should begin late in September 214.[4]
So the earliest possible date of Sotion's death is September 214,
and the latest September 213. We have seen that the Soteria
was celebrated in autumn. If it was held in Pythian years
Sotion could not have announced the festival of 214 unless he
had gone to Egypt several months before his death. On the
other hand, if the Soteria was held in Olympic years it is unlikely that Sotion had gone to proclaim the festival of 212 at
least one year before its celebration. In conclusion, it must be
admitted that nothing definite can in fact be based on the
delicate dating of Sotion as far as the concurrence of the Soteria
with the Olympic or Pythian Games is concerned.

So far we have taken for granted the quadrennial periodicity
of the Aitolian Soteria. Yet one should not fail to note that the

---

[1] *The Reigns of the Ptolemies*, Münchener Beitr. z. Papyrusforschung u. ant.
Rechtsgesch. 39, 1954.

[2] *Ptolemaic Chronology*, Münchener Beitr. z. Papyrusforschung u. ant. Rechtsgesch. 43, 1962, p. 114.

[3] *Ibid.*, p. 108.

[4] According to Samuel (*ibid.*, p. 167, Table D) the ninth year of Philopator
began approximately on Mesore 16, which is equated on Skeat's tables with
September 26, 214.

arrangement of the eleven records of winners at four year intervals over the second half of the third century raises some
difficulties which have made several scholars suggest different
systems (annual, biennial, change from quadrennial to annual,
etc.).[1] Firstly, it presupposes that no list has been lost, and
leaves no room before 208 (or 204?) for any other record that
might incidentally turn up. Nor would the composition of the
Amphictyonic Council recorded in the lists allow the present
arrangement to be stretched over a longer period.[2] Secondly,
none of these inscriptions includes athletes. Yet, as we have
seen, the Aitolians introduced to the Soteria gymnic and hippic
contests modelled after the Nemean Games (ἰσονέμεος ταῖς
ἡλικίαις), and asked the cities to confer upon the victors of the
Soteria the same honours as those accorded to the Nemean
victors (ἰσονέμεος ταῖς τιμαῖς). Now Roussel[3] and Flacelière[4]
may be right in that the Soteria fell short of its founders' ambition to set up and maintain a great and much more important
festival than the Amphictyonic, and that athletic contests did
not take place 'que de loin en loin, faute de concurrents, ou
pour toute autre raison qui nous échappe' (Flacelière). But
such contests did in fact take place. We have a considerable
number of inscriptions commemorating athletic victories at the
Soteria, two of which at least date from the third century,[5] and
also an Amphictyonic decree, dated 215–205, stating that the
honours accorded to a Koan doctor were to be announced at
the gymnic contest of the Soteria.[6] How will these inscriptions
be reconciled with the absence of athletic victors from the

---

[1] See bibliography and discussion in Flacelière, *Aitoliens*, pp. 160–77; Dinsmoor,
List, pp. 127–31.

[2] In fact the last list in Dinsmoor's scheme, *F.D.* iii.4 128, was dated by
Flacelière, *Aitoliens* (1937), p. 407, no. 38a, about 223 on account of the composition of the Amphictyony. In spite of Dinsmoor's argumentation Flacelière retained
his date in *F.D.* iii.4 (1954).

[3] *R.É.A.* 26 (1924), 109.

[4] *Aitoliens*, pp. 169–70.

[5] *I. Olymp.* 176, πένταθλον (?); *S.E.G.* xi.1 338, παῖδας δίαυλον. Cf. *B.C.H.* 5
(1881), 193; *I.G.* ii² 3150; *I.G.* iv 611; *I.D.* 1957; *Didyma* ii 97 b; *Hermes* 49 (1914),
314–15, dating from the second and first century.

[6] *S.I.G.*[3] 538. Cf. *S.I.G.*[3] 579 B in which the word γυμνικός is restored. It has also
been restored in *S.I.G.*[3] 431 which dates from the year of the archon Emmenidas
(255/4?, Daux, *Chronologie*, G 23), that is from the time of the Amphictyonic
Soteria which did not include athletics.

catalogues if we really possess all the records from 248 to 208, or even 204? If we accept an annual or biennial system we get over the obstacle providing that the athletic contests occurred rarely. But the quadrennial system is strongly suggested by *S.I.G.*[3] 402 (see p. 66), and by the fact that each celebration of the festival was proclaimed by *theoroi* like Sotion. Had the festival been annual the *theoroi* would have been incessantly travelling.

It is time now to look at the question of the 'lesser' Soteria which is supposed to have been held in the two intervening years between the penteteric 'great' Soteria. No evidence exists for such festivals in the third century. In the post-Aitolian period a festival called χειμερινὰ Σωτήρια is attested by an inscription.[1] The designation of this festival as 'winter' Soteria implies the existence of some other kind of Soteria differing in the time of celebration. The winter Soteria presents some obvious resemblances to the old Amphictyonic festival. It was held in honour of 'the god', viz. Apollo, it included only musical and dramatic performances, and all performers were recorded. It looks therefore as if it were a revival of the original Soteria. Or could it have been a survival? It has been suggested[2] that the winter Soteria was instituted immediately after the Gallic invasion, and was appropriately held in winter-time since the decisive battle was fought in the winter of 279/8.[3] But we are in a position to know that the Amphictyonic Soteria was held between midsummer and the autumn equinox (see p. 64, n. 1), and it is highly improbable that two festivals of exactly the same character, and differing only in the time of celebration, were simultaneously founded to the memory of the same event. On the other hand Flacelière[4] has expressed the opinion that the winter Soteria may go back to the time of the Aitolian reformation. Perhaps the Amphictyonic Soteria was not abolished then but was transferred to the winter and held as lesser Soteria in the years between the quadrennial festivals. Had there been some concrete evidence for this lesser Soteria

---

[1] *S.I.G.*[3] 690, dated 145–125 B.C., Daux, *Delphes*, p. 359.

[2] Th. Klee, *Zur Geschichte der gymn. Agone an griech. Festen*, p. 69, cf. Pfister, *R.E.*[2] iii 1228.

[3] *F.D.* iii.2 138$_{31-33}$; Flacelière, *op. cit.*, p. 99.

[4] *B.C.H.* 52 (1928), 270–1.

in the third century we should perhaps have been able to attribute our lists to it, thus circumventing the difficulty raised by the absence of athletes. But the whole matter is too uncertain, and Flacelière himself renounced his theory later in favour of an annual scheme of classification of the records.[1]

In conclusion we must admit that at the present stage of our knowledge the problem of the Soteria cannot be convincingly solved. It seems beyond any reasonable doubt that the Soteria was set up in honour of Apollo soon after the Gallic invasion, and held annually in August-September until the middle of the third century, when the Aitolians re-organized it in an effort to create a great panhellenic *panegyris* run by them. Zeus Soter was introduced as an honoured god, and athletic contests were added to the musical ones. Unfortunately the exact date of the reformation and the periodicity of the new festival, together with all their important implications, must remain uncertain. In the second century, after the Aitolians had receded from Delphi, the programme of the Soteria still included athletic contests. Though the Aitolian *agonothetes* must have been replaced by a Delphian by then there is no evidence for other changes. Another festival, the winter Soteria, which resembles the original Soteria in many respects, is attested after the mid-second century. Whether this festival goes back to the date of the liberation of Delphi from the Aitolians (191 B.C.), or to the time of the re-foundation of the Soteria by them, cannot be decided. Until somebody produces new evidence the degree of probability accorded to the various interpretations and suggestions regarding the Soteria will remain a matter of opinion. As I did not aim to present an objective history of the problem I cannot claim that the views summarized in the preceding pages have been expressed in an unbiased way.

AMPHICTYONIC SOTERIA

(1) *Programme*

Ten inscriptions are attributed to this festival. They are records of artists who participated in various performances.

[1] *Aitoliens*, p. 166.

These records, and particularly four which are very well preserved, give a good picture of the celebration of the Soteria in
the middle of the third century. The programme of the festival
comprised musical, cyclic, and dramatic contests. The musical
performers were rhapsodes,[1] kithara-players, singers to the
kithara, and poets of *prosodia*. Two choruses, one of boys and
one of men, each usually consisting of fifteen members, sang the
dithyrambs. Each chorus was accompanied by a flute-player
and had its own instructor (*didaskalos*). Musical and dithyrambic performances were followed by the dramatic productions. Here we are particularly lucky to know not only the
names and the number of artists but also the way they
co-operated in producing the plays. For they are recorded
under a unique arrangement in groups of three actors, a
didaskalos and a flautist. Evidently each group was a company
capable of presenting a certain number of plays. Tragedies
were played by two or three such troupes; comedies by two or
three, and in one case by four troupes. In another case we have
only one *didaskalos* and one flute-player against nine comic
actors. Seven or eight comic choreuts follow the comic groups
in the records. It seems, then, that all comic groups shared the
same chorus. This is hardly surprising since the chorus of New
Comedy had long ago ceased to have any connection with the
plot of the plays. A chorus of professional artists would doubtless
be able to provide interludes for a large number of plays. We
should also expect such a chorus to be independently trained,
since its *entr'acte* appearances had nothing to do with the play
proper. In fact, in one case we have a *didaskalos* and a flautist,
in another case only a flautist, concluding the records (F, G).
These men must be the instructor and accompanists of the
chorus although they are separated from the dancers by the
himatiomisthai, the persons who provided the costumes of the
actors.

There is no sign of a tragic chorus in the inscriptions. It has
been suggested that the dithyrambic chorus of men may have
been also employed by the tragic troupes. This suggestion gains
support from some analogous cases (see p. 116).

---

[1] The rhapsodes were 'musical' performers in the sense that they regularly
participated in the musical festivals (μουσικοὶ ἀγῶνες).

The following table shows the programme of the festival and the number of artists who took part in some of the celebrations between c. 262 and c. 252 B.C.[1]

Music	A	B	C²	D³	E	F	G	H
rhapsodes		2?	2	2?	2	2	3	2
kitharistai	⎫	—		1?	2	—	1	1
kitharodes	⎬ ?	?	2	1?	2	2	—	3
poets of *prosodia*	⎭	2		—	—	—	3	—
Dithyramb								
cyclic flautists	2	?	2	?	2	3	1	2
didaskaloi	2	?	2?	?	2	—	1	2
boy choreuts		c.15		14?	10?	13	15	15
men choreuts		c.15		10?	10?	15	15	15
Drama								
tragic actors	6	9?		6?	9	9	6	6
didaskaloi	2	?			3	3	2	2
flautists	1?	?			3	3	2	2
comic actors	9				12	6	9	9
didaskaloi	3				4	2	3	1
flautists	1?				4	2	3	1
comic chorus					7	8	7	7
didask. of chorus					—	1	—	—
flautists of chorus					—	1	1	—
himatiomisthai					3	3	2	1

A — *S.E.G.* i 187B; *F.D.* iii.1 478 + *S.E.G.* xviii 234. Flacelière, *Aitoliens*, p. 173, 263 B.C.

B — *S.E.G.* i 187A; *F.D.* iii.1 477 + *S.E.G.* xviii 232. Flacelière, 262; Dinsmoor, *List*, p. 115, 263/2; Daux, *Chronologie*, G 17, 263/2? or 262/1?

(continued)

---

[1] On the supposed mistakes of the stone-cutters, which would affect the number of participants and their roles, see E. Capps, *T.A.P.A.* 31 (1900), 124ff.

[2] Ll. 18–22 coming after the list of rhapsodes, kitharodes, and poets of *prosodia*, have been edited by J. Bousquet, *B.C.H.* 83 (1959), 166–8, and in *S.E.G.* xviii 230, as follows: [αὐλη]ταί· Χαρικλῆς Χαιρίωνος [Βοιώτιος.| διδά]σκαλος· ᾿Αλέξανδρος Διο[---|20 Νικοκ]λῆς Τιμοδάμου Σ[ικυώνιος. τραγωι]δός· Νεοπτ[όλεμος ᾿Αθη-ναῖος?| κωμωιδός·] Νεο[πτόλεμος ᾿Αθηναῖος?]. The restoration of this passage cannot stand for many reasons. After the flute-players and instructors of dithyramb the names of choreuts ought to be expected. The list belongs to the Amphictyonic Soteria, and consequently all the actors must have been recorded. The restoration of ll. 20–2 after the model of the Aitolian records of winners is unwarrantable. The name of Nikokles in l. 20 is restored on the ground of *S.G.D.I.* 2568 = *F.D.* iii.4 126₁₁₋₁₂, but the person recorded there (Νικ [c. 4 ll.] Τιμοδήμου Σικυώνιος) is a flute-player and not a *didaskalos*.

[3] It is uncertain whether the last five names of the fragmentary list were actors, as they have been taken to be by the editor of the inscription, or members of the chorus of men.

(continued)

C — *S.I.G.*[3] 489; *S.E.G.* xviii 230. Flac. 259; Dins. 261/0.

D — *B.C.H.* 1928, 259; *S.E.G.* xviii 235. Flac. 258; Dins. 262/1.

— *B.C.H.* 1928, 264, n. 3; *S.E.G.* xviii 231. Flac. 257 (a small splinter).

E — *S.G.D.I.* 2563; *S.I.G.*[3] 424. Flac. 256; Dins. 260/59; Daux, G 21, 257/6?

F — *S.G.D.I.* 2564. Flac. 255; Dins. 259/8; Daux, G 23, 255/4?

G — *S.G.D.I.* 2565. Flac. 254; Dins. 258/7; Daux, G 24, 254/3?

H — *S.G.D.I.* 2566. Flac. 253; Dins. 257/6; Daux, G 25, 253/2?

— *S.E.G.* xviii 236; fragment of a list of names considered to be a record of the Soteria by J. Bousquet, *B.C.H.* 83 (1959), 170–1.

The names of the dramatic artists as grouped together in the records are given in Table 3. Table 4 shows the known provenances of all participants in the Amphictyonic Soteria and the number of artists provided by each place.

(2) *Three actor rule*

The Soteria records of contestants yield some important evidence for the history of later Greek drama. They show for one thing that the rule of three actors was still observed in the mid-third century. It has been argued[1] that this convention would not be applicable to New Comedy, and Pickard-Cambridge[2] suggested in regard to the Soteria that plays requiring more than three actors would be adapted to the possibilities of the troupes, or else avoided. However, there is no Menander scene which cannot be played by three principal actors provided that a character could be split between two actors, and also taken over by an auxiliary actor in scenes where he had no speaking part. Auxiliary actors were needed for mute parts, and might even occasionally speak a few lines if necessary.[3]

It is worth noting that the three principal actors of a tragic group in E (Table 3, E 52, 53, 54) recur in the same order in the record of next year (F 45, 46, 47). A comic troupe including its *didaskalos* in F (66, 67, 68, 70) is repeated in G (68, 69, 70,

---

[1] K. Rees, 'The Three Actor Rule in Menander', *Cl. Phil.* 5 (1910), 291–302; Körte, *R.E.* xv 756; Pickard-Cambridge, *Festivals*, pp. 152–3; cf. K. Schneider, *R.E.* Suppl. viii 190–3.

[2] *Ibid.*, p. 153.

[3] G. P. Goold, *Phoenix* 13 (1959), 145–50; J. G. Griffith, *C.Q.* n.s. 10 (1960), 113–17; Webster, *Studies in Menander*,[2] pp. 225f.; E. W. Handley, *The Dyskolos of Menander*, London, 1965, pp. 25ff.

71). Finally, the first and second actor of another comic group in F (61, 62) were still (or again) working together two years later (H 68, 69).

(3) Dramatic music

The inclusion of a flute-player in every company betrays a new emphasis on music as an element of production. These musicians, apparently called *tragikoi* (cf. *O.G.I.S.* 51 = *S.B.* 885$_{562}$) or *komikoi auletai* (*S.E.G.* xix 335$_{47}$), are for the first time enumerated alongside the actors, and shown to be indispensable members of dramatic troupes. There would have been, of course, nothing extraordinary about it if the Delphian inscriptions had been one hundred and fifty years earlier. But at a time when the lyric element of drama is supposed to have been much restricted, and the chorus reduced to singing *embolima* interjected between the acts of a play, it is hard to see what would be the job of the 'tragic' and 'comic' flautists, particularly if the chorus was common to several companies, and had its own accompanist, as appears to be the case of the comic chorus at the Soteria.

As long as episodes and *stasima* were interwoven with each other in classical drama, spoken, recited or sung parts were interlaced too. The chorus frequently shared the *stasima* with singing actors. But when the chorus was given irrelevant odes to sing between the episodes, the actors could not join the chorus in the *embolima*. Although the decline of the chorus reflects a more general decay of the lyric and musical element a place for non-choral song was still reserved within the episodes. Unhappily, because of the paucity of literary remains we do not know what was the proportion of lyrics in later drama.

It seems, however, that music held an important place in Hellenistic tragedy. A distinction of style between choral and non-choral music had developed in consequence of the clear division of plays into acts and *embolima*. Different musical modes were used for soli, namely the hypodorian and hypophrygian, and for choric odes, mainly the mixolydian. It is most significant that Agathon, who was the first according to Aristotle (*Poet.* 1456 a 26) to introduce the practice of the *embolima*, is also credited with the introduction of the hypodorian and hypophrygian in tragedy by the author (Michael Psellos?) of a Byzantine treatise on tragedy recently published by R. Browning.[1] The explanation for the distinction between choral and non-choral music given in the Aristotelian *Problems* (XIX 30.48) is that the hypophrygian and hypodorian modes are imitative; the first has a character of action, the other is magnificent and steadfast. They are therefore proper for characters on the stage because the actors imitate heroes, and among the ancients only the leaders were heroes. The folk, of whom the chorus consists, were common men. So a human, quiet, mournful kind of music is suitable to the chorus. The mixolydian[2] suggests a passive mood and attitude, whereas the hypophrygian and hypodorian modes urge to action. Therefore the mixolydian is the most suitable to the chorus, for the chorus remains inactive, and simply assumes a friendly attitude towards whatever characters it is present with. This passage of the *Problems* must be dated to the Hellenistic period because its writer has a different idea from Aristotle about the chorus (cp. p. 134).

Two possible examples of actors' soli, most probably Hellenistic although neither seem to be in the modes prescribed by the *Problems*, were published some years ago from an Oslo papyrus.[3] The first is a quasi-messenger's narrative of an epiphany of Achilles in anapaestic metre, the second, immediately following the first on the same piece of papyrus, is an apostrophe to the island of Lemnos in iambic trimeters. Both texts are provided with musical notation. In the first fragment there is an address to Deidameia, which suggests Skyros as the place of dramatic action. The play seems to have been about the delegation sent by the Greeks to summon Neoptolemos to Troy. Ph. J. Kakridis[4] has shown that such an argument is compatible with the epiphany of Achilles, which occurred before the fall of Troy. According to a little known version

---

[1] 'A Byzantine Treatise on Tragedy', in Γέρας G. *Thomson*, Charles University, Prague, 1963, pp. 67ff., §5, l. 39: πρῶτος δὲ ᾽Αγάθων τὸν ὑποδώριον τόνον εἰς τραγῳδίαν εἰσήνεγκεν καὶ τὸν ὑποφρύγιον.

[2] Cf. Browning, *loc. cit.*, §5, l. 34.

[3] S. Eitrem, L. Amundsen, R. P. Winnington-Ingram, 'Fragments of Unknown Greek Tragic Texts with Musical Notation', *Symb. Osl.* 31 (1955), 1–87.

[4] *Wien. Stud.* 77 (1964), 5ff.

Achilles had been killed by Penthesileia but Thetis asked Zeus to let him return from the dead in order to revenge himself on the queen of the Amazons (Ptolemaios Hephaistion in Phot. *Bibl.* 190, 151b 29–32 Henry; Eustath. *Com. ad Od.* XI 538, p. 1696, 51–3). The second fragment seems to contain a reference to the Hephaistos-made armour of Achilles, which was promised to Neoptolemos by Odysseus,[1] and apparently comes from the same play. The papyrus is badly damaged, and it is not evident how the two fragments are related to each other.[2] The anapaestic narrative, treated as monody, is without precedent, so far as we know, in classical tragedy (where, however, a lyric monody could take the place of a messenger's speech, Eur. *Or.* 1369ff.). The musical iambics, on the other hand, show that even purely dialogic metres could occasionally be set to music by a later interpreter.[3] The evidence for apparently non-choral tragic music given by a later writer, Aristides Quintilianus, fits in with that of the Aristotelian *Problems* and the Oslo papyrus: τρόποι δὲ μελοποιίας, says Aristides, γένει μὲν γ'. διθυραμβικὸς νομικὸς τραγικός. ὁ μὲν οὖν νομικός ἐστὶ νητοειδής, ὁ δὲ διθυραμβικὸς μεσοειδής, ὁ δὲ τραγικὸς ὑπατοειδής (I 12, p. 30, Winn.-Ingr.). Professor Winnington-Ingram tells me that the terms νητοειδής, etc., probably refer to general range of pitch, and that the low pitch which is associated with the tragic *tropos* would be less appropriate to choral singing than to the soli of actors. This music appears to have grown into a separate genre, and it is not surprising that

---

[1] Kakridis, *loc. cit.*, p. 13.

[2] The first editors did not think there was any relationship between the two fragments, and considered them as excerpts from different tragedies probably intended for performance as such. The alternative suggestion put forward by Eitrem and Amundsen, *loc. cit.* 26, that the anapaests might come from a poem relative to Lycophron's *Alexandra* is highly improbable because the *Alexandra* was a purely literary product intended for reading, whereas the musical narrative was to be performed. Nobody would ever think of setting the *Alexandra* to music.

[3] It is unfortunate that the date of composition cannot be estimated with safety. The papyrus is dated to the late first or early second cent. A.D., but there are reasons to believe that the music is earlier, for the melody respects the word-accent, as in the Delphic hymns dated in 128 B.C., though rather less strictly (see p. 89). But even if the fragments come from the 'text book' of a *tragodos* of Roman date, or a kitharode (and we need to learn a lot more about the activities of such performers before drawing any definite conclusions), the anapaestic narrative remains an indisputable witness of the importance that non-choral music had in later tragedy.

a separate class of musicians, viz. the tragic flute-players, should respectively specialize in performing it (cf. the *pythikoi auletai* or *pythaulai* and the *kyklioi auletai* or *choraulai* corresponding to *nomikos* and *dithyrambikos tropos*). The term *tragikos auletes* occurs in an inscription from Egypt (*O.G.I.S.* 51) dating from, roughly, the same period as the Soteria records, which in turn supply the evidence that these instrumentalists, significantly associated with the actors and the *didaskalos* of each troupe, accompanied the actors.

We know very little about the music of New Comedy. It is commonly assumed that its musical element still rests with the interludic chorus. On the other hand the chorusless plays of Plautus are rich in lyrics which were sung or recited to flute accompaniment. The gap between Menander and Plautus has been considered too big to be filled with the scanty evidence for Menandrian song.[1] So the origin of Plautine *cantica* has at times been sought in the assumed Hellenistic *Singspiel*,[2] 'music-hall' performers like the *ionikologoi*, *kinaidologoi*, etc., to whom we find references in Plautus himself (*Pseud.* 1274, *Persa* 804, *Stich.* 760, 769),[3] mime, tragedy through earlier playwrights who composed tragedies as well as comedies like Livius Andronicus and Naevius,[4] Old Comedy, inheritance from Etruria, the Latin *satura*, the *phlyakes*, the Atellana, and so on.[5]

However, the *Dyskolos* has now provided us with an ending of a Menander play, which strongly recalls the final scene of

---

[1] *Theophor.* 28 + schol. Eur. *Andr.* 103, fr. 258 (Koe.), cf. Marius Victorinus, *Gr. L.* vi 104 K, Caesius Bassus, *Gr. L.* vi 255 K. On lyric metres in Menander see A. Körte, *R.E.* xv 753–4. However, F. Marx, who made a thorough investigation into the lyrics of later Greek comedy, arrived at the conclusion that we need not look outside the Greek comedy for the origin of *cantica*. See his monumental edition of the *Rudens*, Abh. d. phil.-hist. Kl. der Sächsischen Ak. d. Wiss. Nr. v, Bd. xxxviii, Leipzig, 1928 (repr. Amsterdam, 1959), pp. 254–63.

[2] F. Leo, *Die plautinische Cantica und die hellenistische Lyrik* (Abhandl. d. königlichen Gesellschaft d. Wissenschaften zu Göttingen, N.F. i, no. 7), Berlin, 1897. Cf. O. Immisch, *Zur Frage der plautinischen Cantica* (Sitz. d. Heidelb. Ak., 7. Abhandlung), 1923.

[3] G. Michaut, *Sur les tréteaux latins*, Paris, 1912, pp. 213–14. E. Fraenkel, *Plautinisches im Plautus*, Berlin, 1922, pp. 367ff. (Italian edition, 1960, pp. 348ff.).

[4] Fraenkel, *op. cit.*, pp. 321ff.

[5] G. E. Duckworth, *The Nature of Roman Comedy*, Princeton, 1952, pp. 375ff., with bibliography.

Plautus' *Stichus*.[1] Getas and Sikon certainly recite their iambic tetrameters (cf. l. 910). Sikon probably sings the lines 946ff. A reference is made in the text to the flute-player (880) who seems to be present on the stage from the beginning of the scene. The second century Delos mosaic (see p. 54) representing a slave dancing before a flute-player seated on a rock might be cited as an illustration of this scene. Professor Webster[2] has called attention to some other dramatic monuments[3] showing dancing characters of Middle and New Comedy, which foreshadow the dancers in Plautus' *Stichus, Pseudolus,* and *Persa.*

The Soteria records occur halfway between Menander (died c. 292) and Plautus (*Asinaria* produced in 212).[4] It is to be taken for granted that the comic flute-players, like the tragic, accompanied the actors, even if in some cases they were also to accompany the chorus. Are we, then, to understand here an intermediate stage in the development of non-choral song between Menander and Plautus? I think the answer must be affirmative. After all if Plautus was influenced by various para-theatrical performers, would not the third century Greek poets have received similar influences? Moreover, we can hardly believe that during his long centuries of popularity Menander was uniformly produced. Interpolation, adaptation, various alterations, are all possible. Our terracottas, mosaics, and other works of art representing comic characters and masks show that the actor's appearance changed with the times, and so the whole style of *mise en scène* must have also undergone changes. Such changes would be brought about through fashion, influence from other forms of entertainment, eagerness of the Dionysiac *technitai*—in the ranks of whom Plautus started his career—to satisfy the taste of their public. So Menander may have been μουσικώτερος in the third and second centuries than in his own life-time.

[1] T. B. L. Webster, 'Alexandrian Epigrams and the Theatre', in *Misc. di studi alessandr. in memoria di A. Rostagni*, 541–2; J.-M. Jacques, *Ménandre, Le Dyscolos*, éd. Budé, 1963, pp. 18f.

[2] *Loc. cit.*, p. 542.

[3] *M.O.M.C.* tT 1, CT 3, AT 63 (=Bieber, *Hist. of Gr. and Rom. Theat.*[2], fig. 179); *M.N.C.* TT 27, NM 2 (=Bieber, *ibid.*, fig. 346), MT 1 (=Bieber, *ibid.*, fig. 341), MT 15 (=Bieber, *ibid.*, fig. 342).

[4] K. H. E. Schutter, *Quibus annis comoediae plautinae primum actae sint quaeritur*, Diss. Groningen, 1952, pp. 14–20.

At all events, the significance of the Soteria inscriptions as far as the Roman dramatic *cantica* are concerned should not be overestimated. But if they suggest, as we have assumed, that the music outside the choric *embolima* had a considerable place in Hellenistic theatre production, then this phase of Greek drama has indeed to be accounted among the main influences which contributed to the development of the tuneful Roman drama (cf. p. 78, n. 1).

(4) Didaskaloi, *Artists' changing functions, Costumiers*

If we knew what plays were put on at Delphi, the point we tried to make above might have been better illustrated. (An inscription from Tegea bearing witness to productions of Euripides' *Herakles* and Archestratos' *Antaios* at the Soteria is more likely to refer to the Aitolian festival, see p. 84.) A critical question is, of course, whether the *didaskaloi* were poets or producers. The title *didaskalos* applied to a poet producing his own plays (Photius *s.v.* ὑποδιδάσκαλος). But it might also apply to a producer, particularly in the third century when old plays were frequently revived, and the expansion of the theatre had increased the demand for the services of such professionals.[1] None of our *didaskaloi* is otherwise known as a poet. Three of the comic ones, Kephisodoros (Table 3, E 66, F 65), Diogeiton (E 76), and Thyrsos (H 64), are listed among the comic choreuts at other times (H 76, F 74–G 75, and F 78 respectively), a rather odd job for a poet to perform, all the more if he would not be dancing in his own plays. The same Kephisodoros, Menekrates (E 71), Dionysios (F 70), Moschion (G 61), and Kallikles (G 66), may be identical with homonymous comic actors in Delos and/or Athens, where the patronymic and *ethnikon* are omitted from the records. These bits of information about the other activities of *didaskaloi* do not allow positive conclusions. However, I feel inclined to think of them as producers rather than poets for two additional reasons. First, the

---

[1] It may be true that at Athens, even in late Hellenistic times, the producers were called *hypodidaskaloi*, a title that occurs always in relation to Athenian *technitai*. On *chorodidaskaloi* see pp. 90 and 117–20. Διδάσ]καλοι τῶν τραγωιδῶν καὶ κωμωιδῶν (certainly producers) occur in *I.G.* xii.9 207₂₄. Plutarch, *Mor.* 710 F, mentions *didaskaloi* of tragedies but it is not clear if he means poets or producers.

title *didaskalos* is given both to the instructors of the cyclic choruses and the trainer of a comic chorus (F 83); second, the Aitolian Soteria inscriptions, which are lists of victors, include cyclic flautists, leaders of cyclic choruses, and actors, but neither dithyrambic nor dramatic poets, which shows that competitions of poets were not included among the events of the festival (see p. 83).

It is generally believed that the functions of tragic and comic actors were kept well apart down to the Roman period.[1] Some exceptions to the rule occur in the second half of the second and the first half of the first centuries (cf. p. 93). The Soteria records may provide another. The protagonist of the second tragic troupe in H is Diokles, son of Diokles, Athenian (H 55). The tritagonist of the third comic company in E is – – okles, son of Diokles, Athenian (E 69). The name has been restored to Diokles (Baunack, Pomtow), but there would also be room for a longer name like Philokles, a comic actor known to have won the contest of Dionysia at Athens in c. 282, and that of Lenaia a few years before.[2]

The tragic and comic flute-players were apparently more versatile than the actors. Pantakles played for a tragic group in one year (E 55), and for a comic in another (F 69). Philiskos is comic in E (61) and G (72), but tragic in H (58). Leukippos is tragic in F (58) and comic in G (62).

Another shift of function is noteworthy. Nikon, son of Herakleitos, from Epeiros, was a costumier in F (80) but a comic actor in G (65).

The ἱματιομίσθαι were the persons who hired out theatrical costumes (Pollux VII 78, Anecdota Bekker 100, 24). Pollux adds that the term was used by the νέοι, while the μέσοι used the word ἱματιομισθωτής. In addition to the Soteria inscriptions the term occurs also in *I.G.* xii.9 207$_{22}$ (Euboea, 294–87 B.C.), and *S.E.G.* xix 335 (Tanagra, early first cent. B.C.). In the former the sum of 300 drachmai was laid down as a salary to be paid to the *himatiomisthes* by the cities of Euboea, in the latter a *himatiomisthes* is found among the artists who received money rewards for their contribution to the performances of

---

[1] Plato, *Rep.* 395 a; J. B. O'Connor, *Chapters in History of Actors and Acting*, p. 43.
[2] *I.G.* ii² 2325$_{94, 210}$. Cf. E. Capps, *T.A.P.A.* 31 (1900), 126.

the Sarapeia. It seems therefore that the function of *himatio-misthai* in Hellenistic times was different from what their title implies. Instead of letting out costumes to actors, or *choregoi* (cf. Pollux *loc. cit.*), as they may have been doing at Athens in the fourth century, they hired their services to festival managers for a certain salary, and undertook to provide the artists with all necessary equipment. Several scholars[1] believe that they had become members of the Dionysiac guilds, and this is supported by the fact that an Egyptian guild had a σκευοποιός among its members. Moreover, our costumiers, none of whom is a Delphian, went to Delphi along with the *technitai*, and were included in the records of the artists who participated in the festival of the Soteria.

(5) *The two preambles of the records*

The lists are preceded by two introductory formulae. The first, employed in B and C (the heading of A is missing), reads as follows: ἐπὶ (name) ἄρχοντος ἐν Δελφοῖς, ἱερομνημονούντων (list of names), γραμματεύοντος (name), ἐπὶ ἱερέως δὲ (name) ἐκ τῶν τεχνιτῶν, τὸ κοινὸν τῶν τεχνιτῶν ἐπέδωκε τῷ θεῷ καὶ τοῖς Ἀμφικτύοσιν εἰς τὰ Σωτήρια τὸν ἀγῶνα παντελῆ· ἠγωνίσαντο δὲ οἴδε. The second, used in D, E, F, G, H, reads: ἐπὶ (name) ἄρχοντος, ἱερέως δὲ (name), ἱερομνημονούντων (list of names), οἴδε ἠγωνίσαντο τὸν ἀγῶνα τῶν Σωτηρίων. The apparent interpretation of the first introduction is that one of the Dionysiac guilds—the Isthmian and Nemean it is said—offered a complete programme of performances gratuitously to Apollo and the Amphictyony. But this collective expression of reverence was not repeated every year. In the more frequent type of introduction there is no allusion to free offering of performances, or to a certain *koinon*. However, the priest recorded between the Delphian archon and the hieromnemons was again priest of the *technitai* (cf. E 58), therefore member of a *koinon*. Does this mean that all the artists were members of one guild presided over by the priest? An answer to this question would be very important because it would illustrate the way the Dionysiac guilds functioned, and show whether the Soteria was a prestigious festival

[1] A. Müller, *Lehrbuch der griechischen Bühnenalterthümer*, p. 406; Poland, *R.E.*[2] v 2486; Pickard-Cambridge, *Festivals*, p. 313.

capable of attracting artists from all over Greece. I am inclined to believe that more than one guild is represented in the lists, for reasons discussed in App. II.

AITOLIAN SOTERIA

(1) *Programme*

The programme of the Aitolian Soteria was very similar to that of the previous festival. Unfortunately, the number of artists and the pomp of celebration are not disclosed by the lists of winners attributed to this festival. However, the frequent absence of many items from the programme (b, e, j) implies that the Aitolian fête failed to achieve a panhellenic impact (see p. 69).

The programme of the festival was as follows:

Music

	a	b	c	d	e	f	g	h	i	j
rhapsode		b		d	e	f	g	h		j
kitharistes		}b?		}d?	e	f	g	}h?		—
kitharode					e	f	g			—

Dithyramb

	a	b	c	d	e	f	g	h	i	j
boys: flautist		—	c	d	e	f	g	h		—
leader of chorus		—	c?	d	e	f	g	h		—
men: flautist		—	c	d	e	f	g	h	i	—
leader of chorus		—	c		—		g	h		—

Drama

	a	b	c	d	e	f	g	h	i	j
tragic actor	a	—	c		—	f	g	h		—
comic actor	a	—	c		—		g	h		—

a — *S.E.G.* ii 260, 1. Flacelière, *Aitoliens*, p. 173 C, 240 B.C. Dinsmoor, *List*, p. 140, 248/7 B.C.

b — *Ibid.* 260, 2. Flac. 239,[1] Dins. 244/3; Daux, *Chronologie*, K 5, 240/39? or 244/3?

c — *Ibid.* 260, 3. Flac. 238; Dins. 240/39.
   — *Ibid.* 260, 4. Flac. 235; Dins. 236/5 (traces of one name only).

d — *Ibid.* 260, 5. Flac. 234; Dins. 232/1; Daux, K 7, 228/7 or 232/1?

e — *Ibid.* 260, 6. Flac. 229; Dins. 228/7.

f — *S.I.G.*³ 509; *F.D.* iii.4 125. Flac. 227; Dins. 224/3; Daux, K 9, 220/19? or 224/3?

g — *S.G.D.I.* 2568; *F.D.* iii.4 126. Flac. 226; Dins. 220/19.

h — *F.D.* iii.4 127. Flac. 225; Dins. 216/5.

i — *F.D.* iii.4, p. 202. Flac. 224; Dins. 212/1.

j — *F.D.* iii.4 128. Flac. 223; Dins. 208/7.

---

[1] Flacelière dates 'b' c. 238, *op. cit.* 402, 472. All his dates are approximate.

(2) *Known plays, Actors*

No poets are included in the preserved lists of winners, and this is perhaps an indication that the *didaskaloi* of the Amphictyonic Soteria were not poets either. However, the actors could select their pieces out of a vast number of classical and post-classical plays, although the absence of poets does not necessarily imply that contemporary plays were not produced. We know of a tragic actor from Tegea who acted the title-roles in the *Herakles* of Euripides, and *Antaios* of Archestratos, at the Soteria. He was a very successful actor, as well as a champion pugilist—he had won a boxing contest at Alexandria—specializing in impersonating great heroes. An inscription set up at the theatre of Tegea commemorated his victories (*S.I.G.*³ 1080 = *I.G.* v.2 118). He had carried off the prizes of eighty-eight scenic contests at various cities including Athens, where he did *Orestes*, Delphi, Argos, where he appeared in the *Herakles* and *Archelaos* of Euripides, and Dodona, where he repeated the *Archelaos*, and also played Chairemon's *Achilleus*. The letters of the inscription suggest a late-third-century date but the production of the *Archelaos* in Dodona must have taken place before 219, when the city was sacked by the Aitolians. So perhaps our tragedian appeared at Delphi, which comes before Dodona in the record, some years earlier.

The name of this remarkable Tegean actor is not known. In fact very few names of actors have been preserved in the records of victors. They are as follows:

	Tragic actors	
Antimedes, s. of Herakleitos	Halikarnassos	f 12
Dionysios, Διοφ ––	Rhodes	g 13
		In Delos, Table 1, X A1.
––, ––δου	Syracuse	h 11–12
––, –––,	Kassandreia	c 6–7
	Comic actors	
Amyklas, s. of Euphraios	Histiaia	g 14
		In Delos, Table 1, IX B3
Aristomachos, s. of Philonides	Athens	f 13
		Nationalized Athenian, son of Philonides of Zakynthos, Table 3, E58
Artemon, s. of Diodoros		h 12

WINTER SOTERIA

All we know about this festival derives from an inscription—a decree of the Isthmian and Nemean guild of Dionysiac artists—dated 145–125 B.C. (*S.I.G.*[3] 690; Daux, *Delphes*, p. 359). Three Delphian delegates had been sent to the *technitai* inviting them ὥστε καταγωνίξασθαι τῷ θεῷ τὸν ἀγῶνα (of the Winter Soteria) ἐπιετῆ (i.e. *huius anni*, in that same year). In accordance with the request the *koinon* dispatched a number of artists to Delphi to give gratis performances in honour of Apollo: Two musicians, 1 *kitharistes* and 1 kitharode, a chorus of boys and another of men, each consisting of 2 choreuts and 1 leader (the leader of the men being the same as the kitharode), and a comic group consisting of 1 *komodos*, 2 supporting actors (*synagonistai*), and 4 comic choreuts. These artists could not possibly organize any 'contest', but it is possible that the Delphians had also secured the participation of other *technitai*.

The following artists constituted the comic troupe sent to Delphi by the Isthmian guild:

	Komodos	
Apollas (s. of Bion)	Pheneos	*S.I.G.*[3] 690₁₅ Although under a contract he failed to appear in Epidauros and was fined, *I.G.* iv² 100
	Synagonistai	
Soteles		*ibid.*, l. 17
Theokritos		*ibid.*, l. 17
	Choreuts	
Xenolaos, s. of Sosikrates	Opous	*ibid.*, l. 19
Myrton, s. of Theophilos	Thebes	*ibid.*, l. 20
Aristokleidas	Thebes	*ibid.*, l. 21
Menekrates, s. of Sopatros	Thebes	*ibid.*, l. 22

The significance of this inscription as evidence for dramatic chorus in the second half of the second century is discussed on p. 117.

CHAPTER X

THE PYTHAIDS

TRADITIONAL *THEORIA* OF ATHENIANS
TO DELPHI

In late Hellenistic times the Athenian *technitai* of Dionysos staged numerous musical and dramatic performances at Delphi on three special occasions. In fact they participated in three Pythaids held in 128/7, 106/5, and 98/7 B.C.

The Pythaid[1] (ἡ Πυθαΐς) was a specific Athenian *theoria* to Delphi. Its mission was to offer a *hekatombe* and first-fruits to Apollo Pythios. The Pythaid had nothing to do with the Pythian Games. It was held in the early summer (Athenian month Thargelion, Delphian Herakleios), whereas the Pythia were celebrated in the autumn. Moreover it had no fixed periodicity. In classical times a heavenly sign informed the Athenians that they ought to send their offerings to Apollo: for three days and nights, in three consecutive months every year, the *pythaistai* watched to see whether Zeus would hurl lightning over Harma, a ridge of Mount Parnes near Phyle, their observatory being the hearth of Zeus Astrapaios 'on the wall between Olympion and Python' (Strabon IX 2, 11 [C. 404]).[2]

---

[1] G. Colin, *Le culte d'Apollon Pythien à Athènes*, Paris, 1905; idem., *B.C.H.* 30 (1906), 161–328; idem., *F.D.* iii.2 2–53; Pomtow, *S.I.G.*³ 696–9, 711, 728; A. Boëthius, *Die Pythais, Studien zur Geschichte der Verbindungen zwischen Athen und Delphi*, Diss. Uppsala, 1918; G. Daux, *Delphes*, pp. 521ff., 708ff., A. W. Parsons, *Hesperia* 12 (1943), 233–8.

[2] Apparently the omens were not sent frequently because in the time of Pericles the phrase ὅταν δι' Ἅρματος ἀστράψῃ was a proverbial equivalent of rarely. Strab., IX, 2, 11 (C. 404); Plut., *Mor.* 679 C; Suda *s.v.* ἅρμα; Hesych. *s.v.* ἀστραπὴ δι' Ἅρματος. More references in Boëthius, *op. cit.*, 145–6. As for the location of the hearth of Zeus, scholars cannot agree on whether the Olympion and Python are the shrines by the river Ilissos, or two caves on the north-west slope of the Acropolis, the latter being more likely in view of Eur. *Ion* 285. For modern discussions of this topographical problem see A. W. Gomme, *A Historical Commentary on Thucydides*, ii (1956), pp. 53ff.; R. E. Wycherley, *A.J.A.* 63 (1959), 68ff., 67 (1963), 75ff.; I. Travlos, Πολεοδομικὴ ἐξέλιξις τῶν Ἀθηνῶν, Athens, 1960, pp. 22, 61, 106f.; J. Bousquet, *B.C.H.* 88 (1964), 663ff.; O. Broneer, *Arch. Ephemeris* 1960 (published 1965), 54ff. Bousquet and Broneer rightly put the emphasis on the evidence of the *Ion*.

The tradition was not observed in the third century while Athens was a Macedonian dependency, and Delphi under Aitolian control, nor even in the first part of the second century when both cities were free. The Pythaid was revived in 138/7 B.C. At that time Athens was flourishing again under the auspices of Rome. It seems that no omen was watched for this time. It was repeated ten years later, and then in 106/5, when it was decreed that the *theoria* should be sent at regular eight-year intervals (*enneeteris*) ἀκολούθως τοῖς χρησμοῖς καὶ ταῖς ἱστορίαις. In 98/7 a Pythais was actually sent, but internal political struggles, the involvement of Athens in the first Mithridatic war, and finally the sack of the city by Sulla, brought about the discontinuance of the tradition.

The Pythaid was an act of homage to Apollo who was highly respected by the Athenians. He had passed from Athens on his way to Delphi,[1] and the Pythaists followed the same route through Oinoë on Kithairon, and Thebes. The *theoriai* to Delphi were always important events. The eminent politicians and orators Lycurgus and Demades were among the members of a Pythaid sent most likely in 326 B.C.[2] (*F.D.* iii.1 511, *S.I.G.*[3] 296). But the Pythaids were never so splendidly held as in the second and early first centuries. No other Greek state was in such good relations with Delphi as Athens during that period.[3] Having recovered Delos in 167/6, Athens was trying to extend her influence on the other centre of Apollo's cult. The whole body of the nine Athenian archons led the second (128/7), third (106/5), fourth (98/7), and possibly the first[4] (138/7) Pythaids. Other magistrates were also present, notably the strategus ἐπὶ τοὺς ὁπλίτας who seems to have been in command of the *theoria* in 105 and 97.[5] A whole army of *theoroi*—representing the Athenian people, the Nobles, and the Marathonian tetrapolis[6]—boy pythaists, ephebes, basket-bearers, horsemen,

---

[1] Strabon IX 3, 12, quoting Ephoros, *F. Gr. Hist.* ii A, p. 52, 31b.

[2] D. M. Lewis, *B.S.A.* 50 (1955), 34; 330 B.C. is favoured by S. Charitonides, *Hesperia* 30 (1961), 44.

[3] Daux, *Delphes*, p. 577.

[4] Daux, *ibid.*, pp. 548-9, *contra* Pomtow, *S.I.G.*[3] 696, n. 2, and Boëthius, *op. cit.*, p. 60.

[5] Daux, *ibid.*

[6] The cult of Apollo was particularly strong in the tetrapolis (Marathon,

and *technitai* of Dionysos, followed.[1] The first Pythaid, which included neither horsemen nor *technitai*, consisted of more than a hundred delegates, the second and the fourth of more than two hundred and fifty, and the third of about three hundred and fifty. No doubt the arrival of so many Athenian chief magistrates and feasting pilgrims in Delphi would mark the beginning of a festival. An impressive procession, sacrifices and other ceremonies would be held. The numerous horsemen (88 in 105 B.C.) organized riding contests, and the Dionysiac artists musical and dramatic performances.

THE DIONYSIAC GUILD AT PYTHAID II

The *technitai* did not participate in the first Pythaid except for two of them who went to Delphi as masters of the choir of boy pythaists. But it would have been surprising if they had not been present at the other so magnificently conducted *theoriai*. 'Because the guild of the Athenian *technitai*', we are told, 'has always honoured and revered the gods, and been willing to augment their traditional honours, it has gained immortal glory by the greatest and noblest deeds. And now that the people of Athens have decreed to send the Pythaid after many years, in accordance with the oracles and the traditions, the guild has promptly offered to participate'—by sending to the second Pythaid an *architheoros* and four *theoroi*, a big choir consisting of 39 singers and their master to sing the paean to the god, and 27 musicians and actors to add more lustre to the god's festive days with their performances (ἐξαπέστειλαν δὲ καὶ ἀκροάματα τὰ συναυξήσοντα τὰς τοῦ θεοῦ ἡμέρας[2]). These artists were *auletai* (2), *kitharistai* (7), *aulodos* (1), *kitharodoi* (2), *komodoi* (8), *tragodoi* (3), *chorodidaskaloi tragikoi* (3) and *komikos* (1) (*F.D.*

Tricorynthos, Oinoë, and Probalinthos). There was a Python at Oinoë, and a Delion at Marathon. The tetrapolis dispatched its own *theoriai* to Delphi, also called Pythaids, even when the Athenian Pythaids were suspended. On these *theoriai* see Boëthius, pp. 34ff.; Daux, pp. 532ff.

[1] See Colin's table in *B.C.H.* 30 (1906), 168–9, and *F.D.* iii.2, p. 13.

[2] Pomtow, *S.I.G.*[3], ii, p. 301, had connected these days with the Delphian festival Herakleia, but his thesis was easily subverted by Boëthius, pp. 87–8, and Daux, p. 727.

iii.2 47 = *S.I.G.*³ 698). But in fact the guild's delegation was not
so numerous as it seems, for 11 of the 39 singers of paean had
also other jobs to do. They were comic or tragic actors, singers
to the *aulos* or *kithara*, trainers of dramatic choruses. One of the
theoroi is also recorded as comic actor, and another served as
epimeletes (head of the mission). However, the total number of
technitai at the second Pythaid was no less than 58.

The considerable cost of travel and maintenance for so many
people was defrayed by the guild. In reward the *synodos* as a
whole, and each of the *technitai* who had performed at Delphi,
were awarded the god's crown of laurel; the *asylia*, which had
been conferred on the Athenian *technitai* long ago (see p. 100,
no. 2), was renewed, and all of them were given the privileges
enjoyed by the public friends and benefactors (πρόξενοι and
εὐεργέται) of the city. A copy of the relative Delphian decree was
to be sent to the parliament and assembly in Athens, and
another to the *synodos*.

THE DELPHIAN HYMNS

Among the documents of Pythaids I and II inscribed on the
southern wall of the Athenian Treasury at Delphi the two
hymns to Apollo famous for their musical notation were
recorded. The one conventionally considered as first (*F.D.*
iii.2 137) bears the heading: [ἆισμα μετὰ κιθάρας? ε]ἰς τὸν
θεὸν ὃ ἐ[πόησε – – 'Aθ]ηναῖος. The title of the second (*F.D.* iii.2
138, cf. *S.I.G.*³ 698 C) is restored as follows: [πα]ιὰν δὲ καὶ
π[ροσό]διον εἰς τ[ὸν θεὸν ὃ ἐπό]ησε[ν καὶ προσεκιθάρισε]ν
Λιμήνι[ος Θ]οίνο[υ 'Aθηναῖος]. Limenios, son of Thoinos, was
among the *kithara*-players of 127, so his composition must have
been executed by the choir of the second Pythaid. On palaeo-
graphical grounds, and because of δέ in the heading of Limenios'
paean, the first hymn has also been referred to Pythaid II.
These poems, both in paeonic metre except for the concluding
section (the *prosodion* of the title) which is written in Aeolic
metre, are composed in a grandiose style, and have a moderate
poetic merit. However, they are the longest of the extant Greek
musical documents (33 and 40 lines respectively), and therefore

an invaluable source for the study of ancient music.[1] In both hymns reference is made to the *technitai* of Dionysos, so E. Pöhlmann's[2] suggestion that the first one might be attributed to the first Pythaid cannot stand, since the guild did not take part in Pythaid I. The performance of hymns by the chorus of *technitai*, accompanied by a small orchestra of flutes and *kitharai* (see below), must have been the main musical event of the celebrations.

CHORODIDASKALOI

It would be futile, I think, to speculate on how the eight comic and three tragic actors of the second Pythaid combined forces, or what plays they brought on to the stage. But there is one point deserving special attention, the presence of three tragic chorus trainers (χοροδιδάσκαλοι), and one comic one. Dramatic choruses are not separately recorded, and these persons may have been producers of tragedies and comedies, since two of them, Elpinikos, son of Epikrates, and Philion, son of Philomelos, are referred to as tragic *hypodidaskaloi* in another, slightly earlier, inscription (*I.G.* ii² 1132, Amphictyonic decree). But precisely because they are called *chorodidaskaloi*, while a title more appropriate to a producer existed, and had actually been applied to the very same persons on another occasion, I am inclined to think that these artists were to train dramatic choruses, and probably produce the plays at the second Pythaid. Be that as it may, the choreuts had to be drawn out of the big choir, eleven members of which, including our four *chorodidaskaloi*, were also, as we have seen, allotted other tasks.

THE GUILD AT PYTHAIDS III AND IV

Two Delphian decrees acknowledge the presence of the *technitai* at the third and fourth Pythaids, and praise them for their

---

[1] Th. Reinach in *F.D.* iii.2, pp. 147ff.; E. Martin, *Trois documents de musique grecque*, Paris, 1953, pp. 25–47, 73–8; R. P. Winnington-Ingram, *Symb. Osl.* 31 (1955), 65–7; I. Henderson in *New Oxford Hist. of Music*, vol. i: Ancient and Oriental Music, 1957, pp. 363–9 (where we are told that the first hymn 'must have won a prize in the Pythian festival'); E. Pöhlmann, *Griechische Musikfragmente* (Erlanger Beitr. zur Sprach- und Kunstwissenschaft, viii), 1960, pp. 59ff., cf. Winnington-Ingram, *Lustrum* 3 (1958), 8–9.

[2] *Op. cit.*, p. 61, n. 1.

piety and generosity. The inscription of 105 (*F.D.* iii.2 49, *S.I.G.*³ 728 K) is badly damaged but we can safely restore the opening and closing sections on the grounds of the other decree (*F.D.* iii.2 48, *S.I.G.*³ 711 L + *B.C.H.* 62 [1938], 362ff., 97 B.C.) which is obviously a copy of the earlier one. The middle part with the list of artists is lost except for a few names. It seems, though, that the delegation to Pythaid III was as large as that to Pythaid IV which comprised c. 100 artists. Both delegations were led by Alexandros, son of Ariston, a comic poet, who is called *epimeletes* and *architheoros* of the *technitai*. The contribution of the Dionysiac artists to the celebration of Pythaids III and IV was the same as to Pythaid II. They took part in the processions and made sacrifices, the choir sang τοὺς παιᾶνας καὶ τὸν χορὸν in praise of Apollo, and the rest of them offered ἀπαρχὰς ἀγώνων διὰ τῆς ἑαυτῶν ἐπιστήμης μέλψαντες τὸν θεόν, that is to say they gave gratuitous performances in honour of the god whom they celebrated through their art. The city of Delphi expressed its gratitude by conferring a crown of gold upon the guild. Two 'golden' statues (of the personification?) of the *synodos* were also to be set up, one at a conspicuous place in the sanctuary of Apollo at Delphi, and the other in the precinct of Dionysos at Athens. For the erection of the latter the *technitai* had to obtain the permission of the city of Athens. On the bases of both statues the following inscription was to be written: 'The city of Delphi dedicated the *synodos* of Dionysiac artists in Athens (sc. to Apollo and Dionysos respectively) because of their virtue and piety toward the God.' Daux deduced from the wording of the decree of Pythaid IV that the cost of the statues was to be borne by the guild.[1] He further suggested that the project of setting up the statues was not realized in 105, and so permission to dedicate the statues in the name of Delphi was given to the guild again in 97. However, the two texts were exactly alike, and so Professor Daux may have underrated the ambitions, and the financial capacities of the Athenian guild. The same honours were awarded to Alexander, the *architheoros* and *epimeletes* of the guild. The other *theoroi*, and the master of the choir in 97, were crowned with laurel. The conferring of crowns was to be announced in public at the gymnic contests of Pythia and

[1] *Delphes*, pp. 728–9.

Soteria. The privileges granted to all members of the guild are repeated in both decrees, copies of which were to be sent to the Athenian parliament and assembly, and the guild.

The delegation of the guild to the last Pythaid was led by a group of eight *theoroi* whose specialities were included in the record: 1 comic poet, 1 tragic *hypodidaskalos*, 2 comic actors, 2 tragic poets, and 2 tragic *synagonistai*. The same tragic *hypodidaskalos*, Diokles, son of Aischines, was the master of the choir which consisted of 42 (or 43) singers, and was accompanied by 5 *kithara*-players, 3 ποτικιθαρίζοντες, and 6 flute-players. The ποτικιθαρίζοντες must have been playing a different kind of accompaniment from the *kithara*-players. Since harmony, in the modern technical sense of the word, and counterpoint were alien to Greek music, and certainly one of the ποτικιθαρίζοντες, and possibly the other two as well, is enumerated among the paean singers,[1] one might suggest that these musicians provided a sort of rhythmic support to the melodic line followed by singers and instrumentalists in unison. Instrumental and vocal melody seem to have been identical, since in the musical notation of Limenios' hymn the system of instrumental notation (σήματα τῆς κρούσεως) is employed. This hymn was originally performed in 127, but was probably repeated in the subsequent Pythaids.[2] In addition to the choir and orchestra other artists were also sent to organize a 'thymelic and scenic contest', namely 3 epic poets, 3 rhapsodes, 1 *aulodos*, 1 *kitharistes pythikos*, 3 flute-players, 4 *komodoi*, 6 comic *synagonistai*, 5 poets of satyr plays, 2 *tragodoi*, 7 tragic *synagonistai*, and 2 tragic poets.

How many artists participated in the third Pythaid we do not know. But the delegation apparently included epic poets, comedians, 5 supporting actors of comedy, 4 *tragodoi*, and 8 supporting actors of tragedy.

DRAMATIC ARTISTS AT THE PYTHAIDS

The dramatic artists known to have taken part in the Pythaids are listed in Table 5.

Artists whose names are given in brackets went to Delphi as

---

[1] Διονύσιος Σιμάλου, *F.D.* iii.2 48, ll. 20 and 24.
[2] Daux, *op. cit.*, p. 725.

theoroi of the *synodos*, and did not take part in the performances except for Diokles (IV.30) and Themison (IV.27), conductor and member of the choir respectively.

In all cases the comic artists come before the tragic, and this probably means that comedies were played before tragedies.

Three poets of tragedy among the poets of satyr play in 97 (IV.12, 13, 16) show that the satyric drama remained the domain of tragic poets. It must have been that of tragic actors too, since no specific actors for satyr play are found in the record of Pythaid IV.

The fact that two *theoroi* of the last Pythaid are called *synagonistai* (IV.26, 27) and not *hypokritai*, proves that in Athens too the actor's profession was divided into protagonists and secondary actors.[1] But these artists could easily cross the boundaries of their rank and profession. For instance Diomedes, son of Athenodoros (III.12), a tragic *synagonistes* in Pythaid III became a famous comic poet. Statues of him were erected in Athens and Epidauros, and he was also awarded the citizenship of Pergamon. Praxiteles, son of Theogenes, is comic *synagonistes* in 105 (III.5), but protagonist of tragedy in 97 (IV.18). We also know that he won a second victory as an actor of old comedy, and a first as a *keryx*, at Tanagra a few years later. The comic *synagonistes* Theodoros, son of Theodoros (IV.8), turns up as a tragic *chorodidaskalos* in Argos. In these cases a change from tragedy to comedy or vice versa seems to mark a successful turn in the career of the artists. Another tragic *synagonistes*, Demetrios, son of Aristodemos (IV.19), appeared at Argos as a comic one. Finally, all three rhapsodes at the last Pythaid were also tragic *synagonistai* (IV.21, 24, 25).

The comedian Thymoteles, son of Philokles (II.8), performed at the second Pythaid. Two years earlier he was sent to Delphi as a representative of the guild together with four tragic *hypo-didaskaloi* (p. 101, no. 8). Two copies of the same inscription concerning this delegation were found at Athens and Delphi. It appears from these documents that he was a poet. What kind of poet we do not know because his title is not preserved com-

---

[1] On *synagonistai* see Poland, *R.E.*[2] v 2487-8.

plete. The first editor of the Athenian copy S. A. Kumanudis[1] tentatively restored [τραγωιδίας?]| ποιητοῦ in ll. 45–6, 71–2. Koehler in *I.G.* ii 551 preferred the restoration [τραγικοῦ,– ὸν] (ll. 45 and 71 respectively), which was repeated in the subsequent publications of the inscription,[2] and introduced in the Delphian example.[3] In view of Thymoteles' activity as comic actor at the second Pythaid, only two years after the delegation of 130/29, the restoration [κωμικοῦ, – ὸν] seems more likely.

[1] *Chrysallis* 4 (Athens, 1866), 11–13. Also C. Wescher, 'Étude sur le monument bilingue de Delphes', *Mémoires présentés par divers savants à l'Académie des Inscriptions et Belles-lettres*, 1ère série, 8 (1869), 199ff., and O. Lüders, *Die dionysischen Künstler*, Berlin, 1873, pp. 171–3.
[2] Michel 1009, *I.G.* ii² 1132.
[3] *B.C.H.* 24 (1900), 82ff., *F.D.* iii.2 68₃₂.

CHAPTER XI

OTHER DRAMATIC OCCASIONS

PYTHIA

Default of evidence may not be a decisive criterion, yet it is very doubtful if drama was introduced into the programme of the Pythian Games before the time of the Empire. All our information, literary[1] or epigraphical,[2] about play performances at the Pythia is later than the middle of the first century A.D. Plutarch says that as soon as the *tragodos* was admitted to the Games, all kinds of *akroamata*[3] forced their way in as if through a door that had been opened (*Mor.* 674 D). The Pythian Games thus obtained a not unpleasant variety and greater pomp, but the austere and musical character of the festival was not preserved. Plutarch further reports that at the Pythia of A.D. 99 or 103[4] the question whether these additional competitions (ἐπίθετα ἀγωνίσματα) should be banned was raised and discussed. The sudden introduction of many new events which changed the character of the Pythia points to a late date. Moreover the fact that around the beginning of the second century A.D. the place of these events in the Pythia could still be debated implies that they were established by a not very long tradition, say two centuries. Unless therefore new evidence turns up we could not date the official introduction of drama into the Pythian Games before the end of the pre-Christian era.

However, the Pythia ranked second in importance only to the Olympic Games. Naturally, therefore, it attracted a large number of artists. But not all of them competed for the crown-

---

[1] Philostr. *Apoll. Tyan.* V 7 (193); V 9 (195); VI 10 (238); *Vit. Soph.* II 1 (553); II 27 (616); Plut. *Mor.* 410 A, 414 C; 674 D, F.

[2] E. Bourguet, *De rebus delphicis imperatoriae aetatis* (1905), p. 89, cf. L. Robert, *Étud. épigr. et phil.*, p. 26; *F.D.* iii.4 86, cf. Robert, *ibid.*, p. 30; *Mnemosyne* N.S. 47 (1919), 258.

[3] On *akroamata* see L. Robert, *Hermes* 65 (1930), 116, *R.É.G.* 49 (1936), 236f.

[4] The date is suggested by a reference to Petraios, *agonothetes* of the Pythia, see A. B. West, *Cl. Phil.* 23 (1928), 262ff.

of-laurel prize. Until 310 B.C. at least the musical programme of the Pythia comprised only flute-players, *kithara*-players, and singers to the *kithara* (Pausanias X 7, 2, cf. Plut. *Mor.* 674 D). Other artists gave performances outside the contests for money rewards, or gratuitously, though they were usually awarded the *proxenia* of the city and the consequent privileges (inviolability, right to acquire land, right to consult the oracle first, etc.). At the Pythia of 130 (or 134) B.C., for example, a lady harp-player[1] from Kyme gave a performance as an offering to Apollo, and two or three more at the request of the city. She was given a huge reward, 1000 drachmai, and awarded the exceptional honour of a bronze statue (*S.I.G.*[3] 689). Another lady harp-player, Polygnota of Thebes, went to Delphi in 86 B.C., at the time when the Pythian festival ought to be cele-brated. The festival was not held in that year διὰ τὸν ἐνεστακότα πόλεμον, i.e. because of the first Mithridatic war, but she gave performances for four days, the first being an offering to the god, and was rewarded by 500 drachmai (*S.I.G.*[3] 738 = *F.D.* iii.3 249–50). In 94 B.C. the Delphians even sent a delegation to invite the Cretan organist (ὕδραυλος),[2] Antipatros of Eleu-therna, to exhibit his unusual art at Delphi and thus contribute to the splendour of the festival.[3] At the same Pythaid a certain – ρ[ο]ς, son of Artemon, whose profession is not preserved on the stone, gave ἀκροάσεις and was granted proxenia, etc. (*F.D.* iii.1 263). The most interesting case is, of course, that of Satyros of Samos who was the first flute-player to win the Pythian con-test without competitors in 194 B.C. At the sacrificial ceremony that followed the end of the athletic events he offered to the god and the Greeks gathered in the Pythian stadium a strange performance described as ᾆσμα μετὰ χοροῦ Διόνυσον καὶ κιθάρισμα ἐκ Βακχῶν Εὐριπίδου (*S.I.G.*[3] 648 B). This passage

---

[1] On harp-players see Robert, *Étud. épigr. et. phil.*, pp. 36–8.

[2] On ancient organs see Hero Alex., *Pneumatica* I 42 (Schmidt); Vitruv. X 8; C. Loret, 'Recherches sur l'orgue hydraulique', *Rev. Arch.*, 3ème sér., 15 (1890), 76–102; C.-E. Ruelle in Daremberg and Saglio, *s.v.* hydraulus; W. W. Hyde, 'An Inscribed Water Organ', *T.A.P.A.* 69 (1938), 392–410; W. Apel, 'Early History of the Organ', *Speculum* 23 (1948), 191–216.

[3] *S.I.G.*[3] 737; cf. L. Robert, *B.C.H.* 53 (1929), p. 39, n. 3: 'Il est vraisemblable qu' on a fait venir Antipatros à Delphes pour rehausser l'éclat des Pythia par un récital d'orgue.'

has been the subject of much speculation.[1] Satyros seems to have conducted a musical performance, the details of which cannot be made out with certainty. Nevertheless the important thing is that an excerpt of tragedy could be executed separately as early as the beginning of the second century B.C.[2]

PERFORMANCES OUTSIDE FESTIVALS

Were whole tragedies played at the Pythia in the margin of the contests? Free-lance poets and virtuosi of such rather rare instruments as the hydraulic organ or the harp which had no official place in the programmes of musical festivals would after all be expected to appear in a city on some festive occasion (cf. *B.C.H.* 66–7 [1942–3], 130, l. 6). But the production of a play would involve a whole troupe of Dionysiac *technitai* who were kept busy by numerous dramatic festivals in various cities. However, the tragic actor Nikon of Megalopolis was made *proxenos* of Delphi c. 165 B.C. on account of performances he and his company dedicated to Apollo: καὶ ἐνδαμήσας δὲ ἀξιωθεὶς ἐπέδωκε τῶι θε|⁵ῶι ἁμέραν καὶ ἀγωνίξατο (sc. performed) καὶ εὐδοκίμησε, (ἔδοξε τᾶι πόλει) ἐπαινέσαι Νίκωνα Νικία Μεγαλο-| πολίταν καὶ ὑπάρχειν αὐτῶι καὶ ἐγγόνοις παρὰ τᾶς πόλιος προξενίαν etc.|⁹ καλέσαι δὲ αὐτὸν καὶ τοὺς μετ᾽ αὐτοῦ τοὺς ἄρχοντας καὶ ἐν τὸ πρυτανεῖον (*S.I.G.*[3] 659 = *F.D.* iii.1 48). A separate decree must have been issued in honour of the supporting actors (τοὺς μετ᾽ αὐτοῦ) Echekrates and Philon of Argos whom we find together with Nikon in a list of *proxenoi* of Delphi (*S.I.G.*[3] 585, 128/30). The phraseology of Nikon's inscription is very similar to that employed in the honorary decrees referred to above, but we cannot decide whether he went to Delphi in order to present his performances to Apollo, perhaps timing his visit with the

---

[1] L. Couve, *B.C.H.* 18 (1894), 85–6; Dörpfeld-Reisch, *Das griech. Theater*, p. 259; M. Nilsson, *Zur Geschichte des Bühnenspiels in der rom. Kaiserzeit*, pp. 16ff.; Th. Birt, *Die Schaubauten der Griechen*, p. 27; K. Latte, *Eranos* 52 (1954), 126–7; S. Eitrem-L. Amundsen, *Symb. Osl.* 31 (1955), 27; T. B. L. Webster, *Misc. in memoria di A. Rostagni*, p. 540.

[2] Many other decrees do not mention the occasion on which the honoured artist made ἐπιδείξεις or ἀκροάσεις, but those dated to Pythian years (some of them even to the first semester of the Delphic year, in which the festival was held) are most likely to be connected with the Pythia: *S.I.G.*[3] 452, 254? B.C.; *S.I.G.*[3] 447 = *F.D.* iii.3 217, 246? B.C.; *F.D.* iii.3 119, 130 or 134 B.C.; *F.D.* iii.1 273, 130 or 134 B.C.

celebration of a fête, or if he did so after the conclusion of the Soteria of that year, though the latter alternative seems to me less likely.[1] Another tragic actor, Kleonikos, son of Kleokrates, from Rhodes, was awarded *proxenia*, *asylia*, and so on, early in the second half of the third century B.C., but we are not told how he earned these distinctions (*F.D.* iii.3 382). The same privileges were accorded to him by the city of Oropos because εὔνους ὢν διατελεῖ τῇ τε πόλει κοινῇ καὶ ἰδίᾳ τοῖς δεομένοις τῶν πολιτῶν παρέχεται χρ[εί]ας ἐμ παντὶ καιρῷ (*I.G.* vii 275). This is a general formula repeated in hundreds of proxenic decrees of several cities without really disclosing the particular events which occasioned the conferring of privileges.

---

[1] In two cases it is clearly stated that the kitharodes Menalkes of Athens (*S.I.G.*³ 431, 255/4? B.C.) and Athanadas of Rhegion (*B.C.H.* 73 [1949], 276–7, 153/2–144/3 B.C.) gave performances as an offering to Apollo in addition to their participation in the Soteria contests. Menalkes, son of Speuson, offered his kitharodic performance after his participation in the Soteria as a member of the dithyrambic chorus of men in the year of archon Emmenidas (*S.G.D.I.* 256₄₅; see p. 74). The same man seems to have offered free performances in Delos also, and was rewarded with the *proxenia* of the city (*I.G.* xi 575).

CHAPTER XII

PRIVILEGES OF *TECHNITAI*

GUILDS

Living in an age of most unstable balance of power and incessant warfare, it was natural that the *technitai* of Dionysos should try to take advantage of various measures adopted by the Greek cities in their effort to protect themselves from the evils of war and the dangers which beset their turbulent era.[1] Such measures were the confederations of cities, the recognition of inviolability (ἀσυλία) of certain places—originally sanctuaries, later whole cities—and persons, or classes of persons, warranty of personal safety (ἀσφάλεια) particularly useful to people travelling in the territory of the state granting it, the *proxenia*, unsparingly given to large numbers of individuals by all cities, the conferring of citizenship on distinguished foreigners, or even reciprocity of civic rights agreed and guaranteed by treaty between two states (ἰσοπολιτεία), and so forth.[2]

The *technitai* claimed that they were sacred servants of Dionysos, and in spite of their bad reputation as persons of dubious morals,[3] this was partially true because their performances were a part of the celebration of various religious festivals. On the other hand they deserved some kind of international protection because their profession involved them in ceaseless wandering over alien lands. So they asked for, and obtained, several privileges and assurances of safety from many cities and Hellenistic rulers, who in turn wanted their festivals properly celebrated.[4]

All the guilds tried to be on good terms with Apollo and Delphi, for the guarantees given by the Amphictyons on behalf

[1] Tarn, *Hell. Civil.*[3], pp. 82ff.; Rostovtzeff, *S.E.H.*, i, pp. 194ff.

[2] Tarn, *loc. cit.*, Rostovtzeff, *loc. cit.* (also consult the index); G. Busolt-H. Swoboda, *Griechische Staatskunde* (Handb. d. Altertumswissenschaft, iv, I.1. München, 1926), pp. 1240ff.; V. Ehrenberg, *The Greek State*, Oxford, 1960, pp. 103ff.; H. Francotte, *Mélanges de droit public grec*, Liège-Paris, 1910, pp. 182ff.; E. Schlesinger, *Die griechische Asylie*, Diss. Giessen, 1933.

[3] Athenaeus, VI 254 b; *Probl. Arist.*, XXX 10.   [4] Poland, *R.E.*[2] v 2488ff.

Date	Reference	Issuing body	Contents
1	Before 280	*S.I.G.*³ 460=*F.D.* iii.1, p. 85, n. 1	Delphi	*Promanteia, proedria, prodikia,* to the Isthmian and Nemean guild.[1]
2	279/8?	*F.D.* iii.2 68_{61-94}= *I.G.* ii² 1132_{1-39}= *S.I.G.*³ 399	Amphictyony	The Amphictyony grants *asylia, asphaleia,* immunity from taxation and military service (*ateleia, ateleia strateias*) to the Athenian guild, so that the *technitai* would be able to carry out their sacred mission without any impediment, and the honours and sacrifices to the gods, i.e. the festivals, could be performed. The privileges would not apply to artists failing to observe an agreement.
3	240?– 228?	*F.D.* iii.3 218 B 5– 8=*I.G.* ix² 175= *S.I.G.*³ 507	Aitolians	The guild of Ionia and Hellespontos is given the same privileges (*asylia, asphaleia*), which had already been conferred on the Isthmian and Nemean guild.
4	228–215?	(*a*) *F.D.* iii.1 351= *S.E.G.* xix 379, ll. 11–29. (*b*) *F.D.* ibid., *S.E.G.* ibid., ll. 30–9	Amphictyony	(*a*) At the request of the city of Thebes and the Isthmian and Nemean guild the Amphictyons recognize the sanctuary of Dionysos Kadmeios as *asylon* and guarantee the *asylia* and *asphaleia* of *technitai* going to Thebes for five days before [and five days after] the festival of Dionysos Kadmeios. (*b*) Any artist who, being in good health, does not comply with his appointment by the guild to appear at the festival will be liable to fine and prosecution.

[1] J. Pouilloux, 'Promanties collectives et protocole delphique', *B.C.H.* 76 (1952), 484ff.

	Date	Reference	Issuing body	Contents
5	220? or 224?	*I.G.* vii 4135 = *S.I.G.*³ 635, cf. Feyel, *Contrib. à l'épigr. béot.*, p. 141	Amphictyony	Same protection to the sanctuary of Apollo Ptoios at Akraiphia in Boeotia, and to the *technitai* taking part in the festival of Ptoia, as granted to Thebans.
6	214[1]	*F.D.* iii.1 351 = *S.E.G.* xix 379, ll. 1–10	Amphictyony	Request of Thebans to inscribe no. 4 on the Treasury of Thebans granted.
7	205/4– 203/2 ?	(a) *F.D.* iii.2 134a = *I.G.* ix² 192 (b) *F.D.* iii.2 134b (c) *Ibid.*, 134c	(a) Aitolians (b) Amphictyony (c) Delphi	The city of Teos is proclaimed *asylon* and sacred to Dionysos. The Teians are given all the privileges enjoyed by Dionysiac artists.
8	130/29[2]	*I.G.* ii² 1132, ll. 40–94 = *S.I.G.*³ 692 (ll. 52–94 = *F.D.* iii.2 68, ll. 1–61) + *S.E.G.* xviii 249	Amphictyony	Renewal of privileges given to the Athenian artists by no. 2
9	128/7	*F.D.* iii.2 47 = *S.I.G.*³ 698	Delphi	*Asylia, promanteia, proxenia* to the Athenian guild.

[1] On the date see Flacelière, *Aitoliens*, p. 409, n. 40.
[2] Delphian archon Aristion dated 134/3(?) or 130/29? by Daux, *Chronologie* L 65, cross-dated by the Athenian archon Demostratos, placed in 130/29.

Date	Reference	Issuing body	Contents
10	128/7?	*F.D.* iii.2 50 = *S.I.G.*³ 699	Delphi	Same privileges are bestowed on the association of Athenian epic poets who were later merged in the major guild.
11	c. 125?	*F.D.* iii.2 69 = *I.G.* ii² Amphictyony 1134, ll. 1–63		A panegyric address to Athens, mother of education and culture, and inventor of all kinds of drama. The old privileges of Athenian *technitai* are renewed. The right to wear their traditional crown of gold and other ornaments (χρυσοφορία), and possibly a purple robe,[1] in all cities, is guaranteed to the priests of the guild.
12	117/6	*I.G.* ii² 1134, ll. 77– Amphictyony 109		Renewal of Athenian privileges (*asylia, asphaleia, chrysophoria* and *synergasia*[?] mentioned).
13	106/5	*F.D.* iii.2 49 = *S.I.G.*³ 728 K	Delphi	Privileges of Athenian guild renewed (see p. 92)
14	98/7	*F.D.* iii.2 48 = *S.I.G.*³ 711 L	Delphi	As above.

[1] [πορφυροφ]ορεῖν Colin in *F.D.*, [στεφανηφ]ορεῖν Klaffenbach, *Symbolae*, pp. 37, 40, n. 1, and Wilhelm, *Jahresh.* 17 (1914), 40, adopted in *I.G.* Cf. Poland, *R.E.*² v 2491. Daux, *Delphes*, p. 367, n. 1, defended Colin's restoration.

of their governments would be respected in most parts of Greece. Moreover, the Aitolians who controlled Delphi and the Amphictyony in the third century were famous brigands and pirates, therefore it would be vital to the *technitai* to immunize themselves against Aitolian raids and privateering. That is why in some cases the *technitai* asked the Aitolians directly to guarantee their safety, although the Amphictyonic decisions were supposed to provide protection in Aitolia as well as in many other regions.

The decrees (pp. 100–2) giving privileges to the Dionysiac guilds, have been issued at Delphi.

Decree no. 2 probably coincides with the foundation of the Soteria.[1] No. 3 (cf. no. 7) implies that the Aitolians had already guaranteed the *asylia* and *asphaleia* of the Isthmian and Nemean artists.[2] The Athenian *technitai* organized their spectacular performances at the second Pythaid after the renewal of their privileges in the previous year (no. 8). Decrees 9–10, 13 and 14 were issued after each Pythaid, and mention the privileges among other honours awarded to the artists. Nos. 11 and 12 belong to the dossier of the well-known dispute between the Athenian and the Isthmian and Nemean guilds, which followed the failure of the two associations to co-operate.[3] The artists referred their controversy to the Roman proconsul of Macedonia, and later to the Senate. The Romans justified the Athenians, and the Amphictyons conforming, as it were, to the Roman jurisdiction expressed their admiration for the city in which civilization and drama were born, and confirmed the privileges of the Athenian guild.

INDIVIDUAL ARTISTS

In addition to the above decrees the city of Delphi conferred proxenia and the rights ensuing from it (acquisition of land,

---

[1] Ferguson, *A.J.P.* 55 (1934), 324; Flacelière, *Aitoliens*, pp. 122–3, 143–4.

[2] The Isthmian and Nemean guild had been given various privileges by the Delphians (no. 1) but these privileges were rather nominal than substantial. Such warranties as inviolability, safety of travel, and so on, had to be accorded to by the Aitolians, or the Amphictyony that was again controlled by the Aitolians.

[3] On the dispute of the guilds see Klaffenbach, *Symbolae*, pp. 29ff.; Pomtow, *S.I.G.*[3] 704–5; Poland, *R.E.*[2] v 2504ff; Daux, *Delphes*, pp. 359ff.; Pickard-Cambridge, *Festivals*, pp. 294ff.

immunity from taxation, right to consult the oracle first, and so on) upon a large number of artists who gave free performances at Delphi as offerings to Apollo. Very few of these artists were actors[1] whose immunity was in fact warranted by the Amphictyony. Moreover, the production of drama is a team-work, and indeed the guilds had several times paid tribute to Apollo by organizing free performances for which they were appropriately rewarded. The Delphian *proxenia* was at times granted to lyric poets,[2] epic poets,[3] singers to the *kithara*[4] and other musicians,[5] writers of *enkomia*,[6] harp-players,[7] an organist,[8] and so on.[9] Particularly interesting is a decree for a pantomime dated between 84 and 60 B.C.[10] This inscription together with another from Priene[11] are the earliest inscriptions we have for the pantomimic dancing which borrowed its themes from tragedy (hence τραγικὴ ὄρχησις, τραγικῆς κινήσεως ὑποκριτής).[12] Equally noteworthy is another decree[13] of similar date in honour of a

---

[1] See pp. 97–8. The Athenian hieromnemon at the Pythia of 30(?) B.C., Thrasykles, son of Archikles, was honoured by Delphic proxenia, *F.D.* iii.2 67. He was perhaps a tragic poet who had won a victory at Athens in that same year: ἀγωνισάμενος ἐν τῇ ἰδίᾳ πατρίδι τραγῳδίᾳ καινῇ καὶ νικάσας.

[2] *S.I.G.*³ 449 A=*F.D.* iii.2 190, 337/6–334/3 B.C.; *S.I.G.*³ 450=*F.D.* iii.2 78, 250–225?

[3] *S.I.G.*³ 452, 254/3?; *S.I.G.*³ 447=*F.D.* iii.3 217 (cf. *I.G.* xi 572), 246/5ff.?; *S.I.G.*³ 448=*F.D.* iii.2 75, 245–225?; *S.I.G.*³ 451=*F.D.* iii.2 158, 228–215?; *F.D.* iii.1 273, 130/29?

[4] *S.I.G.*³ 431, 255/4? (cf. *I.G.* xi 575, Delian *proxenia*); *B.C.H.* 73 (1949), pp. 276–7, 153/2–144/3.

[5] *S.I.G.*³ 660=*F.D.* iii.1 49, 161/0?; *B.C.H.* 63 (1939), p. 161, 142/1 or 141/0; *S.I.G.*³ 703, 133–121?; Robert, *Hellenica* ii (1946), 34–6, cf. Daux, *B.C.H.* 73 (1949), p. 287, second century B.C.; Daux, *ibid.*, p. 286, end of first century B.C.

[6] *S.I.G.*³ 702=*F.D.* iii.3, 124, 157/6.

[7] *S.I.G.*³ 689, 130/29?; *S.I.G.*³ 738=*F.D.* iii.3 249–50, 86/5.

[8] *S.I.G.*³ 737, 94/3.

[9] The professions of artists are omitted, or not preserved in *F.D.* iii.3 125, 157/6; *ibid.*, 126, 157/6; *B.C.H.* 66–7 (1942–3), p. 130, 153/144; *F.D.* iii.1 365, letters of second century, B.C.; *ibid.*, 263a, 94/3.

[10] Robert, *Étud. épigr. et phil.*, p. 11, Daux, *B.C.H.* 63 (1939), p. 169.

[11] *Inschr. Priene* 11364–66; L. Robert, 'Pantomimen im griechischen Orient', *Hermes* 65 (1930), 114–16.

[12] On pantomime Robert, *Hermes* 65 (1930), 106–22; O. Weinreich, *Epigramm und Pantomimus*, Sitz.-Ber. d. Heidelberger Akad. d. Wiss., phil.-hist. Kl., 1944–8, 1. Abh.; E. Wüst, *R.E.* xviii (1949), 833–69 (article 'Pantomimus'); V. Rotolo, *Il pantomimo: studi e testi*, Palermo, 1957; M. Kokolakis, *Platon*, fasc. 21 (1959), 3–59.

[13] Robert, *Étud. épigr. et phil.*, p. 7.

magodos,[1] a kind of musical mime mentioned by Hesychius, Strabon, and Athenaeus (quoting Aristoxenos and Aristocles)[2] but formerly unattested in epigraphy. More pantomimes,[3] conjurors,[4] and acrobats[5] in Delphi, as well as musicians[6] and a *tragodos*,[7] are attested by inscriptions of imperial times.

[1] Maas, *R.E.*[2] iii 159–60 (article 'Simodos'); H. Reich, *Der Mimus*, Berlin, 1903, i.1, pp. 13, 233–5, 238–41, 282–3, 344–6, i.2, 531–41, 548–9; Robert, *Étud. épigr. et phil.*, pp. 8–11.

[2] Hesych. *s.v.* μαγῳδή; Strab. XIV 648; Athen. XIV 620 d, 621 c.

[3] *F.D.* iii.2 105, cf. Robert, *Hermes* 65 (1930), 108; *F.D.* iii.2 106, cf. Robert, *ibid.*, 112; *F.D.* iii.1 551, Robert, *ibid.*, 106.

[4] *F.D.* iii.1 469.

[5] *F.D.* iii.1 216, cf. Robert, *Étud. épigr. et phil.*, 102ff.; *F.D.* iii.1 226 (also 225?), Robert, *ibid.*, 104ff.

[6] Singers to the *kithara*: *S.I.G.*[3] 817=*F.D.* iii.4 34; Flacelière, *B.C.H.* 73 (1949), 465; perhaps *F.D.* iii.2 104. Flute-players: *F.D.* iii.3 129; Daux, *B.C.H.* 68–9 (1944–5), 124; *F.D.* iii.2 250; *F.D.* iii.1 547. Trumpet-player: *F.D.* iii.1 554. *Mesochoros*: *F.D.* iii.1 219 (explained as conductor of chorus by Robert, *Étud. épigr. et phil.*, pp. 96ff.). 'Poets': *F.D.* iii.1 206, 210, 542.

[7] Δ – – s, son of Apheles, Athenian, *F.D.* iii.2 101, end of first century A.D.

CHAPTER XIII

ARCHAEOLOGICAL EVIDENCE

THEATRE BUILDING

The theatre of Delphi is one of the best preserved Greek theatres. It occupies the north-western corner of the sanctuary of Apollo, and commands a magnificent view over the sanctuary and the valley of Delphi. The *koilon* whose axis runs from north-west to south-east is divided into two parts by a *diazoma*. The lower tier consists of twenty-seven and the upper of eight rows of seats.[1] The upper part is not fully developed in a semicircle, and has only six *cunei* against seven of the lower *cavea*. The orchestra is laid with polygonal slabs, and circumscribed by a water ditch. The construction of the orchestra and the Parnassos-limestone auditorium is now dated to the late fourth century B.C.[2] The stage building was reconstructed in 160–158 B.C. when the Pergamene king Eumenes II financed an important ἐπισκευή of the theatre and dispatched a number of technicians[3] to Delphi to carry out the work (*F.D.* iii.3 237, 239).

The theatre is mentioned, or briefly described in preliminary reports[4] of the excavations, and in several handbooks on ancient theatres,[5] but no special study of this important architectural monument has appeared so far. Moreover, the student is bewildered by the fact that nearly every time the general plan of the sanctuary area was revised in the past fifty years the ground plan of the stage building was restored in a different way

[1] Arch. reports in *B.C.H.* 75 (1951), 137.

[2] *B.C.H. ibid.*, J. Pouilloux, *F.D.* ii, *La région nord du Sanctuaire* (1960), pp. 108, 117. See Addendum to Ch. XIII, p. 108.

[3] Cf. the painters sent to Delphi by Attalos II, *S.I.G.*[3] 682, 140/39 B.C.

[4] Th. Homolle, *B.C.H.* 21 (1897), 261–3; recent work at the theatre by G. Roux and Chr. Dunant is reported in *B.C.H.* 75 (1951), 136–7.

[5] O. Puchstein, *Die griechische Bühne*, p. 100; H. Bulle, *Untersuchungen*, pp. 257–9; P. E. Arias, *Il teatro greco fuori di Atene*, pp. 58–63; N. Modona, *Gli edifici teatrali greci e romani*, p. 44; cf. F. Schober, *R.E.* Suppl. v 138.

for reasons not explained to the layman.[1] It is clear, however, that the *skene* consisted of a large central room (c. 5 × 2 m), and two small side rooms (c. 2 × 2 m).[2] It must have been at least three storeys high because the ground floor was about 4 m lower than the level of the orchestra (the difference is due to the slope of the hillside), and the second storey was screened by the *proskenion*, the stylobate of which rests on the orchestra level. The façade of the third storey, therefore, was the background of the dramatic action which took place on the *proskenion*. An opening on the roof may have been used for divine appearances as in Corinth and Priene (see p. 129).[3] The internal walls of the *skene* were extended across the *proskenion* area which appears accordingly to have been divided into three parts corresponding to the three sections of the *skene*. But in the latest plan published in *Énigmes à Delphes* (1963) by J. Pouilloux and G. Roux—who has recently conducted new research in the theatre and is preparing with the collaboration of Mlle Chr. Dunant a detailed publication of the monument in the *F.D.* series[4]—the colonnade of the *proskenion* runs between the north ends of these walls and before the central room of the skene only. The two side sections are treated as projecting wings of the *skene* (*paraskenia*) enclosing the *proskenion*, or more precisely, the *hyposkenion*, area. Furthermore, the single eastern ramp shown in earlier designs to lead up to the *logeion* is left out from the new plan. The side entrances to the *logeion* (*ano parodoi*) would be provided through the *paraskenia* which would also embrace the *logeion*. We are looking forward to seeing the evidence on the grounds of which Professor Roux accepted this restoration of the stage plan, which recalls the theatres of Segesta and New Pleuron. At present the plan cannot be unreservedly considered as satisfactory for two reasons. First, the *proskenion* is too short for a theatre as

[1] (a) A. Tournaire, *F.D.* ii, *Relevés et restaurations* (1902), pl. 4; Pomtow, *Berl. Phil. Woch.* 32 (1912), 1173-4; (b) F. Poulsen, *Delphi* (Engl. transl. 1920), p. 52; Pomtow, *R.E.* Suppl. iv 1199; (c) P. de La Coste-Messelière, *Au Musée de Delphes* (1936), pl. 50, retained in subsequent publications until 1960; (d) J. Pouilloux–G. Roux, *Énigmes à Delphes* (1963), plan of the sanctuary.

[2] So Schober, *loc. cit.*

[3] An uncertain restoration, [τῶι ἀρχιτέκτονι τοῦ θεο]λογίου μισθὸς μηνὸ[ς] ῾Ηραίου, has been suggested for *F.D.* iii.5 78₂₁, an account of wages and expenditure on maintenance and repairs of public buildings dated between 327-300 B.C.

[4] Cf. J. Pouilloux, *F.D.* ii, *La région nord du Sanctuaire*, p. 7, n. 1.

big as that of Delphi; to my knowledge, there is no other instance of a *proskenion* shorter than the diameter of the orchestra. Secondly, a ramp is strongly suggested on the east side of the stage (if not on the west) by two walls which look like prolongations of the front wall of the *skene* and the *proskenion* respectively.

In the first century A.D. the *proskenion* was replaced by a lower and deep Roman *pulpitum*, the front of which was decorated by a marble frieze showing the labours of Herakles in relief.[1]

DRAMATIC MONUMENTS

Very few dramatic monuments have been discovered at Delphi. We have already mentioned three Athenian terracottas representing characters of Middle Comedy. They are dated to the second quarter of the fourth century B.C., and are as follows: (*a*) Nurse and baby. Other copies of the same type found at Athens and Tanagra (Webster, *M.O.M.C.*, AT 8; *F.D.* v 202, no. 651, pl. 23/15). (*b*) Herakles standing cross-legged, wearing lion-skin, and lightly leaning on his club. Other copies from Athens, Melos, Thebes, Larissa on Hermos, Crimea, Tarentum, etc. (Webster, *ibid.* AT 24; *F.D.* v 163, no. 294, pl. 22/2). (*c*) Man with short wedge beard, perhaps Pollux' *sphenopogon* (Webster, *ibid.* AT 54; *F.D.* v 204, no. 658).

Two more terracottas, one early Hellenistic and the other late Roman (c. A.D. 250), were also excavated in Delphi. The former is a mask of a *diamitros hetaira* (Pollux no. 41. Webster, *M.N.C.*, XT 6; *F.D.* v 206, no. 684, pl. 24/2), and the latter is a lamp decorated with a mask of a wavy-haired leading slave (*episeistos*, Pollux no. 27. Webster, *M.N.C.*, XL 4; *F.D.* v 188, no. 521, fig. 815).

ADDENDUM

The auditorium of the theatre of Delphi has no *proedria* thrones. The first row of seats is about 2 m higher than the level of the

---

[1] These sculptures were formerly taken as a part of the Hellenistic stage front, and referred to Eumenes' reconstruction, P. Perdrizet, *B.C.H.* 21 (1897), 600–3, Ch. Picard–P. de La Coste-Messelière, *Sculptures grecques de Delphes*, Paris, 1927, p. 41. But P. Lévêque, *B.C.H.* 75 (1951), 247–63, showed that they actually decorated the Roman stage, like the sculptures of the *bema* of Phaidros in the Athenian theatre of Dionysos.

orchestra. In the narrow passage between the wall below the
first seats (*podium*) and the water channel of the orchestra there
is no room for any other seats. In view of the recent dating of
the auditorium to the fourth century this arrangement is
extremely important for the question of the high stage, because
had the stone theatre not been designed with a high stage
from the beginning there would have been no reason for the
first seats to be placed so high. That this is the original arrangement is suggested by the fact that the first row of seats is
different from all the others in a small but significant detail.
On either side of every *kerkis* the first row ends in a kind of
schematic foot in the form of a rectangular slab of the same
thickness as the horizontal overhanging edge of the seats.
The front (vertical) edge of this foot projects as far as the
overhanging edge of the seats with which it forms a right angle
(see *B.C.H.* 75 [1951], 135, fig. 30). In the calculation of the
height of the first seats a difference of 20–25 cm between the
level of the present orchestra, which must have obtained its
polygonal limestone pavement at a late Roman date, and what
seems to have been the level of the original orchestra is taken
into account. The original level is suggested by the stylobate
of the *proskenion* and the top of the walls of the water ditch.

Appendices

HIGH STAGE AND CHORUS IN THE HELLENISTIC THEATRE[1]

THE CHORUS IN THE FOURTH CENTURY

The introduction of the high stage and the position of the chorus in the Hellenistic theatre are two aspects of a most interesting and important problem. Although we possess many theatres, archaeological finds, and inscriptions illustrating the theatrical history of post-classical times, there is a great diversity of opinions among modern scholars on this desperately complicated problem. My ambition does not extend to the belief that I shall loose this Gordian knot; I only wish to make one or two suggestions, with the hope that they will not add to the confusion.

I am mainly interested in the situation created by the erection of the high stage but, since the chorus underwent an evolution, or decline, in the course of the fourth century, I think I have to summarize the main points of this evolution in order to define the chorus' status towards the end of the century when, most probably, the *proskenion-logeion* was inaugurated.

In the early fourth century Aristophanes and Agathon ceased to compose special choral songs for each play, and began the practice of inserting *embolima* between the episodes. The *embolima* could be transferred from play to play, and consequently were irrelevant to the subject of each piece (Arist. *Poet.* 1456 a 26). But we may probably assume that the tragic poets had a stock of songs about the power of God, Fortune, Love, the inevitability of human fate, the punishment of *hubris* and impiety, the contravention or ignorance of laws and so on, and could pick out of them the more suitable for each tragic situation. The chorus was not a stranger to the action, and

---

[1] This is a revised and enlarged form of a paper which was read at the Institute of Classical Studies on 11 March 1963, and published in *B.I.C.S.* 10 (1963), 31–45.

remained present during the episodes. This sort of chorus can be traced in comedy down to the time of New Comedy. The last example seems to be the *Skythai* of Antiphanes, dated after 320 B.C.[1] The evidence for tragedy is very meagre. However, we have an instance of a chorus remaining in the orchestra after their *embolimon*, and being addressed by an actor at the beginning of the next episode. In a fragment of papyrus belonging to a fourth-century *Medeia* (attributed to ?Neophron), after the note χοροῦ, Medeia addresses the chorus: 'My dear women, who inhabit the Corinthian plain of this country, etc.'[2] Furthermore, plural titles like Agathon's Μυσοί, Kleophon's Βάκχαι, Dikaiogenes' Κύπριοι, Timesitheos' Δαναΐδες, etc. can hardly be explained if they are not to be taken as implying choruses of Mysians, Bacchai, and so forth.

In Menander we find the last stage of evolution of the comic chorus. It has invariably become a *komos*, a band of revellers who are not present in the course of the play but enter the scene between the episodes or acts,[3] and have nothing to do with the plot of the play.[4] The question is now whether the

---

[1] T. B. L. Webster, *Studies in Later Greek Comedy*, pp. 58–63.

[2] Milne, *Catalogue of Literary Papyri in the Brit. Mus.*, no. 77. Cf. Ennius' *Medea exul*, fr. v (p. 46 Ribbeck[2], p. 79 Klotz): 'Quae Corinthum arcem altam habetis, matronae opulentae, optumates.'

[3] Probably we cannot say more about the difference between episodes and acts than that the latter are parts of a play divided by *embolima*, while the *stasima*, which sometimes involved actors, connected rather than divided the episodes. There is no point in trying to establish a top date for the five-act division because the transition from the *stasima* to *embolima* was gradual. Nor may we infer anything from that division about the status of the chorus. We shall see that the *embolima*, at least in tragedy, were never reduced to the state of what we nowadays call an interlude, when the conception of 'act' and the manner of act-division is quite different (drop-curtain, lights, programme notes, and so on; cf. R. T. Weissinger, *A Study of Act Division in Classical Drama*, 1940, pp. 1ff., 127; W. Beare, *The Roman Stage*[2], p. 188).

[4] The question whether the chorus in Menander was in any way connected with the plot of all or some of his plays has been raised and discussed by several scholars who found some connections: F. Leo, *Hermes* 43 (1908), 166–7, 308–11; A. Körte, *Hermes* 43, 299–306; F. Skutsch, *Hermes* 47 (1912), 141–5; R. C. Flickinger, *Cl. Phil.* 7 (1912), 24–34. Körte had changed his mind in 1921 when he wrote: 'die ἐμβόλιμα füllen einen Zwischenakt ohne jede Berührung mit der Handlung [...] meine Versuche, ihn auch bei Menander mit der Handlung zu verbinden (Herm. XLIII 299ff.) waren verfehlt' (*R.E.* xi 1268, *s.v.* Komödie); nevertheless his arguments were utilized by K. J. Maidment, *C.Q.* 29 (1935), 16ff. Weissinger, *op. cit.*, 67–8, praises Maidment's conclusions, and further supports a second *chorus*

tragic chorus passed into a further stage of decline in the last quarter of the fourth century. I believe that it did not. The playwrights of New Comedy found in the *komos* a chorus type very suitable for the nature of their plays, in which parties and dinners occurred abundantly, and the ordinary street represented almost always by the scenery made the presence of revellers look normal; they were, after all, nothing else than a reversion to the primitive, as has been pointed out.[1] But what sort of group could be established as a standard chorus for tragedy? Certainly none. And to admit that a standard chorus is impossible for tragedy implies that the tragic chorus never reached the final stage of evolution which we know from New Comedy. The tragic poets had always to provide their pieces with a chorus related in some way or other to the subject of the play. This is supported by the little we know about Hellenistic tragedy, to which we shall come later, and by the fact that the special chorus survived in Roman tragedy,[2] while Roman comedy dropped it altogether.[3]

---

ancillarum, which was suggested by Flickinger (*loc. cit.*, 27), between the second and the third acts of the *Heauton* of Terence. I do not think that, particularly after the discovery of the *Dyskolos*, there are many, or indeed any, scholars still believing in a New Comedy chorus related to the plot of the plays. (Choruses of hunters, corybants, slaves, clansmen or wedding guests, which appeared among the characters of the *Heros*, *Theoph.*, *Perik.*, and *Samia*, in the recent edition of Menander's fragments by J. M. Edmonds, *The Fragments of Attic Comedy*, iii B, need not to be taken seriously.) It should be observed that the poet took care to anticipate any speculations of the audience about the nature of the chorus. It is not a matter of chance that the formula with which the actors introduce the chorus, saying that it is time to go because a crowd of drunken youths are approaching and it would not be wise to be in their way, occurs always, so far as we know, at the end of the first act (*Dysk.* 230–2; *Epitr.* 33–5; *Perik.* 71–2). The poet has thus informed his audience that the chorus has nothing to do with the action of the play. This typical announcement of the chorus before their first appearance must have been necessary in a time when the *komos*-type chorus was not yet established as the normal chorus of comedy (cf. Alexis fr. 107 K). The poet had to make the actors dissociate themselves from the approaching chorus because the spectators, naturally, expected some relationship.

[1] Leo, *ibid.*, 167; Körte, *Hermes* 43, 300; cf. Maidment, *ibid.*, 18.

[2] Ribbeck, *Röm. Tragödie*, pp. 607, 631ff.; Capps, *A.J.A.* 10 (1895), 297ff.; Reisch, *R.E.* iii 2403; Ziegler, *R.E.²* vi 1993ff. Cf. Leo, 'Die Composition des Chorlieder Senecas', *Rhein. Mus.* 52 (1897), 509ff.

[3] Diomedes, *Gr. L.* i 490 K; Reisch, *ibid.*; Beare, *The Roman Stage²*, pp. 19, 199ff.; G. Duckworth, *The Nature of Roman Comedy*, p. 99.

EVIDENCE FOR CHORUS IN HELLENISTIC TIMES

In the following paragraphs we shall see that the evidence for dramatic choruses in the Hellenistic period is by no means negligible.[1]

A common decree of the four major cities of Euboea, dated 294–87 B.C., prescribes how the artists for the dithyrambic and dramatic performances of the Dionysia and Demetrieia were to be hired, the rewards (or prizes?) to be given, and many directions for the transaction of the festivals. In the lines 29–32 we read: ἄρχειν δὲ τοὺς αὐλητὰς [---|-------τὸ]ν χορὸν εἰσάγειν, τοὺς δὲ τραγωιδοὺς τοὺς ἐργολαβήσαντας καταλ[είπ]ειν τοῖς α[ὐ]λη|[ταῖς --ἐπὶ τὴν---]ίαν καὶ *ΤΟΥΣ ΧΟΡΟΥΣ ΤΩΝ ΑΝΔΡΩΝ ΤΡΑΓΩΙΔΩΝ* τοῖς ὑποκριταῖς τὰ ἱμάτια νέα πα|[ρέχειν -- (*I.G.* xii.9 207).

The meaning of the passage is obscure because of the gaps but it seems to me clear that the words τοὺς χοροὺς τῶν ἀνδρῶν τραγωιδῶν hold fast together, and it is impossible to connect τραγωιδῶν with τοῖς ὑποκριταῖς,[2] while χοροὶ ἀνδρῶν τραγωιδῶν may mean choruses of men for dithyramb and tragedy. We shall see presently two other cases of choruses with a double function.

In the series of inscriptions from Delphi recording the artists who took part in the Amphictyonic Soteria we have one comic chorus every year consisting of seven (once eight) members, who, as it appears, provided the interludes for all the comedies of the programme (see p. 72). It is odd that we hear nothing of a tragic chorus. But I think von Jan was right in suggesting that the fifteen members of the dithyrambic chorus of men could very well serve the tragedies also.[3]

---

[1] In the following investigation of epigraphical evidence I have not dealt with inscriptions recording *choregoi* of tragedy and comedy. The complex question of the Hellenistic *choregia* deserves a separate study, which I propose to make at some other time. See, however, the discussion of Delian *choregia*, pp. 31ff., especially p. 34.

[2] *Τραγῳδοί* means (1) tragic chorus, (2) tragic poets, (3) tragic actors, (4) all the performers of a tragedy, (5) an occasion of tragic performances; it never means tragedy in the same sense as σάτυροι means satyr-play. Cf. Pickard-Cambridge, *Festivals*, pp. 128–33.

[3] *Verhandlungen der XXXIX Philologenversammlung zu Zürich*, 87, cp. Körte, *N. Jahrb.* 5 (1900), 86, and Reisch, *R.E.* iii 2402.

Our next case comes from Egypt. It is a decree of the Dionysiac artists of Ptolemais (Menshijeh), dated between 270–246 B.C., in the reign of Ptolemy II and Arsinoe (*O.G.I.S.* 51 = *S.B.* 8855). The decree that honours a patron of the *koinon* is signed by the members of the guild. Between l. 47 and l. 61 we read the names of one tragedian, six comedians, four supporting actors of tragedy (συναγωνισταὶ τραγικοί), and one [χορ]οδιδάσκαλ[ος]. After a few illegible lines a tragic flautist (αὐλητὴς τραγικός) follows. I think it would be reasonable to suppose that the *chorodidaskalos* (or *chorodidaskaloi*?) who is found among the dramatic performers was an instructor of dramatic choruses.

In 127 B.C. the Athenians sent their magnificent *theoria* to Delphi, the so-called Pythaid, which was the second of the four sent between 138/7 and 98/7 B.C. One comic and three tragic *chorodidaskaloi* were among the Dionysiac artists who gave performances in honour of Apollo (*F.D.* iii.2 47, cf. L. Robert *apud* Daux, *Delphes*, 723). Again dramatic choruses are not recorded separately but there are reasons to suppose that they were drawn out of the choir which sang the 'paean of the god' (see p. 90). Apart from the special case of the Pythaid, this inscription mentioning trainers of dramatic choruses among the members of the Athenian guild of Dionysiac *technitai* serves as evidence for Athens itself.

The splendour of the Athenians' celebrations in Delphi was not matched by the performances which the Isthmian and Nemean *technitai* offered τῷ θεῷ δωρεὰν at about the same time, at the festival of the winter Soteria. An inscription, dated 145–125 B.C., gives us the names of the artists who participated on that occasion (see p. 85). It is really striking that we have four comic dancers in a total of twelve performers for music, cyclic, and dramatic performances, while the cyclic dancers were miserably reduced to three in the cases of both boys and men.

But our most interesting case is an inscription from Tanagra dated to the beginning of the first century B.C. It tells us clearly about tragic, satyric and comic choruses, and even discriminates between choruses of old and new plays. The first part, edited in *I.G.* vii 540, gives a list of the victorious poets and artists at the musical and dramatic contests of the festival of Sarapis. Another

part of the stone that was discovered lately and published in
Arch. Ephemeris 1956, pp. 36–8, and *S.E.G.* xix 335, gives us a
financial outline of the festival. A benefactor had dedicated (or
bequeathed) a sum of money to be invested and produce an
interest sufficient for the expenses of the Sarapieia. A special
administrator of the money, appointed every four years, gave
the *agonothetes* the sum he needed for the management of the
festival. In our case the *agonothetes* gives a detailed account how
the amount he had received was spent on the purchase of gold
for making the crowns of the victors, on awarding money prizes
to the runners-up, on sacrifices and a banquet. At the end follow
the rewards of some persons whose contribution to the performances was quite important though they did not contest for any
prize: ἱματιομίσθη [ἀττικοῦ ρ΄.| τ]οῖς τραγικοῖς καὶ σατύροις ἀττι-
κοῦ ρ΄ καὶ κωμικοῖς σὺν χοροδιδ[ασκάλοις| ἀτ]τικοῦ ν΄. χοροδιδα-
σκάλοις τοῖς διδάξασιν καινὰς τραγ[ωδίας καὶ| το]ὺς σατύρους
ἀττικοῦ ν΄ καὶ αὐληταῖς τοῖς τὴν τραγῳδίαν [αὐλήσα|σιν][1] ἀττικοῦ
κη΄ καὶ τοῖς κωμικοῖς ἀττικοῦ ιβ΄ (ll. 43–7). ('To the costumier
100 Attic drachmai; to the tragic [performers, that is besides
the actor] and the satyrs 100 Attic dr., and to the comic together with the *chorodidaskaloi* 50 Attic dr.; to the *chorodidaskaloi*
who produced the new tragedies and the satyr plays 50 Attic
dr.; and to the flautists who provided the music of tragedy 28
Attic dr., and to the comic [flautists] 12 Attic dr.')

A few lines later the *agonothetes* mentions the opportunities he
had to spend his own money: [καὶ] ἄλλα ἀναλώματα γενόμενα
εἴς τε τὰ ὅρκια τὰ καθ᾽ἡμέραν [καὶ τὰς ἐσ|τιά]σεις τῶν καθ᾽ἡμέραν τοῦ
ἀγῶνος τῶν τε κριτῶν [καὶ τεχνιτῶν| καὶ χ]ορῶν καὶ νικησάντων
καὶ εἰς τὸ ἐπίθυμα καὶ ρασ[...... οὐ| λ]ογίζομαι διὰ τὸ δεδα-
πανηκέναι παρ᾽ἐμαυτοῦ (ll. 53–6). Since there is no sign of cyclic
dancers in any other part of the inscription, the choruses here
mentioned are necessarily the dramatic ones. This record of
Sarapieia proves the participation of a chorus in every sort of
drama, old and new, at the beginning of the first century. And
it is noteworthy that the producers of new tragedies are not
called *didaskaloi* or *hypodidaskaloi*[2] but *chorodidaskaloi*.

---

[1] [διδάξασιν] Ch. Christou in *Arch. Eph.* 1956, 37, and in *S.E.G.* xix 335. Cf.
G. M. Sifakis, *B.I.C.S.* 10 (1963), 46.

[2] Pickard-Cambridge, *Festivals*, pp. 92, 312.

The Sarapieia of Tanagra is only one of the many festivals in Boeotia known to us from inscriptions of the beginning of the first century. We have lists recording the winners of the Soteria at Akraiphia, Charitesia and Homoloia at Orchomenos, Amphiaraia at Oropos, Mouseia at Thespiai.[1] All these festivals had exactly the same programme as the Sarapieia. And though none was in honour of Dionysos, dramatic performances occupied a big part of them. Would it be unreasonable to suppose that the record from Tanagra illustrates what happened in the other cities of Boeotia at that time?

An unexpectedly large number of Athenian *tragikoi chorodidaskaloi* (14) are recorded in an inscription of Argos also dating from the beginning of the first century B.C. (*Mnemosyne* N.S. 47 [1919], 254; see App. II, pp. 143f.).

The fact that the same persons are sometimes called *chorodidaskaloi* and sometimes *hypodidaskaloi* raises the question what the exact meaning of these terms is, and to what extent they coincide. Photius gives the following definition for the *hypodidaskalos*: ὁ τῷ χορῷ καταλέγων. διδάσκαλος γὰρ αὐτὸς ὁ ποιητής, ὡς Ἀριστοφάνης. So the *hypodidaskalos* was originally a person with a special knowledge of music and dancing, who helped the poet-producer as chorus-trainer. It seems that in Hellenistic times, when old plays were frequently revived and new ones were most likely repeated by the travelling *technitai* at different places after their original production, the *hypodidaskalos* assumed the role of producer (although many leading actors may also have been producing the plays which they acted). This assumption explains why the more specific term *chorodidaskalos* came into use in regard to tragic and comic chorus trainers. In the second and first centuries B.C. there was apparently some confusion in the use of these terms. The tragic *hypodidaskaloi* Elpinikos and Philion went to Delphi in 130/29 as delegates of the Athenian guild of Dionysos to ask the Amphictyony to renew the privileges of the guild (p. 101, no. 8). Two years later the same men took part in the second Pythaid as tragic *chorodidaskaloi* (*F.D.* iii.2 47, cf. pp. 90 and 168, II.12, 14). Furthermore, Elpinikos together with the tragic *chorodidaskalos* Kleon

[1] *I.G.* vii 2727, 3195–7, 416–20, 1760–62; *B.C.H.* 19 (1895), 321ff.; *Polemon* 3 (1947/8), 73ff.

(p. 168, II.13) conducted the choir of boy pythaists at the first Pythaid (*F.D.* iii.2 11 20-2), and the tragic *hypodidaskalos* Diokles was the master of the choir of *technitai* at Pythaid IV (*F.D.* iii.2 48, cf. p. 171, IV.30). Evidently therefore the *hypodidaskaloi* were qualified musicians, competent to conduct a purely musical performance. On the other hand the *chorodidaskaloi* produced both tragedies and comedies in Tanagra (see above). In conclusion, it seems reasonable to accept that no real difference existed between *chorodidaskaloi* and *hypodidaskaloi* in the second and first century. The fact that these dramatic artists were capable of conducting non-dramatic choirs may mean that in drama they were primarily concerned with training choruses.

A marble relief from Athens showing six identical masks of young women, undoubtedly members of a tragic chorus, belongs probably to the same period.[1]

EVIDENCE FOR CHORUS AFTER THE MID-FIRST CENTURY B.C.

In 53 B.C. a performance of Euripides' *Bacchai* with a regular chorus is reported by Plutarch (*Cras.* 33, 3). It was given in the royal court of Armenia by the tragic actor Jason of Tralles as a part of the festivities that followed the marriage of the sister of Artabazes, king of Armenia, to the son of the Parthian king Orodes, whose army fought against the Romans successfully in Mesopotamia at that time, and defeated Crassus. Plutarch tells us that Jason performed in the *andron*, the men's quarters, after the banquet tables had been removed. And he was paid a whole talent for being cunning enough to sing together with the chorus the alternating verses where Agave vaunts the laceration of Pentheus, holding, from l. 1179ff., the real head of Crassus, which had just been brought from Mesopotamia.

From now on it is very difficult to follow the traces of the chorus. The little evidence we have is contradictory, and indicates that what happened at one place did not happen at others. First, Philodemos, the Epicurean philosopher and poet, expresses the view that no dance was ever of any help towards the

---

[1] I. N. Svoronos, *Τὸ ἐν 'Αθήναις 'Εθνικὸν Μουσεῖον*, pp. 241–2, no. 22, pl. 43; *M.T.S.* AS 27.

good and the noble, so nothing is lost now that dancing has been banished from drama.[1] Philodemos came to Rome about 75 B.C., and lived in Italy till his death c. 40–35 B.C. teaching Greek literature and philosophy in Herculaneum and Naples. He knew, then, what happened in Italy. The Roman chorus always stood on the same platform as the actors.[2] And at his time the permanent Roman stage building was fully established in Pompeii and Rome.[3] Therefore it seems to me that even if Philodemos refers to performances of Greek tragedies, he implies a chorus on the *pulpitum*, which, though wider than the *proskenion*, was not convenient for choral dancing.

Many decades later the poet Lucillius, who lived in the time of Nero, expected a tragedian to be surrounded by a chorus:

$$Οὐκ ᾔδειν σε τραγῳδόν, Ἐπίκρατες, οὐδὲ χοραύλην,$$
$$οὐδ' ἀλλ' οὐδὲν ὅλως, ὧν χορὸν ἔστιν ἔχειν.$$

(*Anth. Pal.* XI 11)

Similarly Plutarch (died c. A.D. 127) and Epictetos (died c. A.D. 135) speak of tragic chorus in a way suggesting living practice.[4] But their contemporary Dio Chrysostom (died after A.D. 112) gives an entirely different picture: τὰ μὲν τῆς κωμῳδίας ἅπαντα· τῆς δὲ τραγῳδίας τὰ μὲν ἰσχυρά, ὡς ἔοικε, μένει· λέγω δὲ τὰ ἰαμβεῖα· καὶ τούτων μέρη διεξίασιν ἐν τοῖς θεάτροις· τὰ δὲ μαλακώτερα ἐξερρύηκε τὰ περὶ τὰ μέλη (XIX 5, 487 R).

To what degree is this statement of Dio to be taken as illustrating the general practice of theatre production during

---

[1] *De mus.* 70 (Kemke): καὶ διότι περιῃρημένης τῆς ὀρχήσεως ἐκ τῶν δραμάτων οὐδὲν ἔχομεν ἔλαττον, ἐπειδήπερ οὐδὲν ἦν ἐν οὐδεμιᾷ πρὸς τὸ καλὸν καὶ γενναῖον συνέργημα. This statement was wrongly attributed to Diogenes of Babylon by E. Reisch (Dörpfeld-Reisch, *Das griech. Theater*, p. 260, *R.E.* iii 2402), and subsequently taken as evidence for the abolition of dancing from drama in the second century B.C.
[2] Cp. Vitruvius V 6, 2.
[3] M. Bieber, *The History of the Greek and Roman Theater*[2], pp. 174, 181.
[4] Plut. *Mor.* 63 A: ὥσπερ οἱ τραγῳδοὶ χοροῦ δέονται φίλων συναδόντων, ἢ θεάτρου συνεπικροτοῦντος; Epict. *Diss.* III 14, 1: ὡς οἱ κακοὶ (καλοὶ cod.: corr. Wolf) τραγῳδοὶ μόνοι ᾄσαι οὐ δύνανται, ἀλλὰ μετὰ πολλῶν, οὕτως ἔνιοι μόνοι περιπατῆσαι οὐ δύνανται. ἄνθρωπε, εἴ τις εἶ, καὶ μόνος περιπάτησον καὶ σαυτῷ λάλησον καὶ μὴ ἐν τῷ χορῷ κρύπτου. I 24, 15: ἐν τοῖς πλουσίοις καὶ βασιλεῦσι καὶ τυράννοις αἱ τραγῳδίαι τόπον ἔχουσιν, οὐδεὶς δὲ πένης τραγῳδίαν συμπληροῖ εἰ μὴ ὡς χορευτής.

imperial times? He must have known what happened in many places because he spent a good part of his life wandering around the vast empire; on the other hand it is an indisputable fact that the tragic chorus survived in some places for more than half a century after Dio. This is affirmed by a wall painting from a tomb in Cyrene showing a chorus of young men behind three tragic actors, dated to the time of the Antonines,[1] and by an inscription from Aphrodisias in Caria, dated after A.D. 180, in which the money prizes of a musical and dramatic contest, instituted by a rich citizen called Flavius Lysimachos, are recorded; among those prizes 500 denarii were to be given to the tragic chorus.[2] In any case, theatrical activity in the time of the Roman empire constitutes a long and complicated story that ends in the modern Greek words τραγουδῶ and τραγούδι for 'sing' and 'song', and the folk ballads in which a good many tragic motifs have been preserved.[3]

FRAGMENTS OF HELLENISTIC TRAGEDY

If we turn to the history of literature seeking an answer to our problem in the scanty remains of Hellenistic tragedy, we shall find ourselves on much less firm ground. Nevertheless we have to remark that: (1) Some plural titles of tragedies like Moschion's *Pheraioi*,[4] and Lycophron's *Marathonioi, Hiketai, Kassandreis* suggest choruses. (2) It is probable that the drama *Exagoge* by the hellenized Jew Ezekiel,[5] in which he treated the story of Moses and the exodus of the Jews from Egypt in the form of tragedy, had a chorus consisting of the six sisters of

---

[1] A. Pickard-Cambridge, *The Theatre of Dionysus in Athens*, fig. 120; Bieber, *op. cit.*, fig. 787; *M.T.S.* FP 1.

[2] *M.A.M.A.* viii 85–6, no. 420.

[3] S. Menardos, 'Ιστορία τῶν λέξεων τραγῳδῶ καὶ τραγῳδία, 'Αφιέρωμα εἰς Γ. Ν. Χατζιδάκιν, Athens, 1921, pp. 15ff.; S. Kyriakidis, Αἱ ἱστορικαὶ ἀρχαὶ τῆς δημώδους νεοελληνικῆς ποιήσεως, Thessaloniki, 1954. Cf. B. Hemmerdinger, 'Τραγοῦδι et l'histoire du texte des tragiques', *Glotta* 43 (1965), 298–301, who gives an impossible interpretation of the passage of Dio Chrysostom quoted above.

[4] If Moschion is Hellenistic as F. Schramm, *Tragicorum Graecorum hellenisticae quae dicitur aetatis fragmenta*, Monasterii Westfalorum, 1929, pp. 82–3, plausibly suggested.

[5] 269 verses of the *Exagoge* are preserved in the *Praeparatio evangelica* (IX 28–9) of Eusebius quoting Alexander Polyhistor (*De Judaeorum, F.H.G.* iii 211ff., F. Gr. Hist. iii A 273, F 19).

Sepphora, the daughters of Raguel, king of Madiam; Sepphora in the course of the play becomes wife of Moses. The drama was divided into five acts, and the unity neither of space nor of time was observed. A long time elapsed between the meeting of Moses and Sepphora, with which the play begins, and the safe delivery of the Jews across the Red Sea, after which it ends (cf. *Exod.* II 23). The first act is supposed to be played near the well where Moses met Sepphora and her sisters, and rescued them from the bad shepherds; the second in front of the palace of Raguel, the priest-king of Madiam or Libya; the third on Mount Horeb, where Moses conversed with God; the fourth before the palace of Pharaoh, and the fifth somewhere in the desert on the other side of the Red Sea after the successful passage of the Jews. At first sight the play seems desperately difficult to stage, and the subject itself could hardly be interesting to a Greek audience. But the technical problems are not really insoluble—we shall come to them later—and a Jewish audience and theatre is not unlikely, say, in Alexandria, since a Jewish amphitheatre is known in Berenice (Benghazi).[1] Anyhow the play by the 'author of Jewish tragedies', as Clement of Alexandria (*Strom.* I 23, 155) calls Ezekiel, is considered as a real tragedy composed in order to be produced, and is supposed to reflect the evolution of the technique of tragic composition in Hellenistic times.[2] Consequently the position of the chorus in it is most important from our point of view. The six maidens must have been the chorus. The number six does not indicate any reduction of the chorus' size, because it comes from the Bible (*Exod.* II 16). (After all the Suppliants of Euripides were 'seven', and those of Aeschylus 'fifty'.) They entered after the prologue of Moses, but we cannot tell for how long they stayed there. It has been said that their presence during the conversation of Moses with God, and later in the Egyptian court (third and fourth acts) would not be justified. In fact the problem lies in the many changes of place required. Did the chorus go out together with Moses and Sepphora at the end of the first act,

---

[1] *C.I.G.* iii 5361/2; *S.E.G.* xvi 931; G. Caputo, *Anthemon* (Scritti. . . .in onore di Carlo Anti), 1955, 283–5; cp. J. and L. Robert, *R.É.G.* 68 (1955), 284, n. 278.

[2] A. Kappelmacher, *Wien. Stud.* 44 (1925), 69ff.; K. Ziegler, *R.E.*[2] vi 1979ff.; A. Lesky, *Hermes* 81 (1953), 8–9; P. Venini, *Dioniso* 16 (1953), 7.

and come back at the beginning of the next act, after the scene of action had been transferred to the court of Raguel? Then who filled the gap between the acts? We shall try to give an answer later when we come to speak about the position of the chorus in the theatre with high stage.

Very little can be based on the papyrus fragment dealing with the story of Gyges and Kandaules, which is now believed to be Hellenistic. Maas found some traces of a choral song (the *parodos*?) in the first column, in which only the ends of some lines are preserved, while Latte and Kakridis argued that the narration of the Queen is made in front of a chorus of women. (On the other hand R. Cantarella suggested that the fragment does not belong to a tragedy at all but to a novel!)[1]

CHORUS OF SATYRS

It is worth while to pay a little more attention to the satyric drama. At the beginning of the Hellenistic age mythological comedy, which had taken the place of satyr play to a large degree in the fourth century, was definitely out of fashion. On the other hand the nostalgia for the rustic life that created bucolic poetry was a most favourable atmosphere for the satyr play to flourish in. Contests among poets of new, and actors of old plays now took place everywhere, for the first time in the history of Greek theatre.

It goes without saying that a satyr play without satyrs is inconceivable. Besides, the official name for satyric drama is σάτυροι, and its poet is called ποιητὴς σατύρων. 'Poets of satyrs' occur in catalogues of winners from Teos,[2] Magnesia on Maeander,[3] Samos,[4] Delos,[5] and the Boeotian cities which we referred to above. And we have already discussed the record from Tanagra, in which the chorus of satyrs is explicitly mentioned together with the tragic and comic.

Some more evidence comes from literary sources. Lycophron

---

[1] Maas, *Gnomon* 22 (1950), 142; Latte, *Eranos* 48 (1950), 140; Kakridis, *Hellenika* 12 (1953), 8–9; Cantarella, *Dioniso* 15 (1952), 8ff.

[2] Le Bas-Wadd. 91.

[3] *I. Magn.* 88=*S.I.G.*[3] 1079.

[4] Michel 901.

[5] *I.D.* 1959.

wrote the satyr play *Menedemos*, 'an encomium of the philosopher' (Diog. L. II 140), probably before he went to Egypt (c. 285–3). Athenaeus has preserved a fragment which he introduces saying: 'Lycophron from Chalkis has written the satyrs *Menedemos*, in which (ἐν οἷς) Silenos says to the satyrs: "children of a noblest father most depraved etc."' (X 420 b). Silenos is therefore in Lycophron's play exactly what he is in Euripides' *Cyclops* and Sophocles' *Ichneutai*: a special link between the characters and the chorus; a character himself, and at the same time the father of the chorus.

Another poet of the Pleiad, Sositheos, is praised by the epigrammatist Dioscorides because he restored the satyr play to its ancient vigour:

Κἠγὼ Σωσιθέου κομέω νέκυν, ὅσσον ἐν ἄστει
ἄλλος ἀπ᾽ αὐθαίμων ἡμετέρων Σοφοκλῆν,
Σκίρτος ὁ πυρρογένειος. ἐκισσοφόρησε γὰρ ὡνὴρ
ἄξια Φλιασίων, ναὶ μὰ χορούς, σατύρων
κἠμὲ τὸν ἐν καινοῖς τεθραμμένον ἤθεσιν ἤδη
ἤγαγεν εἰς μνήμην πατρίδ᾽ ἀναρχαΐσας,
καὶ πάλιν εἰσώρμησα τὸν ἄρσενα Δωρίδι μούσῃ
ῥυθμόν, πρὸς τ᾽αὐδὴν ἑλκόμενος μεγάλην
εὔαδέ μοι θύρσων τύπος εὖ χερὶ καινοτομηθεὶς
τῇ φιλοκινδύνῳ φροντίδι Σωσιθέου.

(*Anth. Pal.* VII 707 Waltz)

'I am also watching over the corse of Sositheos, as in the city another of my brothers over Sophocles, I, Skirtos the red-bearded. For he bore the ivy that man, yea by the choruses, in a way worthy of the Phliasian satyrs, and by giving me, already bred in new manners, my old character brought back to memory our fatherland; I urged again the male rhythm on the Dorian Muse, and being drawn to a grand tone I delighted in the beat of thyrsus beautifully cut by a new hand with the care of the venturesome Sositheos'.[1] All the 'venturesome' innovations or reinstatements Sositheos is credited with by the satyr Skirtos concerned, of course, the chorus of satyrs.

[1] On the various interpretations of this epigram see Webster, in *Misc. di studi alessandrini in memoria di A. Rostagni*, pp. 535–6.

I do not think I need insist more on the satyric chorus. I only want to say that the composition of new satyr plays was carried on down to the late second century A.D.,[1] and we have some monuments showing stage *papposilenoi* or satyrs dated a century later.[2]

PROSKENION: STAGE AND NOT BACKGROUND

Up to now we have seen that the chorus did not disappear after the erection of the high stage[3] but, on the contrary, its life was longer than that of the *proskenion*, which was replaced by the *pulpitum* in Roman times. But what was the position of the chorus in the theatre with a high stage? All possible combinations have been put forward by modern scholars trying to reconcile the new development in stage building with the need for intercommunication between actors and chorus. So it has been suggested that: (1) the *proskenion* was never a stage but only a background; actors and chorus performed in the orchestra[4]; (2) the *proskenion* was at first a background but in late Hellenistic times the performance was transferred to it[5]; (3) it had a double function, that is, it served as a stage for the

---

[1] *Satyrographoi* occur among the victors of the Mouseia at Thespiai, *I.G.* vii 1773, *S.E.G.* iii 334.

[2] Webster, *M.T.S.* AT 28–9, FM 1, FS 3.

[3] As Bethe, *Prolegomena zur Geschichte des Theaters im Alterthum*, Leipzig, 1896, pp. 242ff.; *N. Jahrb.* 19 (1907), 84ff.; cf. Christ-Schmid, *Gesch. d. Griech. Lit.* II⁶, i, p. 173; Pickard-Cambridge, *The Theater of Dionysus*, p. 190.

[4] W. Dörpfeld–E. Reisch, *Das griechische Theater* (1896), pp. 379ff.; Dörpfeld, *Ath. Mitt.* 28 (1903), 383, 411ff., 49 (1924), 50ff. Dörpfeld, whose theory had been known for some years before the publication of his book, was followed by E. Capps, 'Vitruvius and the Greek Stage', *The University of Chicago Studies in Classical Philology*, I (1895), 93–113 (first published as a preprint from the *Studies* in 1893), *A.J.A.* 10 (1895), 287–325; T. D. Goodell, *A.J.P.* 18 (1897), 1–18; F. Noack, *Philologus* 58 (1899), 1–24, who did not rule out that the *proskenion* may have occasionally been used as a stage in late Hellenistic times, but believed that it could not have been devised for that purpose; cf. his Σκηνή τραγική, Tübingen, 1915, pp. 55ff., where he suggested that the origin of the *proskenion*-background is to be sought in 'die Schranken der Telesterionhalle'; R. C. Flickinger, *The Greek Theater and its Drama*⁴, pp. 69ff., and others. Dörpfeld was opposed by many scholars and archaeologists who believed that the *proskenion* was designed as a stage from the beginning: Müller, Haigh, Bethe, Navarre, Puchstein, Fiechter, Bulle, Bieber, Dinsmoor, etc. (see Bibliography).

[5] A. v. Gerkan, *Das Theater von Priene*, pp. 73ff., 123ff., and in *Das Theater von Epidauros* by v. Gerkan and W. Müller-Wiener, p. 80; Frickenhaus, *R.E.*² iii 485, 492.

new plays and as a background for the old tragedies and the satyr plays[1]; (4) actors and chorus performed on the *logeion*.[2] Where does the truth lie?

The *proskenion* occurs in an inscription from Delos in 282 B.C. when the making and painting of some panels for it was commissioned (*I.G.* xi 158 A 67–9). Three years later, in 279 B.C., its roof, the *logeion* or the place where one speaks from, is mentioned (*I.G.* xi 161 D 125–7). It is perfectly clear that we are being told about the acting platform and not the background. The distinction between the terms 'scenic' and 'thymelic' has been claimed[3] to go as far back as the fourth century. And Vitruvius says about this distinction: 'The Greeks have a roomier orchestra, as well as a stage of less depth. They call this the λογεῖον, for the reason that there the tragic and comic actors perform on the stage, while other artists give their performance in the entire orchestra; hence from this fact they are given in Greek the distinct names "scenic" and "thymelic"' (V 7, 2—trans. M. H. Morgan; cf. Pollux, IV123, Phrynichos, p. 163 Lob.). A number of scholia on comedies of Aristophanes, derived probably from Alexandrian sources, regard the *logeion* as a stage.[4] And I do not see how the ancient scholiast would have wondered whether, for instance, Dionysos and Xanthias in the *Frogs* make their journey to Hades on the *logeion* or across the orchestra, if the old tragedies and satyr plays were still played in the orchestra. Pollux who also draws upon Alexandrian sources says that 'the stage is appropriated to the actors and the orchestra to the chorus' (IV 123). The *proskenion* as a

---

[1] C. Robert, *Hermes* 32 (1897), 450ff.; H. Bulle, *Das Theater zu Sparta*, pp. 91ff., cf. Pickard-Cambridge, *The Theatre of Dionysus*, p. 196, who finds also probable that they chose old tragedies that could be played on two separated levels without serious loss. Von Gerkan, *Das Theater von Epidauros*, p. 81, accepts the possibility that even after the middle of the second century when, he thinks, the dramatic performances were transferred on to the stage old plays with large choruses could still be produced in the orchestra.

[2] Navarre, *Le théâtre grec*, pp. 60–2; Pickard-Cambridge, *ibid.*, pp. 195–7; Webster, *Greek Theatre Production*, pp. 21–2; P. Venini, *loc. cit.*, p. 4.

[3] By J. Frei, *De certaminibus thymelicis*, Diss. Basle, 1900, pp. 14f., quoted by Pickard-Cambridge, *The Theatre of Dionysus in Athens*, p. 168, and H. Lloyd-Jones, *J.H.S.* 83 (1963), 82. I have not been able to see Frei's book. The earliest inscriptional evidence for the distinction is *S.I.G.*[3] 457, dated c. 220–208 B.C., cf. M. Feyel, *Contribution à l'épigraphie béotienne*, p. 116; see p. 144.

[4] Sch. *Ran.* 183, 299; *Equit.* 149; cp. A. E. Haigh, *The Attic Theatre*[3], p. 149.

stage is referred to also by Polybius (XXX 22 and fr. 212, Büttner-Wobst) and later writers like Plutarch (*Mor.* 1096 b, cf. *Demetr.* 34), and Athenaeus (*Deipn.* XII 536 a, cf. XIV 631f.), while Plautus freely uses the word *proscaenium* for 'stage' (*Amph.* 91; *Poen.* 17, 57; *Truc.* 10). So all the ancient authorities are unaware of the *proskenion* as background. On the contrary, they give evidence for the *logeion*-stage.[1]

Moreover, the remains of many theatres suggest that the *proskenion* was used as a stage.[2] In the theatre of Akrai, Sicily, a large area of the *hyposkenion* is occupied by living rock, that has never been removed. No traces of a door have been found on the stylobate of the *proskenion*. The theatre is dated by Brea to the time of Hieron II, that is 275–215 B.C.[3] Fiechter dates the second reconstruction of the theatre of Eretria c. 300 B.C.[4] The orchestra was removed several metres toward the auditorium, and at the same time it was excavated and sunk more than 3 m below the old level. The space thus created between the stage building and the edge of the old level above the orchestra

---

[1] It has been traditionally believed that a passage of Athenaeus (XIII 587 b) quoting Antiphanes, Περὶ ἑταιρῶν (cf. Harpocration, Suda, Photius *s.v.* Νάννιον), suggests a sort of decorated background: 'Ἀντιφάνης δὲ ἐν τῷ περὶ ἑταιρῶν, Προσκήνιον, φησίν, ἐπεκαλεῖτο ἡ Νάννιον, ὅτι πρόσωπον ἀστεῖον εἶχε καὶ ἐχρῆτο χρυσίοις καὶ ἱματίοις πολυτελέσιν, ἐκδῦσα δὲ ἦν αἰσχροτάτη. This passage does not in fact imply any other kind of *proskenion* because it means nothing more than that the *proskenion* could be 'dressed' (i.e. with *pinakes*) and 'undressed' like Nannion, or that it was a 'Träger der Dekoration' as Fensterbusch puts it (*R.E.* xxiii 1291). It is also clear that a wooden *proskenion* is implied, which would look very much like a scaffold without its decorative panels. The date of Nannion does not raise any difficulty, as Fensterbusch thinks, because this famous lady lived long enough to become very ugly. She was probably alive after 321 B.C. (Menander, *Pseudher.* 456 Koe.=524 K), and surely at the time of Alexis' *Tarantinoi* (330–320 B.C., T. B. L. Webster, *C.Q.* 1952, 21). She could well be the same person as Menander's Nannarion (*Kolax*, fr. 4 Koe.=295 K, produced after 312 B.C.), if the great beauty she is credited with is ironically spoken of. If they were two different persons, how can we be sure that the so-called Proskenion was the first one? Our authority, Antiphanes, is much later than the fourth century. Athenaeus (XIII 567 a) mentions him with Aristophanes (of Byz.), Apollodorus, Ammonius, Gorgias, all of them later authors of books about hetairai. (Bieber, *op. cit.*, p. 115, and H. Kenner, *Das Theater und der Realismus in der griech. Kunst*, p. 93, take him as the poet of Middle Comedy!) However, even the older Nannion falls within the limits of the period of the creation of the high stage. For later references like Synesius, *Aegypt.* 128 C, Suda, etc., see Fensterbusch, *loc. cit.*

[2] See Addendum to ch. XIII, p. 108.

[3] L. B. Brea, *Akrai*, Catania, 1956, p. 39.

[4] *Das Theater in Eretria*, Stuttgart, 1937, p. 41.

was from now on the *acting place*. Except for a vaulted passage leading from behind the stage building to the orchestra, the earth under the *skene* was not removed. So as early as the beginning of the third century Eretria had its high *logeion*. The theatre of Sikyon, which also belongs to the first part of the third century,[1] had its lower floor partly occupied by rock. Two rock ramps led to the *logeion*. Had it been the place of gods' appearances the hard work of cutting the ramps in the rock would have been done in vain. Also unexplainable would be the ramps of Epidauros, which go back to the early third century,[2] of Corinth, the Hellenistic theatre of which dates back to the first half of the third century or even before,[3] and of Oropos, also third century.[4] Furthermore that same theatre of Priene, the *proskenion* of which served according to von Gerkan as a background during its first Hellenistic period, was equipped with a special opening on the roof of the stage building for the appearances of gods, which renders the roof of the *proskenion* purposeless. A similar opening has been found in Corinth, and it seems to have been a quite usual feature of Hellenistic theatre buildings.

As regards the other modern view that the chorus, perhaps diminished in number, went up on to the high stage, our ancient authorities do not seem to have known such a thing. The orchestra is always considered the appropriate place for the chorus.[5] And once more the archaeological remains are in agreement with the literary evidence. In Sikyon, Corinth, Eretria, Philippoi, and Segesta underground passages have been found leading from the *hyposkenion* to the orchestra.[6] These passages, which are not earlier than the third century B.C., are called by Pollux Χαρώνιοι κλίμακες, 'Charon's stairs', and their

---

[1] E. R. Fiechter, *Das Theater in Sikyon*, Stuttgart, 1931, p. 32.

[2] A. v. Gerkan–W. Müller-Wiener, *Das Theater von Epidauros*, p. 80.

[3] R. Stillwell, *Corinth* ii, *The Theatre*, p. 132.

[4] Fiechter, *Das Theater in Oropos*, Stuttgart, 1930, p. 27.

[5] Pollux IV 123 quoted on p. 127; Photius *s.v.* τρίτος ἀριστεροῦ· ἐν τοῖς τραγικοῖς χοροῖς τριῶν ὄντων στοίχων καὶ πέντε ζυγῶν, ὁ μὲν ἀριστερὸς πρὸς τῷ θεάτρῳ ἦν, ὁ δὲ δεξιὸς πρὸς τῷ προσκηνίῳ.

[6] Corinth: Stillwell, *op. cit.*, pp. 39–40; Sikyon: Fiechter, *Das Theater in Sikyon*, p. 25; Eretria: Fiechter, *Das Theater in Eretria*, pp. 27, 38; Philippoi: Flickinger, *The Greek Theater and Its Drama*[4], p. 362; Segesta: Bulle, *Untersuchungen an griechischen Theatern*, pp. 115–16.

function was 'to send up the phantoms'.[1] Such supernatural appearances in the middle[2] of an empty and unused orchestra, close to the spectators and far from the actors, would certainly look absurd. The use of this device presupposes an orchestra occupied by the chorus, and probably not only by the chorus. It also implies a chorus present during the episodes and connected with the subject of the play.

INTERCOMMUNICATION BETWEEN ACTORS AND CHORUS

I have tried to show that the *logeion* always belonged to the actors and the orchestra to the chorus. It is time now to face the problem of the supposed abolition of intercommunication between the two levels of performance. And let us say straight away that intercommunication was not abolished when the high stage was introduced: a staircase provided the necessary connection. I should not like to go into the question whether there was a low stage in classical times and the fourth century that would of course have been connected with the orchestra by some steps.[3] I am only concerned with the Hellenistic *logeion*.

Pollux, our chief authority on the ancient theatre, in the same paragraph in which he describes the *periaktoi* says: 'of the *parodoi* that on the right leads from the country or the harbour or the city (to the theatre); but people arriving on foot from abroad enter through the other; and when they enter the orchestra they go up the stage by means of stairs' (IV 126-7). Pollux lived in the time of the emperor Commodus to whom he

---

[1] IV 132: αἱ δὲ Χαρώνιοι κλίμακες, κατὰ τὰς ἐκ τῶν ἐδωλίων καθόδους κείμεναι, τὰ εἴδωλα ἀπ' αὐτῶν ἀναπέμπουσιν.

[2] The Charonian stairs were in the middle of the orchestra in Eretria, Philippoi, and Sikyon; in Segesta near the corner of the auditorium; in Corinth there were two also near the corners of the auditorium, cf. the passage of Pollux.

[3] For the stage in the classical period see Haigh, *The Attic Theatre*[3], pp. 112–20, 165–74; Müller, *Lehrbuch der griech. Bühnenalterthümer*, pp. 53–60, 107–10, *Untersuchungen zu den Bühnenalterthümern*, pp. 35–57; Navarre, *Dionysos*, pp. 87–109, Daremberg-Saglio v 195–7 (*s.v.* theatrum), *Théâtre grec*, pp. 44–9; L. Roussel, *Rev. Arch.* 31/2 (1949), 892–5; Webster, *Greek Theatre Production*, pp. 7, 11; P. Arnott, *Greek Scenic Conventions*, ch. 1–2. Also now N. C. Hourmouziades, *Production and Imagination in Euripides*, Athens, 1965, pp. 58–74.

addresses his book. But he is not speaking about the Roman theatre, which had a small semicircular orchestra occupied by seats and not used at all. Nor is he speaking about the classical theatre, because although he does not discriminate between the upper and lower *parodoi* of the Hellenistic theatre building, he is by no means saying that everybody made his entry through the orchestra. Only persons coming from abroad, when or if they entered the orchestra, used the stairs to go up on to the stage, presumably after they had asked the chorus about the place, the palace, and its tenants.

Fortunately we do not rely only on Pollux. Athenaeus Mechanicus who wrote a book on siege machines 'towards the end of the third century B.C.'[1] gives us the following information: 'some people', he says, 'made in time of siege some kinds of *klimakes* similar to those which they place in the theatres against the *proskenia* for the actors'.[2] It should be mentioned here that the length of siege ladders (many of which could be joined together) prescribed by Apollodoros is 12 feet, which is the same as Vitruvius' maximum height for the Hellenistic *proskenion*.[3]

Some more evidence, epigraphical this time, comes from Delos. In an inventory of a storehouse containing various objects handed over by the administrators of Apollo's treasure in the year 189 B.C. to their successors of 188 a panel of scenery

---

[1] So Susemihl, *Gesch. d. griech. Lit. in d. Alex.*, i, p. 733, because Athenaeus dedicates his book to somebody called Marcellus, who is identified with the sacker of Syracuse (died in 208 B.C.). The argument is not considered convincing by Christ-Schmid, *Gesch. d. griech. Lit.*, II⁶.i, p. 448, who however remark that his examples are taken from the time of the Successors. F. Hultsch, *R.E.* ii 2033f., dated him to the second century B.C. because he knew Ktesibios the Engineer who, as Hultsch thought, had been active early in the second century. In *R.E.* Suppl. i 220–1 Hultsch assumed that Athenaeus lived shortly after Ktesibios the 'Barber' whose *floruit* was placed around the middle of the second century B.C. However, the two Ktesibioi are now believed to have been one and the same person, who actually lived in the reign of Ptolemy Philadelphos, Christ-Schmid, *op. cit.*, p. 283; Orinsky, *R.E.* xi 2074f.; Lesky, *Gesch. d. griech. Lit.*², pp. 847f. A date as late as the third quarter of the first century B.C. was assigned to Athenaeus by Cichorius, *Rom. Studien*, p. 271, followed by Kroll, *R.E.* Suppl. vi 16f.

[2] *De mach.* 29 (Wescher): κατεσκεύασαν δέ τινες ἐν πολιορκίᾳ κλιμάκων γένη παραπλήσια τοῖς τιθεμένοις ἐν τοῖς θεάτροις πρὸς τὰ προσκήνια τοῖς ὑποκριταῖς.

[3] Apollodoros 176, 4: R. Schneider, *Griechische Poliorketiker*, Abh. d. kön. Gesellschaft d. Wiss. zu Göttingen, Phil.-hist. Kl., N.F. x, Nro. 1, Berlin, 1908, p. 38. Vitruvius V 7, 2.

and a staircase occur. They were dedicated by someone called Alexander, and were kept together with other pieces of scenery old and new (*I.D.* 40344–5). This Alexander must be the same person as Alexander the tragedian who is known from another inscription as dedicator of a mask (*I.D.* 1421 Bb 19–20). It seems to me, then, that our Alexander was also an ambitious producer who, being hired to perform in Delos, did not content himself with the equipment provided by the theatre, but got a panel of scenery and a staircase made in order to have his play staged in his own way. That play was probably an old one since it required intercommunication between the stage and the orchestra. The important implication of this inscription is that already at the beginning of the second century B.C. the theatre of Delos was no longer equipped with a staircase, which is found in inscriptions of the third century. In 274 B.C., for instance, a carpenter repaired the old panels of scenery, the *ekkyklemata*, the *klimax*,[1] and the altars (*I.G.* xi 199 A 95–6). In 269 B.C. a new staircase was made in the theatre (*I.G.* xi 203 A 43).

When did the *klimax* cease to be an indispensable part of the stage? For almost every stone *proskenion* a wooden predecessor has been claimed. Wooden stairs, like those of Delos, put against a wooden platform would not seem odd to anybody, but leaning on the epistyle of a marble *proskenion* would certainly look awkward. And indeed traces of stairs have not been discovered in any theatre. We may assume then that the stairs disappeared when the wooden *proskenia* were turned into stone. But we must be very careful before drawing any further conclusions as regards the abolition of intercommunication between orchestra and *logeion*. In the first place the reconstructions of the *proskenia* in stone did not take place everywhere at the same time. Besides, the case of Alexander in Delos was taken to show that wooden stairs were occasionally used in theatres with stone stages. And such wooden movable stairs are implied by Athenaeus when, in order to illustrate some sort of siege ladders, he refers to those 'which they (usually) place against the *proskenia*'.

---

[1] This *klimax* may have been inside the scene building (Dörpfeld, *B.C.H.* 20 [1896], 579), but it could as well be a visible feature of the stage (Navarre, *Dionysos*, p. 311; Chamonard, *B.C.H.* 20 [1896], 310; Haigh, *The Attic Theatre*[3], p. 381).

ADVANTAGES OF THE HIGH STAGE

So far we have seen that the intercourse between actors and chorus did not stop after the introduction of the high stage, though it was much restricted. But did the new development not offer any advantages? I am not talking about the improvement of view for the upper circle, so to speak, nor the better opportunities for ostentatious stars to display their skill.[1] I mean advantages offered to the playwright, which could also afford a more likely explanation of the change. It cannot be doubted that the raised stage was very convenient for the New Comedy[2] but it is doubtful whether comedy could produce a new type of stage that would raise difficulties for the production of satyr plays, old and new tragedies, and sometimes old, that is to say middle, comedies. And if we learn from the history of literature that later times brought forth better comic than tragic poets, only because we happen to possess very few tragic fragments after the mid-fourth century, we certainly do not expect such appreciation from ancient audiences and political authorities. After all comic poets had previously often taken advantage of scenic conventions and machinery that were primarily designed to meet the requirements of tragedy.[3] We must therefore turn to tragedy to seek for the cause of this radical change in the stage building.

Euripides was the first poet who showed heroes thinking and behaving like ordinary men. He was the most popular of all the classical dramatists throughout the Hellenistic and Roman eras, and the new poets imitated him. The time was highly unfavourable for the great step towards the 'human' tragedy that would draw inspiration from the life, fate, passions, and sufferings of common men. So the poets continued to present the traditional legends before an audience whose idea of religion had been dulled by the worship they offered to innumerable new gods and kings, and reduced to a series of festivals, processions, sacrifices, and other opportunities for entertainment. How could such an audience recognize the

---

[1] Pickard-Cambridge, *The Theatre of Dionysus*, pp. 190–2.

[2] Bieber, *History*[2], p. 115.

[3] Cf. *Ach.* 407ff., *Peace* 82ff., *Thesm.* 1098ff., where Aristophanes uses the *mechane* and the *ekklyklema* in scenes parodying Euripides.

divine status of the tragic heroes who talked and acted like men? It was up to the producer to emphasize that status by making the actors look like heroes. Thus, at the time of the Lycurgean reconstruction of the theatre of Dionysos in Athens, a new type of tragic mask was introduced bearing the so-called '*onkos*', a tower of hair dressed over the forehead.[1] In the late second century B.C. thick-soled shoes were introduced.[2] Later in imperial times the appearance of the tragic actor became really frightful. His *cothurni* were one foot high, the *onkos* of hair bigger than the face of the mask, the mouth a gaping chasm, and a sort of padding round his chest and belly made his figure rise bulkily on the platforms of his shoes.[3]

I venture to suggest that the raised stage belongs to this line of evolution, and comes between the *onkos* masks and the high *cothurni*. The chorus ought to be separated from the actors, 'for the characters on the stage are imitating heroes; and in the old days only the leaders were heroes, but the rest of the folk, to whom the chorus belong, were only men' (*Probl. Aristot.* XIX 48—trans. W. S. Hett). And the writer of the *Problems* goes on to state a few lines later that 'under the influence of the hypo-dorian and hypophrygian modes we are inclined to action which is not appropriate to the chorus. For the chorus is an inactive watcher of events; for its only function is to display a friendly attitude to those who are on the stage at the same time.' So the *Problems* are not in agreement with the *Poetics*, where Aristotle demands that the chorus should be treated as one of the actors.[4] But the author of the *Problems* belongs to different times. New aesthetic trends now dominate the theatrical productions. The chorus and actors are definitely separated; the action is concentrated on the upper level of the performance; the chorus has come closer to the spectators; the development of the plot may completely ignore the lower level, the orchestra, which is hardly a part of the place of action any more. And here

[1] Webster, *Greek Theatre Production*, 43–4.

[2] Webster, *ibid.*, p. 44.

[3] The literary evidence is collected by M. Kokolakis, *Lucian and the Tragic Performances in His Time*, Athens, 1961, pp. 36ff. Cf. Pickard-Cambridge, *Festivals*, figs. 59, 63, 66, 67, 79; Bieber, *History*[2], figs. 568, 594, 787, 802–3, 811.

[4] *Poet.* 1456 a 25; cf. A. Gudeman, *Aristoteles περὶ ποιητικῆς*, Berlin und Leipzig, 1934, p. 326.

comes the great advantage of the high stage. As soon as the space of action was detached from the orchestra the chorus ceased to be an obstacle to the change of scene. The heroes could now pursue their adventures in places differing from one act to another, and be seen there by the spectators, while the chorus would remain in the orchestra making comments on what they saw from their neutral position. The revolving prisms, the *periaktoi*, were added to the stage machinery in order to provide the necessary changes of scenery.

This development in playwriting, radical though it may seem at first sight, was in fact well prepared by the fourth century poets. For the change of scene, not at all unknown to poets of older generations, was nothing more than a step beyond tragedy which was clearly divided into separate episodes.[1] It was however a step difficult to make before the introduction of the high stage, because it would entail μετάστασις of the chorus exactly when the poets needed it to be present, that is between the episodes.

We have seen already that the tragedy of Moses by Ezekiel, which is supposed to reflect the technique of Hellenistic tragedy writing, has five changes of scene. The first, third and fifth acts are played somewhere in the country of Madiam, on Mount Horeb, and in the desert beyond the Red Sea respectively, the second and fourth acts in the courts of Raguel and Pharaoh. Some pieces of landscape painted on the revolving *periaktoi* would inform the audience that the country scenes were set in different places each time, and some symbols also painted on the *periaktoi* would differentiate the palace of Madiam from that of Egypt. During the other acts the palace would be ignored.

So the later tragic poets never dispensed with the chorus. Nonetheless they released tragedy from its immediate presence, which hampered the development of the plot, by splitting the performance into two levels, on the excuse that 'the characters on the stage are imitating heroes; and in the old days only the leaders were heroes, but the rest of the folk, to whom the chorus belong, were only men'.

[1] Cf. the 'episodic' and 'epic' tragedies which Aristotle finds fault with, *Poet.* 1451 b 33, 1456 a 11.

ORGANIZATION OF FESTIVALS AND THE DIONYSIAC GUILDS[1]

PROBLEM RAISED BY THE SOTERIA INSCRIPTIONS

The variety of nationalities represented among the participants in the Amphictyonic Soteria (see Table 4) was used by W. Kolbe[2] as an argument against Roussel's theory about the Aitolian reformation of the festival. Kolbe maintained that the Soteria was from the beginning a festival of panhellenic importance, founded by the Aitolians after the Gallic invasion, and celebrated at quadrennial intervals. W. S. Ferguson[3] reversed the argument claiming that the artists did not come to the Soteria from their distant homes but from the neighbouring centres of the Dionysiac associations which drew their members from all over the Greek world. He also pointed out that 'in two cases it is expressly recorded that a *koinon* of *technitai* provided the programme of the Amphictyonic Soteria' (cf. p. 82), and concluded that the guild in question must be that of Isthmos and Nemea.[4]

Now that the Athenian archon Polyeuktos is firmly dated after 250 B.C., and the reformation of the Soteria is proved beyond doubt, the multitude of nationalities of the *technitai* has lost its value as an argument for dating the Soteria. The question, however, whether all these artists belonged to one guild still remains open. G. Klaffenbach[5] suggested that the three major guilds shared the same festivals, and furthermore, inferred from the Soteria inscriptions that the guild of Teos had not yet been founded because very few artists from Asia Minor

---

[1] First published in *C.Q.* 15 (1965), 206–14.
[2] *Hermes* 68 (1933), 441–3, cf. 69 (1934), 217–22
[3] *A.J.P.* 55 (1934), 323–4.
[4] Cf. Pickard-Cambridge, *Festivals*, p. 291.
[5] *Symbolae*, p. 21.

are included in the four complete records. But Pomtow[1] decided that from 268 until 130 B.C. the Isthmian and Nemean guild monopolized the Delphic festivals. The renewal of the privileges of the Athenian artists in 130 marks a shift of the Delphian favour from the Isthmian to the Athenian *synodos*, which in turn expressed its gratitude by offering the magnificent performances of the second Pythaid. The guild of Isthmos was turned away, and this was presumably one of the causes of the dispute between the two guilds. F. Poland[2] accepted Pomtow's theory and treated the Soteria inscriptions as documents concerning the Isthmian *koinon*. Ferguson and Flacelière[3] followed the same line, though for different reasons.

The question has a general significance. Was there a division of territories between the guilds? Did the guilds undertake the organization of musical and dramatic performances at various festivals and were certain festivals dominated by certain *koina*? And is it likely that the Isthmian *koinon* was as widely international as the Soteria records would suggest? I think such views are not in harmony with the evidence. In the following paragraphs the whole problem of organization of festivals in connection with the guilds of Dionysiac artists is examined, and the view that the various musical and dramatic festivals were open to artists of all guilds is maintained.

ORGANIZATION OF FESTIVALS

The festivals were a public business conducted by a magistrate usually called *agonothetes*. This title underlines the fact that either the festivals were actually ἀγῶνες, 'games', contests, or contests were their main events. It is understandable that a great number of the participants in these festivals would come from local or neighbouring guilds (branches of the Isthmian and Nemean guild were established at Argos, Thebes, Thespiai, Chalkis, etc.), but I do not see how these guilds could prevent foreign artists from taking part in contests set up and governed by the cities. After all, the wider the participation in a competi-

---

[1] *S.I.G.*[3] 424, not. 1, 489, not. 6, 690, not. 1, 692, com.
[2] *R.E.*[2] v 2473-4, 2486, 2502-3.
[3] *Aitoliens*, pp. 143ff.

tion the greater its success. We must, nevertheless, recognize here an important difference between athletic and musical competitions. The athletes were officially amateurs,[1] the musicians and actors were professionals. Moreover, the dramatic performances involved many people who did not compete for any prize: secondary actors, choreuts, flute-players, and so on. A certain amount of preparatory work and consultation between the cities and the artists was therefore necessary before the festivals (Le Bas-Wadd. 1620 C, cf. *M.A.M.A.* viii 492$_{17-19}$). At this point we must make another distinction. The *koina* of *technitai* were guilds, trade unions, and not theatrical companies, a fact whose importance has, I think, been underestimated. It was not the artists who served the *koina*, but the *koina* which served the artists. Consequently, the artists were free to make their own arrangements, and the guilds did not bear any responsibility for the way their members conducted themselves. Artists who failed to comply with a contract to appear in a city were liable to be prosecuted by the city and made to pay heavy fines.[2] Now why should the cities be troubled at all if the *koina* undertook the organization of festivals? In that case the artists would be responsible to their guild and the guild to the cities. In fact we know of such a case—a special one—from a decree of the Ionian and Hellespontian *synodos*. A group of artists were sent by the guild to Iasos to organize the contests of the Dionysia, presumably free of charge, at the appropriate time and in accordance with the laws of the city, as an expression of good will, and because of the traditional friendship between the guild and the city.[3] The decree prescribes the fine of 1000 Antiochian drachmai payable to the guild by any of the appointed artists who failed to go to Iasos or take part in the contests, unless prevented by illness or bad weather.

How the festival managers arranged for the participation of a sufficient number of artists in their festivals is not very clear.

---

[1] A. H. M. Jones, *The Greek City from Alexander to Justinian*, Oxford, 1940, p. 231.

[2] See p. 100, nos. 2, 4; p. 85 (Apollas), cf. *I.G.* iv² 99, and *I.G.* xii.9 207$_{61, 65}$, which perhaps antedates the guilds.

[3] Ὅπως [συν]άγωσι τῶι θεῶι τοὺς [χ]ορούς κατὰ τὰς πατρίας αὐτῶν διαγραφάς, and ἐπιτελεῖσαι τοὺς τῶν Διονυσίων ἀγῶνας ἐν τοῖς ὡρισμένοις καιροῖς πάντα παρασχόντας ἀκολούθως τοῖς Ἰασέων νόμοις (Le Bas-Wadd. 281 = Michel 1014).

In some cases we hear of personal contracts between artists and cities: ἐὰν ἰδίου ἦι συν[βολαί]⌐ου ὑπόχρεος (sc. πόλει) ὁ τεχνί⌐τας (*F.D.* iii.2 68₇₉₋₈₀; *I.G.* ii² 1132₂₁₋₂). A series of inscriptions from Iasos (the earliest c. 190 B.C.)[1] shows that certain magistrates, namely the *stephanephoros* (eponymous archon), *agonothetes*, and *choregoi*, hired one artist each to perform for one or more days at the Dionysia. The method changed about 175 B.C. or a little later, and the same magistrates contributed a fixed amount of money apparently administered by the *agonothetes*.[2] In Euboea each artist had to be backed by a guarantor (*I.G.* xii.9 207₁₇). However, contractors or impresarios of some kind, distinct from the *technitai*, are also mentioned by the same inscription: τοὺς δὲ διδόντας τὰ ἔργα οὓς ἂν κρίνωσιν τῶν τεχνιτῶν ἢ τῶν ἐργολάβων etc. (l. 70).[3] Finally, the members of the Isthmian and Nemean *koinon* taking part in the trieteric festival of Dionysos Kadmeios at Thebes were appointed by the guild, though they were personally responsible to the city, and liable to prosecution by the Theban *agonothetes* in case they did not appear at the festival (*S.E.G.* xix 379₃₄₋₉). In conclusion it seems fair to accept that, although the *koina* could act as a link between the festival authorities and the artists, they were not responsible for the organization of festivals since they were not responsible for the behaviour of the *technitai*.

THE FÊTES OF THE IONIAN *TECHNITAI*

However, the *technitai* of Ionia and Hellespontos ran their own *panegyris* in Teos through an *agonothetes* whom they elected every year (*I.G.* xi 1061₃₋₆). They also celebrated another annual fête in honour of Eumenes II conducted by an *agonothetes* who was priest of the king as well (ὁ ἑκάστοτε γινόμενος ἀγωνοθέτης

---

[1] A. Brinck, *Inscr. graecae ad choregiam pertinentes*, Diss. Halenses, 1899, p. 222.

[2] Le Bas-Wadd. 252–8, 259–99=Brinck, *loc. cit.*, 107–13, 114–53; *Annuario* N.S. 23–4 (1961–2), 582ff., nos. 12, 13.

[3] *I.G.* xii. 9 207 may perhaps antedate the guilds; however, ἐργολάβοι operated in Athens long before the formation of the Dionysiac *koina* (Plato, *Rep.* 373 b, cf. Pollux VII 182). They are also mentioned in an inscription from Kerkyra dated to the beginning of the second century B.C.: εἰ δὲ... μὴ ἀποστείλαι ἡ πόλις ἐπὶ τοὺς τεχνίτας κατὰ τὰν περίοδον ἑκάσταν, ἢ παραγενομένων τῶν ἐργολάβων μὴ μισθώσαιτο τοὺς τεχνίτας etc. (*I.G.* ix.1 694₃₀₋₃₂).

καὶ ἱερεὺς βασιλέως Εὐμένου ἐν τῆι βασιλέως Εὐμένου ἡμέραι, C.I.G. 3068 A, 3070 = O.G.I.S. 325). These festivals had nothing to do with the Dionysia of Teos, which was evidently conducted by Teian magistrates (οἱ καθ᾽ ἕκαστον ἔτος ἀγ[ωνοθέται ἐν τῆι τοῦ κοινοῦ| π]ανηγύρει, καὶ ὅταν ἡ Τηΐων πόλις συντελῇ Διονύσια, I.G. xi 1061, ll. 23–4 = B.C.H. 59 [1935], 212, ll. 27–8). The Teians even interfered with the *panegyris* of the *technitai*, and the latter had to refer the case to the king Eumenes who confirmed the right of the guild to celebrate and conduct its own *panegyris*, but also acknowledged the right of the Teians to have a say, in so far as the *panegyris* affected the revenues[1] of the city (*I. Perg.* 163 = C. B. Welles, *Royal Correspondence*, no. 53, I C 8–9, II B 4–7). Another passage of the same inscription—a letter of Eumenes—seems to advise the *technitai* to respect the laws of the cities in which they conducted festivals: [-- τοὺς πανηγυριάρχας ἐκ τῶν ὑμετέ]|ρων νόμων καὶ ἐθισμ[ῶμ μόνον συντελεῖν τὴν]| πανήγυριν μὴ ὑπευθύνους [ὄντας τοῖς τῆς]| πόλεως εἰς ἣμ πάρεισιν κε[ιμένοις νόμοις]| οὐ φαίνεταί μοι ἀγνωμονεῖ[ν. (III B, cf. Welles' interpretation). The inscription is very badly pre-served, and one wonders how much one should trust the restorations. In any case, it is possible that the Teian *koinon*—the only guild of Asia Minor—undertook to organize the con-tests at certain festivals. But the individual hiring of artists in Iasos, and the widespread institution of *agonothesia*[2] in Asia Minor show that this was not the rule.

THE GUILD OF TEOS IN GREEK MAINLAND AND DELOS

In what follows we shall examine some pieces of straightforward evidence showing that members of different guilds appeared at the same festivals.

I.G. xi 1061 (= *Choix* 75, improved text re-edited by Daux, *B.C.H.* 59 [1935], 210ff.), earlier than 166 B.C., is a decree of

---

[1] The festivals were opportunities for trade, and the cities profited from sales taxes; Strab. X 5, 4 (486); *S.I.G.*³ 695₃₄₋₆; G. McL. Harper, *Yale Class. Studies*, I. (1928), 155; C. B. Welles, *Royal Correspondence*, pp. 234, 286.

[2] E.g. Pergamon, *I. Perg.* 167 = *O.G.I.S.* 299; Priene, *I. Pr.* 4, 8, 17, 50, 109₂₆₁ etc.; Ephesos, *Ephesos* ii, p. 151, n. 30; Ilion, *C.I.G.* 3599, 3601; Sardis, *Sardis* vii 4; Nakrasa, *O.G.I.S.* 268; Laodikeia, *M.A.M.A.* vi 5.

the guild of Ionia and Hellespontos in honour of its leading member the flute-player Kraton of Chalkedon. Kraton had been elected priest of Dionysos and *agonothetes* of the guild twice, and proved himself worthy of this office, and worthy of the *synodos*, by surpassing all his predecessors in generosity and magnificence, and doing his best for the glory of Dionysos, the Muses, Apollo Pythios and all other gods, the kings and queens,[1] the brothers of King Eumenes, and the *technitai* whom καὶ θεοὶ καὶ βασιλεῖς [κ]α[ὶ πάντες οἱ ἄλλοι "Ελ]|ληνες τιμῶσιν δεδωκότες τήν τε ἀσυλίαν καὶ ἀσφάλειαν πᾶσι τ[οῖ]ς τεχν[ί]ται[ς καὶ πολέμου καὶ εἰ]|ρήνης, κατακολουθοῦντες τοῖς τοῦ 'Απόλλωνος χρησμοῖς δι'οὖς [κ]αὶ ἀ[γωνίζονται τοὺς ἀγῶνας τοῦ]| 'Απόλλωνος τοῦ Πυθίου καὶ τῶν Μουσῶν τῶν 'Ελικωνιάδων καὶ τοῦ Διον[ύσου, ἐν Δελφοῖς μὲν τοῖς]|[20] Πυθίοις καὶ Σωτηρίοις, ἐν Θεσπιαῖς δὲ τοῖς Μουσείοις, ἐν Θήβαις δὲ τοῖς 'Αγρ[ιανίοις, εἶναι δοκοῦντες]| ἐκ πάντων τῶν 'Ελλήνων εὐσεβέστατοι (ll. 16–21).

It has been suggested[2] that the *technitai* referred to in this passage are the Dionysiac artists in general and not specifically those of Ionia and Hellespontos. But even if this were true the value of the inscription as evidence for the participation of the Asian guild in the festivals of the Greek mainland is not diminished. For it is unthinkable that the Ionians should speak on behalf of other guilds if they were themselves banned from Greece, or had no interest in her festivals. On the contrary, the fact that in a decree of the artists of Teos the festivals of Delphi, Thebes and Thespiai—and none of Asia Minor—are mentioned shows that the Ionians were keenly interested in the festivals of Greece. It also looks as if the Teians met with some opposition at first on the part of the mainland *technitai*, and had to seek Apollo's authorization for their activities in Greece (τοῖς τοῦ 'Απόλλωνος χρησμοῖς δι' οὖς καὶ ἀγωνίζονται[3] etc.). In any case their *asylia* and *asphaleia* were guaranteed by the Aitolians between 240 and 228 B.C. (see p. 100, no. 3).

Another passage of the same inscription, which was found in

---

[1] On the Pergamene royalty referred to by this decree see Daux, *B.C.H.* 59 (1935), 220ff.

[2] Klaffenbach, *Symbolae*, p. 20, cf. Daux, *B.C.H.* 59 (1935), 218.

[3] I do not see how this reference to Apollo's oracle can apply to the *technitai* in general and not to the guild of Teos, cf. n. 2.

Delos, testifies to the guild's presence in the island. Three statues of Kraton were to be erected by the *koinon*: τὴν μὲν μίαν ἐν Τέωι ἐν τῶι θεάτρωι etc. τὴν δὲ ἄλλην ἐν Δήλωι ὅπως καὶ ἐκεῖ στεφανῶται ὑ[πὸ τῶν περὶ τὸν Διόνυσον τε]χνιτῶν, τὴν δὲ τρίτην οὗ ἂν ἀναθῇ Κράτων etc. (ll. 27–31).[1] For Isthmian artists in Delos see p. 21.

MAINLAND ARTISTS IN ASIA MINOR

Another document (an inscription from Teos) concerning Kraton gives further evidence that the Ionian and Isthmian guilds encountered each other at various festivals, and were not on bad terms at all. It is a decree of the Isthmian and Nemean *koinon* honouring Kraton: τῶν ἐν Ἰσθμῶι καὶ Νεμέαι τεχνιτῶν.| ἐπειδὴ Κράτων etc. πρότερόν τε πολλὰς καὶ μεγάλας παρέσ|χηται χρείας κατ᾽ ἰδίαν τε τοῖς ἐντυγχάνουσιν – – – – (*C.I.G.* 3068 C = Michel 1016 C).

One cannot help thinking that the likeliest way in which Kraton would prove so helpful to members of the other guild is when the latter happened to go to places normally frequented by Ionian artists, i.e. the cities of Asia Minor rather than to places like Delphi or Delos. Indeed we find a number of artists from Greece at Eastern festivals (though the place of origin is very often omitted from the epigraphical records). E.g. Mnasias, son of Pyrrilos, Boeotian flautist, in Iasos (Le Bas-Wadd. 253); Satyros, son of Aristokles, Boeotian flautist, in Iasos (Le Bas-Wadd. 255; Kraton performed at the same festival); Asklepiades, son of Herakleides, satyric actor from Chalkis, in Teos (Le Bas-Wadd. 91); Socrates, son of Zocharis, Athenian flautist, in Miletos (*Rev. Arch.* N.S. 28 [1874], 108; originally Rhodian, *I.G.* ii² 3081 [Athens], also at the Delphic Soteria, *S.G.D.I.* 2564₁₄); Heragoras, son of Poseidonios, *didaskalos* of dithyramb(?) from Macedonia, in Miletos (*C.I.G.* 2868).

FOREIGN ARTISTS IN ATHENS

We know of the activities of many artists recorded at places allegedly belonging to the dominions of different guilds. First

---

[1] This passage is wrongly taken by E. V. Hansen, *The Attalids of Pergamon*, Cornell Univ. Press, 1947, p. 417, as evidence for a branch of the Ionian guild in Delos.

of all the famous tragic actor of Tegea, winner of 88 different scenic contests including the Dionysia at Athens, the Soteria at Delphi, the Heraia at Argos, and the Naia at Dodona (see p. 84). A considerable number of actors at the Dionysia and Lenaia in Athens have been identified with non-Athenian artists also found at other cities, although the Dionysiac association of Athens is shown by all relevant documents to have consisted of Athenian citizens exclusively.[1] See Table 3, E 49, 58, 66, F 61, 66, 83, H 54, cf. G 61.

In the fourth and third centuries foreign flute-players and instructors of dithyrambic choruses were employed at Athens to such an extent that from about the middle of the fourth century onwards the *ethnikon*, Athenaios, was added to the names of Athenian artists in the dedications of *choregoi* and *agonothetai* (*I.G.* ii² 3038ff.). The influx of chorus-trainers and flautists into Athens went on even after the foundation of the local Dionysiac guild (*I.G.* ii² 3081, 3082, 3083, 3085). Foreign poets were of course traditionally welcome to stay in Athens or simply take part in the contests (e.g. Diphilos, Diodoros, Philemon, the Apollodoroi, and so on; Phanostratos of Halikarnassos won a tragic victory in 307/6, see p. 29; a statue of Phanes, son of Deinias, from Chios, who was granted proxenia by the Aitolians in 214/3 B.C., *I.G.* ix.1² 31 154, was erected at the theatre of Dionysos, *I.G.* ii² 3778).

ATHENIANS IN ARGOS AND BOEOTIA

The number of Athenians recorded outside Athens is by no means negligible. Apart from those found in the Soteria records, others known to have been members of the guild of Athens occur in places which were strongholds of the Isthmian and Nemean *koinon*.

From Argos, where a branch of the guild of Isthmos had its headquarters (*I.G.* iv 558), comes an inscription of uncertain character, apparently a list of artists gathered there for the celebration of a festival. It was published by G. Vollgraff in

---

[1] Klaffenbach, *Symbolae*, pp. 47–9; Poland, *R.E.*² v 2492. Foreign artists who had become naturalized Athenians were apparently admitted to the guild, cf. p. 157, E 49, p. 164, H 51; p. 84 (Aristomachos).

Mnemosyne N.S. 47 (1919), 252ff., and dated to the beginning of the first century B.C. The front part of the stone contains the names of thirty-four artists who came from Argos (7), Thebes (7), Sikyon (3), Elis (2), Hermione (2), Sparta (2), Pheneos, Aigeira, Kyparissia, Phigaleia, Megara, Tanagra, Taras, and Teos. One is called 'Rhomaios', and the provenance of two others is not preserved. On the left side of the stele twenty-six names without *ethnika* are recorded. Six come under the heading κωμικ[οὶ συναγωνισταί], thirteen under the heading τραγικοὶ χοροδιδάσκαλοι, one is described as κιθαρῳδός and another as τραγῳδός. The remaining five seem to be comic actors. A tragic poet from Chalkis, and five Theban 'singers' (ᾠδοί) concluded the list. All the artists whose origin is omitted were in fact Athenian. Most of them are also found in other documents of the Dionysiac guild of Athens, mainly in the records of the last two Pythaids (see Table 5, II.3, III.2, IV.1, 4, 8, 17, 19; for other cross-references see Vollgraff, *loc. cit.*).

Many Athenians are included in the victor lists of the Mouseia in Thespiai, the home of another branch of the Isthmian and Nemean *koinon* (*B.C.H.* 19 [1895], 334, n. 8, *Polemon* 3 [1947/8], 73). The festival of Muses was reformed between 211 and 208 B.C.[1] The confederation of Boeotians and the city of Thespiai dispatched delegates to the cities, and the guilds of *technitai*, asking them to recognize the thymelic contest of the Mouseia as an ἀγὼν στεφανίτης and ἰσοπύθιος. The central Isthmian guild—the local branch had probably not been established yet—replied with a decree of acceptance, which is actually our principal source of information about the reorganization of the festival (*S.I.G.*[3] 457). Another fragmentary inscription of a similar character (*I.G.* vii 1735), which had been considered as a decree of Athens, was claimed by M. Feyel[2] to have emanated from the Athenian guild of Dionysos. In any case the frequent presence of Athenian poets and artists at the Mouseia is attested by the lists of victors (*B.C.H.* 19 [1895], 335ff., n. 10$_{12}$, n. 11$_{2,4}$; *I.G.* vii 1760 = Michel 892$_{10, 18, 28}$; *I.G.* vii 1761$_{10}$).

Technitai from Athens are likewise recorded in the preserved

[1] A. Schachter, *Num. Chronicle* 7th s. 1 (1961), 67–9.
[2] *Contribution à l'épigraphie béotienne*, pp. 90ff.

agonistic inscriptions of other Boeotian towns, Tanagra, Orchomenos, and Oropos. A number of Athenian poets and artists in the festivals of Boeotia, who are also known to have been members of the Dionysiac *synodos* in Athens, or in three cases Athenian magistrates, are listed below:

(i) Alexandros, comic poet, in Orchomenos, and at Pythaids III and IV, see p. 169, III.7.

(ii) Ariston, son of Poses, comic poet, in Oropos, *I.G.* vii 416, *prytanis* in Athens, *I.G.* ii² 1756; cf. p. 29.

(iii) Asklepiades, tragic poet, hieromnemon of Athens and delegate of the guild to Delphi; also in Delos and Tanagra, see p. 25.

(iv) Demetrios, comic actor, in Tanagra, and at Pythaid IV, see p. 170, IV.2.

(v) Eubios, son of Eubios, kitharode, in Oropos, *I.G.* vii 416, and at Pythaid IV, *F.D.* iii.2 48₂₆.

(vi) Philotas, son of Theokles, *keryx*, in Thespiai, *B.C.H.* 19, p. 336, n. 10, and at Pythaid II, *F.D.* iii.2 47₁₀.

(vii) Poses, comic poet, *thesmothetes* in Athens, also in Delos and Tanagra, see p. 28.

(viii) Praxiteles, actor of old tragedy and *keryx* in Tanagra, comic *synagonistes* at Pythaid III, *tragodos* at Pythaid IV, see p. 169, III.5.

(ix) Sophocles, tragic poet, in Orchomenos, and at Pythaid IV, see p. 170, IV.16.

(x) Theodotos, rhapsode in Thespiai, Michel 892, rhapsode and tragic *synagonistes* at Pythaid IV, see p. 171, IV.24.

PRIEST OF *TECHNITAI*

From the evidence presented above it can be inferred that all contests were frequented by artists from all major guilds. There remains, however, an obstacle which must be removed before it can be decided if the Athenians at the Soteria came to Delphi from Athens. Does the inclusion of the priest of *technitai* in the opening section of the records really imply that all the performances of the Soteria were carried out by the Isthmian and Nemean guild? The clue for answering this question is the decree by which the Isthmian *koinon* accepted the reformation of the Mouseia at Thespiai, in the winner lists of which a priest of *technitai* is also recorded among the city magistrates (archon of Thespiai, *agonothetes*, priest of Muses, *pyrphoros*, secretary):

δεδόχθαι τοῖς | 40 τεχνίταις ἐπαινέσαι μὲν τὴν | πόλιν τῶν Θεσπιέων καὶ τὸ κοινὸν | τῶν Βοιωτῶν ἐπὶ τῆι φιλοτιμίαι, | ἧι ἔχουσιν εἴς τε τὸ ἱερὸν τῶν | Μουσῶν καὶ τὸ κοινὸν τῶν τε | 45 χνιτῶν· ἀποκρίνασθαι δὲ αὐτοῖς, | ὅτι καὶ πρότερον οἱ τεχνῖται, | κοινὸν ὑπολαμβάνοντες | εἶναι τὸν ἀγῶνα τῶν Μουσῶν | τῆι τε πόλει Θεσπιέων καὶ αὐ | 50 τοῖς, τὴν πᾶσαν προθυμίαν | ἐνεδείξαντο καὶ συνθύοντες | καὶ ἱερέα ἐξ αὐτῶν αἱρούμενοι | καὶ θεωροὺς ἀποστέλλοντες | etc. ἐμφανί | ζειν δὲ αὐτοῖς ὅτι καὶ νῦν πρῶτοι | 60 τὸν ἀγῶνα ταῖς Μούσαις στεφα | [νί]την ἀποδέχοντ[αι --] (*S.I.G.*³ 457).

Evidently, therefore, the priest of the *technitai* was a special delegate who together with a number of *theoroi* simply represented the Isthmian guild, and had nothing to do with the organization of festivals. A priest of the *technitai* is also found at the Agriania in Thebes (*I.G.* vii 2447), and we may assume that the guild sent such representatives to all festivals in which it had a special interest, much in the same way as the Greek cities sent *theoroi* to each other's festivals.

The ambiguous preamble of the Soteria inscriptions B and C (τὸ κοινὸν τῶν τεχνιτῶν ἐπέδωκε τῷ θεῷ καὶ τοῖς Ἀμφικτύοσιν εἰς τὰ Σωτήρια τὸν ἀγῶνα παντελῆ) deserves a separate mention. Both inscriptions are in a very bad state, and it is impossible to form an idea as to the proportion of Athenian participation. Is the Isthmian guild meant here? I should rather understand τὸ κοινὸν τῶν τεχνιτῶν as meaning the *technitai* in general, acting as a unity, and not a certain *koinon*, guild, in the technical sense of the word.[1]

---

[1] Cf. τὸ κ. τῶν ἀρχόντων = οἱ ἄρχοντες, τὸ κ. τῆς κώμης = ἡ κώμη, τὸ κ. τῆς πόλεως = ἡ πόλις, τὸ κ. τῶν Μακεδόνων = οἱ Μακεδόνες, etc., Kornemann, *R.E.* Suppl. iv 914–15.

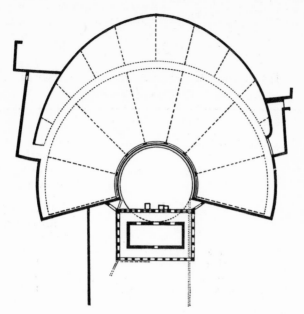

Ground plan of the theatre of Delos

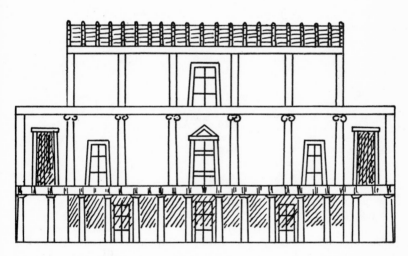

A reconstruction of the stage building at Delos
(See pp. 43ff.)

TABLES

TABLE I. Dramatic poets and actors recorded in inscriptions
of Delian archons

		I. 284 B.C., *I.G.* xi 105	
A. *Trag. actors*	1. Theodoros	Megara	Cf. below II A1, V A1, VII A1
	2. Philokleides	Chalkis	Awarded Delian proxenia, *I.G.* xi 567
B. *Com. actors*	1. Telestes	Athens	In Delphi, see p. 163, G 58, below VI B4
	2. Sannion (twice)		
	3. Dexilaos		
	4. Diodoros	Athens	See p. 26
	– Diodoros	Sinope	Cf. III B6

		II. 282 B.C., no. 106	
A. *Trag. actors*	1. Theudoros	Megara	Cf. I A1, V A1, VII A1
	2. Themistonax	Paros	Cf. III A1
	3. Nikostratos	Kassandreia	
B. *Com. actors*	1. Phaidros	Athens	
	2. Kephisios	Histiaia	Acted the *Mainomenos* by Diodoros (I B4) at Athens in 285/4, *I.G.* ii² 2319₆₄, cf. IV B3

		III. 280 B.C., no. 107	
A. *Trag. actors*	1. Themistonax		Cf. II A2
	2. Dionysios		
	3. Aristarchos		
	4. Hegesippos		
	5. .ΑΣ. ΑΜΙΡΕΥΣ		
B. *Com. actors*	1. Telesis	Paros	
	2. Hieronymos		Vict. at Lenaia, Athens, 286/5, *I.G.* ii² 2319₅₈, 2325₂₀₆

TABLE I   149

III. 280 B.C., no. 107 (*cont.*)

B. *Com. actors* (cont.)	3. Polykles		Vict. at Dionysia and Lenaia, Athens, *I.G.* ii² 2325₉₇, ₂₁₆·
	4. Menekles		Vict. at Lenaia, Athens, *I.G.* ii² 2325₂₂₂; cf. VI B1
	5. Simias	Athens	Cf. IV B2
	6. Diodoros	Sinope	Cf. I B4f.
C. *Com. poets*	1. Philemon		See p. 29
	2. Nikostratos		See p. 27
	3. Ameinias		See p. 24

IV. 279 B.C., no. 108

A. *Trag. actors*	1. Nikolaos (twice)	Epeiros	
	2. Drakon	Taras	In Delphi, p. 160, F50, cf. p. 22
	3. Akesios	Rhodes	
	4. Kleodoros		Vict. at Lenaia, Athens, *I.G.* ii² 2325₂₉₈?
B. *Com. actors*	1. Teleson	Megara	
	2. Simias	Athens	Cf. III B5
	3. Kephisios	Histiaia	Cf. II B2
	4. Aristophanes	Soloi	

V. 268 B.C., no. 110

A. *Trag. actors*	1. Theodoros		Cf. I A1, II A1, VII A
	2. Dionysodoros		
	3. Eukles		In Delphi, p. 157, B19
	4. Oikiades		In Delphi, p. 157, E42
B. *Com. actors*	1. Ergophilos		Cf. VII B1
	2. Hierotimos		In Delphi, p. 164, H60
	3. Choregion		
	4. Kallippos		? Idem K. the 'younger', vict. at Dionysia, Athens, 313/2, *I.G.* ii² 2323a₃₈, 2325₂₀₀·
	5. Kleoxenos		In Delphi, p. 159, E72

VI. 264 B.C., no. 112

A. *Trag. actors*	1. Alexandros (two days)		In Delphi, p. 164, H50, vict. at Lenaia, Athens, *I.G.* ii² 2325₃₀₅.
	2. Kreon		In Delphi, p. 162, G53
	3. Himeros (two days)		
	– Alexandros		
	– Kreon		
	4. Peisikrates		
B. *Com. actors*	1. Menekles (two days)		Cf. III B4
	2. Sosigenes		
	3. ...ὄφρων		
	– Sosigenes		
	4. Telestes (two days)		Cf. I B1
	– Menekles		

VII. 263 B.C., no. 113

A. *Trag. actors*	1. Theodoros		Cf. I A1, II A1, V A1
B. *Com. actors*	1. Ergophilos		Cf. V B1
	2. Phanylos		
	3. Parion		
	4. Eritimos		
	5. Philonides		In Delphi, p. 158, E58, in Athens, *I.G.* ii² 2325₉₃, ₂₁₄.
	6. Nikolochos	Arkadia	
C. *Com. poets*	1. Nikomachos	Athens	Cf. VIII B6; See p. 27

VIII. 259 B.C., no. 115

A. *Trag. actors*	1. Sotion (twice)	Akarnania	His son in Delphi (?), p. 162, G54
	2. Paramonos	Chalkis	
B. *Com. actors*	1. Πο[λύ]κριτος? (twice)	Κασσ[ανδρεὺς]	See p. 28, no. viii
	2. Menekrates		In Delphi, p. 159, E71

TABLE 1   151

VIII. 259 B.C., no. 115 (*cont.*)

B. *Com. actors* (cont.)	3–4. . . . .ǫϛ *ΛΙΦΝΙΩ* – – –		
	5. . . . . . .ηϛ *Κεῖοϛ*		
	6. Nikomachos	Athens	Cf. VII C1 and p. 27
	7. *Πολύνι*[*κοϛ* . . . .]*ου Χαλκιδεύ*[ϛ		
C. *Com. poets*	1. Chrysippos		See p. 30

IX. 236 B.C., no. 120

A. *Trag. actors*	1. Kallikles, son of Nikostratos	Boeotia	In Athens(?) *I.G.* ii² 2325₃₀₆, cf.
	?		Wilhelm, *Urkunden*, p. 141
B. *Com. actors*	1. . .ωμ – –		
	2. Mnesikles		
	3. Amyklas		In Delphi, see p. 84
	4. *Αὐτο* – –		Cf. p. 161, F66
	?		
C. *Trag. poets*	1. – – – [*Δ*]ελφόϛ?		
	2. Philteas		See p. 30
	?		
D. *Com. poets*	1. – – –αϛ (twice)		
	2. Aristeides		See p. 25
	?		

X. 224 B.C.?, no. 123

A. *Trag. actors*	1. Dionysios *ΡΕ*.	Probably to be restored Ῥ[όδιοϛ], cf. Delphi, p. 84
	2. Diophantos (twice)	
	3–4. *ΠΟΛΥΩΝΤΟΣΑΣ* – –|.*ΝΗ*.*ΑΣ*	
B. *Com. actors*	1. *Κ*[λ]ευδημ[οϛ]	
	2–3. . .*ΟΝΔΡΟΜΑΧΛΤΟΥ* – – – –|μοϛ	

XI. 200 B.C., no. 128

A. *Com. actor*	1. Eudemos (thrice)

	XII. 171 B.C., no. 132	
A. *Trag. actors*	?	
B. *Com. actors*	1. Theodoros	Idem in Iasos, Le Bas-Wadd. 256
	– c.45 ll. –	
	2. – – ωπας	
	3. Tharsynon	Cf. XIII B1

	XIII. 170 B.C., no. 133	
A. *Trag. actors*	1. Menedemos	
	2. Eukrates	
	3. – – ων	
	4. Philon	
	5. Autokrates	
	6. ΛΓΜ – – –	
B. *Com. actors*	1. Tharsynon	Cf. XII B3
	2. Herostratos	
	3. – – – ος	

TABLE 2   153

TABLE 2. Inscriptional passages relevant to *choregikon* money

	Date	Reference	Description	Amount	Depositors	Month	Kept until
I	279	I.G. xi 161 A27	(εἰσῆλθε) καὶ τὸ χορηγικὸν ἀργύριον	2056 dr. 4 ob.			
II	279	ibid. l. 39	(εἰστήκει) παρὰ βουλευτῶν τῶν ἐπ' ἄρχοντος Χάρμου (280 B.C.) τοῦ χορηγικοῦ ἀργυρίου δραχμὰς	1482 dr. 3 ob.	bouleutai		
III	274	I.G. xi 199 A16	(παρελάβομεν) τοῦ χορηγικοῦ[.]				
IV	258	I.G. xi 224 A8	π]αρελάβομεν μηνὸς Ἀπατουριῶνος [δ]εκάτ[ηι ἱστα]μένου τοῦ χορηγικοῦ δραχμὰς	50 dr.		Apatourion	
V	before 180	I.D. 442A8-10	(παρελάβομεν ἐν τεῖ κιβωτῶ τεῖ ἱερᾶ) ἄλλον στάμνον ἐπιγραφὴν ἔχοντα· «μηνὸς Ποσιδεῶνος τόδε ἐχώρισαν ἀργύριον τοῦ χορηγικοῦ ἀπὸ τοῦ ἱεροῦ ἀργυρίου ᾿Απολλόδωρος Μαντιθέου, Φιλοκλῆς Φιλοκλέους αἱρεθέντες ὑπὸ τοῦ δήμου κατὰ τὸ ψήφισμα, ἐν ὧι ἐπεγέγραπτο· «λοιπὸν ἔνει FIIIT».	5 dr. 3¼ ob.	commissaries elected by decree of demos	Posideon	169 B.C., I.D. 461Aa9-10 (cf. 453A10, 455Aa8)

TABLE 2. (cont.)

	Date	Reference	Description	Amount	Depositors	Month	Kept until
VI	before 180	ibid. l. 10	ἄλλον στάμνον ἐπιγραφὴν ἔχοντα· «χορηγικὸν θέντων [Φ]ωκαιέως τ[οῦ] Ἀπολλοδώρου καὶ Διαδήλου τοῦ Διαδήλου ΗΡΔΗΙΤ‖».	162 dr. 1¼ $\frac{2}{12}$ ob.	ditto?		ditto
VII	180	ibid. ll. 32-3	ἐπὶ Φωκαιέως, Ποσιδεῶνος, ἔθεσαν ταμίαι Καββαν καὶ Μνησικλείδης εἰς τὸ ἱερὸν τὸ χορηγικὸν	486 dr. 4 ob.	treasurers	Posideon	173 B.C., I.D. 455Aa20*
VIII	179	ibid. l. 46	ἐπὶ Δημάρου, Ποσιδεῶνος, ἔθεσαν [τα]μίαι Μένυλλος καὶ Φωκαιεὺς τὸ χορηγικὸν	486 dr. 4 ob.	ditto	ditto	? 169 B.C., I.D. 461Aa69-70 (cf. 453A24, ? 455Aa19)
IX	178-6	I.D. 453A28	--τὸ χορηγικὸν τῶν τραγωιδῶν ΗΗΗΗ--	400...dr.			
X	175	I.D. 461Aa 43-4	ἄλλην (κοτύλην) ἐν ᾗ ἐν[ῆσ]αν ΡΔΔΙΙΙC‖, ἀπὸ τῆ[s Νυμφοδώ-ρου καὶ Ἡρακλείδου†, ἣν ἔθεσαν τ]αμίαι Βόηβος καὶ Φᾶνος τοῦ χορη-γικοῦ	81 dr. 2½ $\frac{2}{12}$ ob.	treasurers		169 B.C., I.D. 461Aa43-4

TABLE 2   155

	Date	Reference	Greek text	Category	Amount	Date & reference
XI	178–6 or 174	*I.D.* 455Ab4 173 B.C.	τὸ χορηγικὸν τὸ παρὰ -- --			
XII		*I.D.* 455Aa 19	[ἔθεσαν ταμίαι ------- τὸ χο]ρη-γικόν‡		486 dr. 4 ob.	
XIII	172	*I.D.* 461Aa 42–3	ἄλλην (κοτύλην), ἐν ἧι ἐνῆσαν ΗΓΔΓΙΤ|, [ἀπὸ τῆς Νυμφοδώρου καὶ Ἡρακλείδου, ἣν ἔθ]εσαν ταμίαι Ἀναξίθεμις καὶ Σωτίων τοῦ χορηγι-κοῦ, καὶ ὃ κατέβαλε Θρασυμήδης	treasurers	162 dr. $1\frac{1}{4}\frac{1}{12}$ ob.	169 B.C., *I.D.* 461Aa42–3
XIV	171	*ibid.* l. 46	ἄλλον (στάμνον) ἐν ὧι ἐνῆσαν ΓΔΔΔΓC|, ἀπὸ τῆς Νυμφοδώρου καὶ Ἡρακλείδου, ὃν ἔθεσαν τα[μ]ίαι Λάμπρων καὶ Ἐπιτροφῶν χορ[ηγι-κοῦ]	ditto	81 dr. $\frac{1}{2}\frac{1}{12}$ ob.	169 B.C., *ibid.* l. 46
XV	178–6 or 174–3 or 170	*ibid.* l. 30–1	ἄλλον (στάμνον), ἐν ὧι ἐνεῖσαν ΗΗΗΗΓΔΔΔΗΗΙΙΙC|, ἀπὸ τῆς Νυμφοδώρου καὶ Ἡρακλείδου, ὃν ἔθεσαν ταμ[ίαι ------- τὸ περιὸν ἀπὸ τῶ]ν τεχνιτῶν καὶ τὸ χορηγικὸν τὸ παρὰ Σώσου	ditto	394 dr. $4\frac{1}{4}\frac{1}{12}$ ob.	169 B.C., *ibid.* l. 30

* Cf. *I.D.* 461 Aa 69 (169 B.C.) where the sum ΓΗΗΗΗΓΔΔΔΓΗΙC must be corrected into ΙΗΗΗΗ etc.

† These two people were bankers. For the role of banks in the financial life of Delos see Durrbach, *I.D.*, com. on 399 A 1–73.

‡ If this label is not the same as VII or VIII it must be dated 178–6 or 174.

TABLE 3. Dramatic artists at the Amphictyonic Soteria
(Cf. p. 74)

Line		Name	Origin
		A. TRAGEDIES	
17	I Actors	a ’Ἀρχε. AN – –	⎫
18		b ?	⎬ Histiaia
19		c [Νί?]καρχος Ελ – –	⎭
20	Didask.	E.π – –	
	Flautist		
21	II Actors	a Charikleides, s. of Phrikon	
22		b ..I.ας Φιλονικ.ος A – –	
23		c Εἰρανίων? EI – –	
24	Didask.	Eχ – –	
25	Flautist	?......δη[s] ‘Ηγησ.....	
		A. COMEDIES	
26	I Actors	a ’Ἀμφομ/	
27		b ’Ἐχεμᾶς? ’Ἀλέκου?	
28		c Κάμπος A..ΛΖΑΣ	
29	Didask.	ΠΡΟΓ	
	Flautist	—	
30	II Actors	a – – μω Λυκάωνο[s]?	
31		b – – ήδους ’Ἀργεῖος	(Argos)
32		c ‘Η[ρ]ακλεί[δης – –	(Athens?)
			? Idem victor at Lenaia, Athens, c. 260, I.G. ii² 2325₂₂₅
33	Didask. ⎫ ?	..ΔΛ..ΧΑΛΓΗ	
34	Flautist ⎭		
35	III Actors	a Hierotimos, s. of Hierokles	(Tegea) Cf. H60
36		b [Φι]λοκύδ[ης]? (s. of Philagros)	(Athens) Cf. F67, G69
37		c Aristion	(Athens?)
			? Idem victor at Dionysia, Athens, I.G. ii² 2325₉₂.
38	Didask.		
39	Flautist		

Line		*Name*	*Origin*
		B. TRAGEDIES	
19	I Actors	a Eukles, s. of Dionysios	Argos ? Idem Eukles *tragodos* in Delos, 268 B.C., *I.G.* xi 110
		b	
20	Didask. Flautist	c } ? Lykeion, s. of Lykeion	Boeotia
	II Actors	a	
21		b, c } ? . . . . αῖος *Λευκάρου*	Pella
	Didask.		
	Flautist		
22	III Actors	a Agathophanes, s. of Agathokles	Boeotia
		b	
		c	
23	Didask. Flautist	} ? Diogenes, s. of Thodeoros	Athens
		E. TRAGEDIES	
42	I Actors	a [*Οἰ*]*κιάδ*[*η*]*ς*, s. of Nikandros	Kassandreia ? Idem in Delos, 268 B.C., *I.G.* xi 110
43		b Eucharides, s. of Epichares	Opous
44		c Damon, s. of Eudemos	Megara
46	Didask.	Satyros, s. of Simakos	Argos Cf. Simakos F68
45	Flautist	Diophantos	Chios
47	II Actors	a Harmoxenos, s. of Theotimides	Histiaia
48		b Eraton, s. of Philon	Thessalia
49		c Herakleitos, s. of Dion	Argos Idem H51, victor at Lenaia, Athens, *I.G.* ii^{2} 2325$_{304}$
51	Didask.	Isylos, s. of Chrysolaos	Bosporos
50	Flautist	Chariades, s. of Chariades	Athens G52

Line	Name		Origin
		E. TRAGEDIES *(cont.)*	
52	III Actors	a Ouliades, s. of Kallikrates	Miletos F45
53		b Sotylos (s. of Philoxenos)	Aitolia F46
54		c Aristippos, s. of Kallikrates	Miletos F47 (? brother of Ouliades)
56	Didask.	Lykon, s. of [Glauk?]etes	Athens
55	Flautist	Pantakles (s. of Daalkes)	Sikyon F69 (com. fl.)
		E. COMEDIES	
58	I Actors	a Philonides, s. of Aristomachos	Zakynthos Priest of *technitai* E-H, victor at Dionysia and Lenaia, Athens, *I.G.* ii^2 2325$_{93, 214}$; in Delos 263 B.C., *I.G.* xi 113. Possibly producer of his company
59		b Lykidas, s. of Thrasyxenos	Zakynthos
60		c Herakleitos, s. of Herakleides	Elis
	Didask.	omitted(?)	
61	Flautist	Philiskos, s. of Philon	Boeotia G72 (com. fl.), H58 (trag. fl.)
62	II Actors	a Dion, s. of Theudoros	Achaia
63		b Dionysios, s. of Simos	Herakleia H66
64		c Nikomachos, s. of Polykleides	Boeotia
66	Didask.	Kephisodoros, s. of Kallias	Boeotia F65 (com. did.), H76 (com. chor.); ? idem at Dion., Athens, *I.G.* ii^2 2325$_{103}$

TABLE 3   159

Line		Name	Origin
		E. COMEDIES (*cont.*)	
65	Flautist	Klytios, s. of Mendaios	Naukratis
67	III Actors	a Polyaratos, s. of Eudoxos	Kyrene Cf. *S.E.G.* xv 265 (Oropos)
68		b – – –, s. of Hegesias	Athens
69		c Di]okles, s. of Diokles	Athens ? Idem H55
71	Didask.	Menekrates, s. of Potidaios	Megara ? Idem M. com. actor in Delos, 259 B.C., *I.G.* xi 115
70	Flautist	Xanthippos, s. of Moiragenes	Bocotia
72	IV Actors	a Kleoxenos, s. of Achaios	Chalkis In Delos, 268 B.C. *I.G.* xi 110
73		b Epitimos	Ambrakia
74		c Philiskos, s. of Dareikos	
76	Didask.	Diogeiton (s. of Euarchides)	Boeotia F74–G75 (com. chor.)
75	Flautist	. . . . χος – – –	Athens
78	Comic chorus	Dromares, s. of Teisamenos	Abydos
79		Theodotos, s. of Theodotos	Athens F71, G73
80		Thersinous, s. of Nikonides	Sikyon F73, H74
81		Aristokles, s. of Kallias	Boeotia
82		Dionysodoros, s. of Pamphilos	Megara H77
83		Sosikrates, s. of Leptines	Sikyon F75
84		Moschos (s. of Sosikleides)	Sikyon F72, G77

Line		Name	Origin

E. HIMATIOMISTHAI

Line		Name	Origin
85		Stratokles, s. of Apollodoros	Salamis G80, H78
86		Nilon, s. of Menekles	Soloi
87		Dionysios, s. of Dionysodoros	Herakleia

F. TRAGEDIES

Line		Name	Origin
45	I Actors	a Ouliades, s. of Kallikrates	Miletos E52
46		b Sotylos, s. of Philoxenos	Aitolia E53
47		c Aristippos, s. of Kallikrates	Miletos E54
49	Didask.	Satyros, s. of Demochares	Athens
48	Flautist	Lysandros, s. of Dexitheos	. . . . $\alpha\chi\epsilon\acute{\upsilon}s$
50	II Actors	a Drakon, s. of Lykon	Taras In Delos, 279 B.C. *I.G.* xi 108, 161 A86, cf. p. 22
51		b Apollogenes, s. of Orthagoras	Arkadia
52		c Mnesiphon, s. of Euphragoras	Troezen
54	Didask.	Hierokles, s. of Nikon	Athens G51
53	Flautist	Alexias, s. of Asklapichos	Arkadia
55	III Actors	a Peithanor	Sikyon
56		b Neokles, s. of Eudemos	Argos
57		c Agimenes, s. of Philomenes	Sikyon
59	Didask.	Moschion, s. of Epainetos	Arkadia
58	Flautist	Leukippos, s. of Philonides	Boeotia G62 (com. fl.)

TABLE 3   161

Line		Name	Origin
		F. COMEDIES	
61	I Actors	a Lykiskos, s. of Lykos	Kephallenia H68, idem (?) Athens, *I.G.* ii^2 2325$_{217}$ (Lenaia)
62		b Dionysodoros, s. of Asklepiades	Boeotia H69
63		c Euarchides, s. of Amphistratos	Boeotia
65	Didask.	Kephisodoros, s. of Kallias	Boeotia E66 (com. did.), H76 (com. chor.)
64	Flautist	Melon, s. of Melon	Herakleia G67
66	II Actors	a Autolykos, s. of Aston	Aitolia G68, idem (?) victor at Lenaia, Ath., *I.G.* ii^2 2325$_{213}$
67		b Philokydes, s. of Philagros	Athens G69, A36?
68		c Simakos, s. of Menekrates	Argos G70, cf. E46, (Menekrates, com. act. in Delos, 259 B.C., *I.G.* xi 115)
70	Didask.	Dionysios, s. of Philokydes	Athens G71, com. act. (?) at Dion. Athens, *I.G.* ii^2 2325$_{105}$
69	Flautist	Pantakles, s. of Daalkes	Sikyon E55 (trag. fl.)
71	Comic chorus	Theodotos, s. of Theodotos	Athens E79, G73
72		Moschos, s. of Sosikleides	Sikyon E84, G77
73		Thersinous, s. of Nikonides	Sikyon E80, H74
74		Diogeiton, s. of Euarchides	Boeotia E76 (com. did.), G75 (com. chor.)
75		Sosikrates, s. of Leptines	Sikyon E83
76		Agathokles, s. of Meliton	Boeotia
77		Pasikles, s. of Pasikles	Athens G74

Line	Name	Origin

Line		Name	Origin
78		Thyrsos, s. of Kriton	Ephesos H64 (com. did.)
83	Didask.	Pronomos, s. of Diogeiton	Boeotia Cyclic *chorodidaskalos* at Athens, 271/0, *I.G.* ii² 3083
82	Flautist	$--o\ddot{\iota}\sigma\kappa o[\varsigma]\ M\epsilon\nu\acute{\alpha}\lambda\kappa[ov]^1(?)$	

F. HIMATIOMISTHAI

Line	Name	Origin
79	Ilisos, s. of Ilioneus	Herakleia
80	Nikon, s. of Herakleitos	Epeiros G65 (com. actor)
81	Menedemos, s. of Ergoteles	Herakleia

G. TRAGEDIES

Line			Name	Origin
48	I	Actors	a Erginos, s. of Simylos	Kassandreia B13 (boy choreut)
49			b Nikophon, s. of Theokles	Athens
50			c Asklapon, s. of Apollodoros	Megara
51		Didask.	Hierokles, s. of Nikon	Athens F54
52		Flautist	Chariades, s. of Chariades	Athens E50
53	II	Actors	a Kreon, s. of Euphanes	Athens In Delos, 264 B.C., *I.G.* xi 112
54			b Aristokrates, s. of Sotion	Akarnania
55			c Moiragenes, s. of Anaxilas	Kassandreia
56		Didask.	Arkesilaos, s. of Hieron	Corinth
57		Flautist	Orsilaos, s. of Hermaion	Boeotia H53

¹ Line 82 is problematic; see Baunack, *S.G.D.I.* 2564, com. on l. 82; Pomtow, *S.I.G.*³ 431, n. 3; E. Capps, *T.A.P.A.* 31 (1900), 130ff.

TABLE 3   163

Line		Name	Origin
		G. COMEDIES	
58	I Actors	a Telestes, s. of Theokleides	Athens In Delos, 284 B.C., *I.G.* xi 105
59		b Nikon, s. of Eumathidas	Sparta
60		c Philon, s. of Straton	Ambrakia
61	Didask.	Moschion, s. of Euboulos	Gargara Com. act. (?) at Lenaia, Athens, *I.G.* ii^2 2325$_{204}$
62	Flautist	Leukippos, s. of Philonides	Boeotia F58 (trag. fl.)
63	II Actors	a Lysimachos, s. of Eukrates	Boeotia
64		b Demeas, s. of Anaxikrates	Athens
65		c Nikon, s. of Herakleitos	Epeiros F80 (*himatiomisthes*)
66	Didask.	Kallikles, s. of Saon	Boeotia
67	Flautist	Melon, s. of Melon	Herakleia F64
68	III Actors	a Autolykos, s. of Aston	Aitolia F66
69		b Philokydes, s. of Philagros	Athens F67, A36?
70		c Simakos, s. of Menekrates	Argos F68
71	Didask.	Dionysios, s. of Philokydes	Athens F70
72	Flautist	Philiskos, s. of Philon	Boeotia E61 (com. fl.), H58 (trag. fl.)
73	Comic chorus	Theodotos, s. of Theodotos	Athens E79, F71
74		Pasikles, s. of Pasikles	Athens F77
75		Diogeiton, s. of Euarchides	Boeotia E76 (com. did.), F74 (com. chor.)
76		Archedamas, s. of Aristokritos	Sikyon H71
77		Moschos, s. of Sosikle[ides]	Sikyon E84, F72
78		Kallimedon, s. of Kallimedon	Sikyon
79		Herakleides, s. of Lykos	Ambrakia H75
82	Flautist	Epikrates, s. of Asopon	Boeotia

Line		Name	Origin
		G. HIMATIOMISTHAI	
80		Stratokles, s. of Apollodoros	Salamis E85, H78
81		Kleon, s. of Kleinos	Athens
		H. TRAGEDIES	
50	I Actors	a Alexandros, s. of Demetrios	Athens In Delos, 264 B.C., *I.G.* xi 112, vict. at Lenaia, Athens, *I.G.* ii^2 2325$_{305}$
51		b Herakleitos, s. of Dion	Athens Idem E49 (Argive)
52		c Phrasilaos, s. of Teisikrates	Athens
54	Didask.	Peithias, s. of Exainetos	Arkadia Died at Athens, *tit. sep. I.G.* ii^2 9282
53	Flautist	Orsilaos, s. of Hermaion	Boeotia G57
55	II Actors	a Diokles, s. of Diokles	Athens ? E69 (3rd trag. actor)
56		b Archias	Aigina
57		c Kleonymos	Achaia
59	Didask.	Philesios, s. of Kallias	Boeotia
58	Flautist	Philiskos, s. of Philon	Boeotia E61–G72 (com. fl.)
		H. COMEDIES	
60	I Actors	a Hierotimos, s. of Hierokles	Tegea A35 In Delos, 268 B.C., *I.G.* xi 110
61		b Noumenios, s. of Hermonax	Argos
62		c Damotimos, s. of Timon	Ambrakia
64	Didask.	Thyrsos, s. of Kriton	Ephesos F78 (com. chor.)

TABLE 3

165

Line		Name	Origin
		H. COMEDIES (*cont.*)	
63	Flautist	Philoxenos, s. of Hellan	Tegea
65	II–III Actors	a Astias, s. of Apollodoros	Boeotia
66		b Dionysios, s. of Simos	Herakleia E63
67		c Sosikrates, s. of Mnasion	Sikyon
68		a Lykiskos, s. of Lykos	Kephallenia F61
69		b Dionysodoros, s. of Asklepiades	Boeotia F62
70		c Praxias, s. of Krateas	Tegea
71	Comic chorus	Archedamas, s. of Aristokritos	Sikyon G76
72		Stratios, s. of Komon	Argos
73		Chairichos, s. of Archelochos	Boeotia
74		Thersinous, s. of Nikonides	Sikyon E80, F73
75		Herakleides, s. of Lykos	Ambrakia G79
76		Kephisodoros, s. of Kallias	Boeotia E66–F65 (com. did.)
77		Dionysodoros, s. of Pamphilos	Megara E82

		H. HIMATIOMISTHAI	
78		Stratokles, s. of Apollodoros	Salamis E85, G80

TABLE 4. Provenances of participants in the Amphictyonic Soteria
(Cf. p. 74)

	A	B	C	D	E	F	G	H
		(*fragmentary*)				(*complete*)		
Abdera								1
Abydos					1			
Achaia								1
Aigina					2			1
Aitolia			1		1	2	2	1
Akarnania							1	
Ambrakia					1		2	2
Argos	1	1			2	2	2	4
Arkadia		1	2		2	12	1	6
Athens		2		2	9	9	15	5
Boeotia	2	5	1	10	12	12	20	14
Bosporos					1			
Byzantion			1		1			1
Chalkis					3	1	2	1
Chios					1			
Corinth	1					1	2	
Delphi		1						
Elis					1			
Epeiros						1	1	
Ephesos						1		1
Gargara							1	
Herakleia					2	3	1	1
Hermione	2	2	2	1		2		
Histiaia	1				1			
Kassandreia	1	1			1		2	
Keos					1	1	1	1
Kephallenia						1		1
Kleitorion				6				4
Knidos								2
Kynaitha								2
Kyrene					1			
Kythera						1	1	
Megalopolis		1		3				
Megara			1		3	1	2	1
Messene								1
Miletos				1	2	2		
Myrina					1			
Naukratis					1			
Opous					1			

TABLE 4   167

	A	B	C	D	E	F	G	H
			(*fragmentary*)			(*complete*)		
Pella		1						
Pellene					1	1		2
Philippoi				1		1	1	
Rhodes	1					1		
Salamis					1		1	1
Samos								1
Sikyon	1	1	1	3	4	11	9	8
Sinope						1		
Soloi					1			
Sparta							1	
Stymphalos		1		2				
Syracuse		1	1					
Taras						1		1
Tegea						1	1	3
Tenedos							1	
Tenos							1	
Thessalia					1			
Thronion					1			
Troezen						1		
Zakynthos					2	1	1	1
?		2		4	2	3	3	1

TABLE 5. Dramatic artists at the Pythaids
(Cf. p. 92)

Komodoi (8)

1. Apollodoros, s. of Nikanor, 25	Paean singer, 12.
2. Damon, s. of Bion, 25	Paean singer, 10; ? idem at Dionysia 168/7, 155/4, *I.G.* ii² 23²3₂₀₉,₂₁₃,₂₃₃,₂₃₇,₂₃₉.
3. Dion, s. of Dion, 25	Paean singer, 11; in Argos, *Mnemosyne* 1919, 253, B3; idem or his son among the ephebes of Pythaid III, *F.D.* iii.2 25₁₃.
4. M ---, 26	
5. Menophilos, s. of Hipponikos, 25	Paean singer, 16.
6. Noumenios, s. of Alexandros, 26	*Theoros*, 7.
7. Rhadamanthys, 25	Horseman at the same Pythaid, *F.D.* iii.2 27₂₈.
8. Thymoteles, s. of Philokles, 26	Cf. p. 93.

Tragodoi (3)

9. Apollodoros, s. of Chrysippos, 27	Paean singer, 11.
10. Sarapion, s. of Agelaos, 27	Paean singer, 10.
11. ---, 27	

Tragic chorodidaskaloi (3)

12. Elpinikos, s. of Epikrates, 28	Paean singer, 15; *didask.* of choir of boy pythaists 138/7, *F.D.* iii.2 11₂₀₋₂₂; tragic *hypodidask.*, *I.G.* ii² 113₂₄₆,₇₂.
13. Kleon, s. of Eumelos, 28	Paean singer, 14; *didask.* of choir of boy pythaists 138/7, *F.D.* iii.2 11₂₀₋₂₁.
14. Philion, s. of Philomelos, 28	Paean singer, 14; tragic *hypodidaskalos*, delegate sent to Delphi, *I.G.* ii² 113₂₄₇,₇₂.

(*Trag. poet*)

15. (Menelaos, s. of Ariston)	*Theoros*, 8; known to be tr. poet from *I.G.* ii² 1330₇,₆₇; cf. below IV.13.

Com. chorodidaskalos (1)

16. Basileides, s. of Poseidonios, 29	Paean singer, 16.

TABLE 5   169

Komodoi (?)

1. Herostratos s. of Leonidas, 30

Com. synagonistai (5)

2. Demon, s. of Eugeiton, 31 — In Argos, *Mnemosyne* 1919, 253, B8; paean singer, 18.

3. Myron, s. of Philetairos, 30
4. Philotas, s. of Philotas, 30 — Paean singer in 97, *F.D.* iii.2 48_{26}.
5. Praxiteles, s. of Theogenes, 30 — *Tragodos* in Pythaid of 97, IV.18; actor of old trag. and *keryx* in Tanagra, *S.E.G.* xix $3354_{4,39}$; ephebe 117/6, *I.G.* ii² 1009, col. II 82.

6. – – –, s. of Dorotheos, 31 — ? Idem Theophilos, s. of Dorotheos, paean singer in 97, *F.D.*, *ibid.*, l. 28.

(Com. poet)

7. (Alexandros, s. of Ariston) — *Architheoros, epimeletes* of *techn.* l. 39; cf. IV.11; idem (?) com. poet A., s. of Aristion, in Orchomenos, *I.G.* vii $3197_{33,51}$.

Tragodoi (4)

8. Eugeiton, s. of Eumedes, 31 — Cf. Eumedes, s. of Eugeiton, paean singer in 127, *F.D.* iii.2 471_{6}; *tit. sep. I.G.* ii² 6730.

9. Herakleitos, s. of Herakleitos, 31 — Boy pythaist in 137, *F.D.* iii.2 111_{11}.
10. Hieron, s. of Hieron, 31 — Ephebe 119/8, *I.G.* ii² 1008, col. IV 94.

11. – – –, 31

Trag. synagonistai (8)

12. Diomedes, s. of Athenodoros, 33 — Comic poet victor at Romaia in Magnesia on Maeander, *S.I.G.*³ 1079_{20}; statues of him at Epidauros, *I.G.* iv 1146, *I.G.* iv² 626, and Athens, *I.G.* ii² 4257; awarded citizenship of Pergamon, *S.I.G.*³ 1079.

13. Dionysios, s. of Demokles, 32
14. Kriton, s. of Nikodemos, 33
15. Mentor, s. of Protogenes, 32
16. Metrodoros, s. of ʻH – –, 32
17. Π – – –, 32
18. Timon, s. of Eukleides, 32 — Paean singer, 17.
19. – – –, s. of Dionysodoros, 32 — Probably the same as Dionysodoros, s. of Dion., paean singer, 18.

PYTHAID IV: *F.D.* III.2 48

Komodoi (4)

1. Agathokles, s. of Sokrates, 33 — Theoros, 16; paean singer, 22; in Argos, *Mnemosyne* 1919, 253, B1.

2. Demetrios, s. of Demetrios, 33 — Winning actor of new comedy at Tanagra, second in old comedy, *S.E.G.* xix $335_{15,41}$; boy pythaist in 137, *F.D.* iii.2 11_{11}; ephebe in Pythaid III, *F.D.* iii.2 25_9.

3. Glaukias, s. of Herakleidas, 33 — *Theoros*, 16; paean singer, 21; cf. Her., s. of Gl., *architheor.* in 127, *F.D.* iii.2 47_7.

4. Kallikrates, s. of Kallikrates, 33 — Paean singer, *B.C.H.* 62 (1938), 363, l. 3. In Argos, *Mnem.* 1919, 253, B 4; ephebe in 119/18, *I.G.* ii² 1008, col. IV 92.

Com. synagonistai (6)

5. Pausanias, s. of Lykiskos, 35

6. Philoxenos, s. of Philoxenos, 34 — Paean singer, *B.C.H.* 62 (1938), 363, l. 3.

7. Solon, s. of Solon, 34 — Paean singer, *B.C.H.* 62, 363, l. 5.

8. Theodoros, s. of Theodoros, 34 — Paean singer, *B.C.H.* 62, 363, l. 3. Tragic *chorodidaskalos* in Argos, *Mnem.* 1919, 254, l. 23; ephebe 101/0, *I.G.* ii² $1028_{118,120}$.

9. Theodotos, s. of Basileides, 34 — Cf. II.16.

10. Thoas, s. of Noumenios, 35

(Com. poet)

11. (Alexandros, s. of Ariston) — *Architheoros* and *epimeletes* of *techn.*, 3, 15, 47, cf. III.7.

Satyric poets (5)

12. Aristomenes, s. of Aristomenes, 35 — *Theoros*, tragic poet, 16; paean singer, 22.

13. Ariston, s. of Menelaos, 35 — *Theoros*, tragic poet, 17; paean singer, 23; epic poet, 30; cf. II.15.

14. Diogenes, s. of Diogenes, 36

15. Dionysios, s. of Kephisodoros, 36

16. Sophocles, s. of Sophocles, 35 — Paean singer, *B.C.H.* 62, 363, l. 10; tragic poet, winner at Orchomenos, *I.G.* vii 3197_{28-9}.

TABLE 5   171

PYTHAID IV: *F.D.* III.2 48 (*cont.*)

Tragodoi (2)

17. Demetrios, s. of Theodosios, 36   In Argos, *Mnemosyne* 1919, 254, l. 31.
18. Praxiteles, s. of Theogenes, 36   Comic *synagonistes* in 106/5, cf. III.5; paean singer in 97, *B.C.H.* 62, 363, l. 4.

Trag. synagonistai (7)

19. Demetrios, s. of Aristodemos, 38   Comic actor at Argos, *Mnemosyne* 1919, 254, l. 12.
20. Eudikos, s. of Alkimos, 38
21. Kallon, s. of Kallon, 37   Rhapsode, 31; paean singer, *B.C.H.* 62, 363, ll. 4–5.
22. Nikon, s. of Aristion, 37
23. Philonikos, s. of Hermon, 37   Paean singer, *B.C.H.* 62 363, l. 7.
24. Theodotos, s. of Pythion, 37   Paean singer, 26; rhapsode, 31; rhapsode at Thespiai, *I.G.* vii 1760_{18}.
25. Xenophantos, s. of Eumachos, 38   Paean singer, 25; rhapsode, 31.
26. (Chairestratos, s. of Philagros)   *Theoros*, trag. *synagon.*, 17.
27. (Themison, s. of Poseidonios)   *Theoros*, trag. *synagon.*, 17; paean singer, *B.C.H.* 62, 363, l. 5. cf. J. Bousquet, *ibid.*, p. 366.

Trag. poets (2)

28. Antiochos, s. of Antiochos, 38
29. Apollonios, s. of Kallistratos, 38   Paean singer, 24.

(Trag. hypodidaskalos)

30. (Diokles, s. of Aischines)   *Theoros*, trag. *hypodid.*, 15; master of the choir, 18, 48.

BIBLIOGRAPHY

The following list is selective, and includes only works which were used fairly extensively, or have a direct connection with the questions discussed in this book. For more bibliographical information on topics loosely connected with the subject of this work the reader is referred to the footnotes. A general bibliography on the ancient theatre is to be found in M. Bieber, *The History of the Greek and Roman Theater* (1961).

ALLEN, J. T., *Problems of the Proskenion*, Berkeley, California, 1923.
—, *Stage Antiquities of the Greeks and Romans and their Influence*, New York, 1927.
AMUNDSEN, L., see Eitrem, S.
ARIAS, P. E., *Il teatro greco fuori di Atene*, Firenze, 1934.
ARNOTT, P., *Greek Scenic Conventions*, Oxford, 1962.
BAUNACK, J., *S.G.D.I.* ii, *Die delphischen Inschriften* (nos. 1683–2504 A), Göttingen, 1899.
BEARE, W., '*Χοροῦ* in the *Heautontimoroumenos* and the *Plutus*', *Hermathena* 74 (1949), 26–38.
—, *The Roman Stage*, 2nd ed., London, 1955.
BÉGUIGNON, Y., REPLAT, J., 'Le tracé du théâtre de Délos', *B.C.H.* 51 (1927), 401–22.
BELOCH, K. J., *Griechische Geschichte*, 2nd ed., i.1–iv.2, Berlin–Leipzig, 1912–27.
BETHE, E., *Prolegomena zur Geschichte des Theaters im Alterthum*, Leipzig, 1896.
—, 'Das griechische Theater Vitruvs', *Hermes* 33 (1898), 313–23. (Cf. Dörpfeld, W., 'Das griechische Theater Vitruvs', *Ath. Mitt.* 22, 439–62 and 23, 326–56.)
—, 'Die hellenistische Bühne und ihre Dekorationen', *J.d.I.* 15 (1900), 59–81.
—, 'Thymeliker und Skeniker', *Hermes* 36 (1901), 597–601.
BIEBER, M., *Die Denkmäler zum Theaterwesen im Altertum*, Berlin–Leipzig, 1920.
—, *The History of the Greek and Roman Theater*, 2nd ed., Princeton, 1961.
BIRT, TH., *Die Schaubauten der Griechen und die attische Tragödie*, Schriften der Gesellschaft für Theatergeschichte, Band 42, Berlin, 1931.

BIZARD, L., LEROUX, G., 'Fouilles de Délos, II. Monuments de sculpture', *B.C.H.* 31 (1907), 504–25. (Choregic monument of Karystios and the sculptures of the Dionysiac Stibadion.)

BOËTHIUS, A., *Die Pythaïs. Studien zur Geschichte der Verbindungen zwischen Athen und Delphi*, Diss. Uppsala, 1918.

BOURGUET, E., *F.D.* iii.1, *Inscriptions de l'entrée du Sanctuaire au Trésor des Athéniens*, Paris, 1929.

—, *F.D.* iii.5, *Les comptes du IVᵉ siècle*, Paris, 1932.

BOUSQUET, J., 'Inscriptions de Delphes. Catalogues des Sôtéria', *B.C.H.* 83 (1959), 166–74.

BRINCK, A., *Inscriptiones graecae ad choregiam pertinentes*, Diss. Halle, 1899.

BULLE, H., *Untersuchungen an griechischen Theatern*, Abh. d. Bayer. Ak. d. Wiss., xxxiii, München, 1928.

—, *Das Theater zu Sparta*, Sitz.-Ber. d. Bayer. Ak. d. Wiss., 1937, Heft 5, München, 1937.

CAPPS, E., 'Vitruvius and the Greek Stage', Univ. of Chicago Studies in Classical Philology, I, 1893.

—, 'The Chorus in the Later Greek Drama with Reference to the Stage Question', *A.J.A.* 10 (1895), 287–325.

—, 'Studies in Greek Agonistic Inscriptions', *T.A.P.A.* 31 (1900), 112–37.

CHAMONARD, J., 'Théâtre de Délos', *B.C.H.* 20 (1896), 256–318.

—, *Délos* xiv, *Les Mosaïques de la Maison des Masques*, Paris, 1933.

CHRIST, W. V., *Geschichte der griechischen Litteratur* (320 v. Chr.–100 n. Chr.), sechste Auflage bearbeitet von W. Schmid, Handb. d. klas. Altertums–Wiss., vii 2.1, München, 1920.

COLIN, G., *Le culte d'Apollon Pythien à Athènes*, Paris, 1905.

—, 'Inscriptions de Delphes. La théorie athénienne à Delphes', *B.C.H.* 30 (1906), 161–328.

—, *F.D.* iii.2, *Inscriptions du Trésor des Athéniens*, Paris, 1909–13.

DAUX, G., 'Craton, Eumène II et Attale II', *B.C.H.* 59 (1935), 210–30.

—, *Delphes = Delphes au IIᵉ et au Iᵉʳ siècle* (191–31 av. J.-C.), Bibliothèque des Écoles françaises d'Athènes et de Rome, fasc. 140, Paris, 1936.

—, *F.D.* iii, *Chronologie delphique*, Paris, 1943.

—, *F.D.* iii.3, *Inscriptions depuis le Trésor des Athéniens jusqu'aux Bases de Gélon*, Paris, 1943.

DEONNA, W., *Délos* xviii, *Le mobilier délien*, Paris, 1938.

DINSMOOR, W. B., *List = The Athenian Archon List in the Light of Recent Discoveries*, Columbia Univ. Press, 1939. (On the dating of the Soteria.)

—, *The Architecture of Ancient Greece* (revised and enlarged edition based on the first part of *The Architecture of Greece and Rome* by W. J. Anderson and R. Phené Spiers, 1927), London–New York, 1950.

DÖRPFELD, W., REISCH, E., *Das griechische Theater*, Athens, 1896.

—, 'Le Théâtre de Délos, et la scène du théâtre grec', *B.C.H.* 20 (1896), 563–80.

—, 'Das griechische Theater Vitruvs', *Ath. Mitt.* 22 (1897), 439–62. (Cf. Bethe, E., 'Das griechische Theater Vitruvs', *Hermes* 33, 313–23, and Dörpfeld's reply in *Ath. Mitt.* 23 [1898], 326–56.)

—, 'Die optischen Verhältnisse der griechischen Theaters', *Ath. Mitt.* 24 (1899), 310–20. (Against A. Müller, *Untersuchungen* ..., see below.)

—, 'Thymele und Skene', *Hermes* 37 (1902), 249–57. (Answer to E. Bethe, 'Thymeliker und Skeniker', *Hermes* 36, 597ff.)

—, 'Die griechische Bühne', *Ath. Mitt.* 28 (1903), 383–436.

—, 'Das Theater von Priene und die griechische Bühne', *Ath. Mitt.* 49 (1924), 50–101.

DUCKWORTH, G. E., *The Nature of Roman Comedy*, Princeton, 1952.

DUNANT, CHR., see ROUX, G.

DURRBACH, F., *I.G.* xi.2, *Inscriptiones Deli liberae, tabulae archontum, tabulae hieropoeorum annorum 314–250*, Berlin, 1912.

—, *I.D.*, *Comptes des hiéropes* (*nos. 290–371*), Paris, 1926.

—, ROUSSEL, P., *I.D.*, *Actes des fonctionnaires athéniens préposés à l'administration des sanctuaires après 166 av. J.-C.* (*nos. 1400–1479*), Paris, 1935.

EITREM, S., AMUNDSEN, L., WINNINGTON-INGRAM, R. P., 'Fragments of Unknown Greek Tragic Texts with Musical Notation', *Symbolae Osloenses* 31 (1955), 1–87.

FENSTERBUSCH, C., 'Σκηνή bei Pollux', *Hermes* 60 (1925), 112.

—, 'Proskenion', *R.E.* xxiii 1287–96.

—, 'Theatron', *R.E.*, 2e Reihe, v 1384–1422.

FERGUSON, W. S., *Hellenistic Athens*, London, 1911.

—, *Athenian Tribal Cycles in the Hellenistic Age*, Harvard Univ. Press, 1932.

—, 'Polyeuktos and the Soteria', *A.J.P.* 55 (1934), 318–36.

FEYEL, M., *Contribution à l'épigraphie béotienne*, Paris, 1943.

FIECHTER, E. R., *Antike griechische Theaterbauten*, Stuttgart, 1930–50. 1. Das Theater in Oropos, 2. Die Theater von Oiniadai und

Neupleuron, 3. Das Theater in Sikyon, 4. Das Theater in Megalopolis, 5–7. Das Dionysos-Theater in Athen, 8. Das Theater in Eretria, 9. Nachträge. Piraieus, Thera.

FLACELIÈRE, R., 'Remarques sur les Sôtéria de Delphes', *B.C.H.* 52 (1928), 256–91.

—, *Aitoliens = Les Aitoliens à Delphes*, Bibliothèque des Écoles françaises d'Athènes et de Rome, fasc. 143, Paris, 1937.

—, *F.D.* iii.4, *Inscriptions de la Terrasse du Temple et de la région nord du Sanctuaire*, Paris, 1954.

FLICKINGER, R. C., 'Χορου̂ in Terence's *Heauton*', *Class. Philology* 7 (1912), 24–34.

—, *The Greek Theater and its Drama*, Univ. of Chicago Press, 4th ed., 1936.

FOUCART, P., *De collegiis scenicorum artificum apud Graecos*, Diss. Paris, 1873.

FRAENKEL, E., *Plautinisches im Plautus*, Berlin, 1922. (Italian ed.: *Elementi plautini in Plauto*, Firenze, 1960.)

FREI, J., *De certaminibus thymelicis*, Diss. Basle, 1900.

FRICKENHAUS, A., 'Skene' in *R.E.*, 2e Reihe, iii 470–92.

—, *Die altgriechische Bühne*, Schriften der Wissenschaftlichen Gesellschaft in Strassburg, 31. Heft, 1917.

GERKAN, A. VON, *Das Theater von Priene*, München, 1921.

—, MÜLLER-WIENER, W., *Das Theater von Epidauros*, Stuttgart, 1961.

HAIGH, A. E., *The Attic Theatre*, 3rd ed. revised by A. W. Pickard-Cambridge, Oxford, 1907.

HANDLEY, E. W., 'Χορου̂ in the *Plutus*', *C.Q.* N.S. 3 (1953), 55–61.

—, *The Dyskolos of Menander*, London, 1965.

HOMOLLE, TH., 'Comptes et inventaires des temples déliens en l'année 279', *B.C.H.* 14 (1890), 389–511.

—, *B.C.H.* 18 (1894), 162–8. (On the theater of Delos.)

—, *B.C.H.* 21 (1897), 261–3. (On the theatre of Delphi.)

IMMISCH, O., *Zur Frage der plautinischen Cantica*, Sitz. d. Heidelb. Ak., 1923, 7. Abhandlung.

KAHRSTEDT, U., 'Zu den delphischen Soterienurkunden', *Hermes* 72 (1937), 369–403.

KAKRIDIS, I., ''Η γυναίκα του̂ Κανδαύλη. Μιὰ ἄγνωστη τραγωδία', 'Ελληνικά 12 (1953), 1–14.

KAKRIDIS, PH. J., 'Frauen im Kampf', *Wiener Studien* 77 (1964), 5ff.

KAPPELMACHER, Z., 'Zur Tragödie der hellenistischen Zeit', *Wiener Studien* 44 (1925), 69–86. (On Ezekiel's *Exagoge*.)

KENNER, H., *Das Theater und der Realismus in der griechischen Kunst*, Wien, 1954.

KIRCHNER, J., *P.A.* = *Prosopographia attica*, Berlin, 1901–3.

—, *I.G.* ii–iii.2, 2, *Inscriptiones atticae Euclidis anno posteriores* (*nos. 1696–2776*), Berlin, 1931.

KLAFFENBACH, G., *Symbolae ad historiam collegiorum artificum bacchiorum*, Diss. Berlin, 1914.

KLEE, TH., *Zur Geschichte der gymn. Agone an griech. Festen*, Leipzig–Berlin, 1918.

KOKOLAKIS, M., 'Pantomimus and the Treatise περὶ ὀρχήσεως', Πλάτων, fasc. 21 (1959), 3–59.

—, *Lucian and the Tragic Performances in his Time*, Athens, 1961 (= Πλάτων, fasc. 23/4, 67–109).

KOLBE, W., 'Die Stiftung der aitolischen Soterien in Delphi', *Hermes* 68 (1933), 440–56.

—, 'Zu den aitolischen Soterien', *Hermes* 69 (1934), 217–22.

KÖRTE, A., 'Das Fortleben des Chors im griechischen Drama', *Neue Jahrbücher* 5 (1900), 81–9.

—, 'Χοροῦ', *Hermes* 43 (1908), 299–306.

—, 'Komödie' in *R.E.* xi 1207–75.

—, 'Menandros' in *R.E.* xv 707–61.

LAIDLOW, W. A., *A History of Delos*, Oxford, 1933.

LATTE, K., *De saltationibus Graecorum capita quinque*, Religionsgeschichtliche Versuche und Vorarbeiten, Band xiii, Heft 3, Giessen, 1913.

—, 'Ein antikes Gygesdrama', *Eranos* 48 (1950), 136–41.

LAUMONIER, A., *Délos* xxiii, *Les figurines de terre cuite*, Paris, 1953.

LAUNEY, M., see ROUSSEL, P.

LEHMANN-HARTLEBEN, K., 'Zum griechischen Theater', *J.d.I.* 42 (1927), 30–40.

LEO, F., *Die plautinische Cantica und die hellenistische Lyrik*, Abhandl. d. königlichen Gesellschaft d. Wissenschaften zu Göttingen, N.F. i, no. 7, Berlin, 1897.

—, 'Die Composition des Chorlieder Senecas', *Rheinisches Museum* 52 (1897), 509–18.

—, 'Χοροῦ', *Hermes* 43 (1908), 308–11.

LEROUX, G., see BIZARD, L.

LESKY, A., 'Die *Theophoroumene* und die Bühne Menanders', *Hermes* 72 (1937), 123–7.

—, 'Das hellenistische Gyges-Drama', *Hermes* 81 (1953), 1–10.

—, *Geschichte der griechischen Literatur*², Bern–München, 1963.

LÉVÊQUE, P., 'La date de la frise du théâtre de Delphes', *B.C.H.* 75 (1951), 247–63.

LEWIS, D. M., 'The Chronology of the Athenian New Style Coinage', *Numismatic Chronicle*, 7th s., 2 (1962), 275–300. (Cf. Thompson, M.)

LÜDERS, O., *Die dionysischen Künstler*, Berlin, 1873.

MAAS, P., 'E. Lobel: A Greek historical drama, London, 1950', *Gnomon* 22 (1950), 142–3.

MAIDMENT, K. J., 'The Later Comic Chorus', *C.Q.* 29 (1935), 1–24.

MARTIN, E., *Trois documents de musique grecque*, Paris, 1953.

MARX, F. *Plautus, Rudens,* Abh. d. phil.-hist. Kl. der Sächsischen Ak. d. Wiss., Nr. v, xxxviii Band, Leipzig, 1928 (repr. Amsterdam, 1959).

MODONA, N., *Gli edifici teatrali greci e romani*, Firenze, 1961.

MÜLLER, A., *Lehrbuch der griechischen Bühnenalterthümer*, Freiburg, 1886.

—, 'Untersuchungen zu den Bühnenalterthümern', *Philologus* Supplementband 7 (1899), 1–116.

—, 'Noch einmal die Sehverhältnisse im Dionysostheater', *Philologus* 59 (1900), 329–43. (Answer to Dörpfeld, 'Die optischen Verhältnisse...', *Ath. Mitt.* 24, 310ff.)

MÜLLER-WIENER, W., see GERKAN, A. VON.

NAVARRE, O., *Dionysos. Étude sur l'organisation matérielle du théâtre athénien*, Paris, 1895.

—, 'Theatrum' in Daremberg and Saglio, *Dictionnaire des antiquités grecques et romaines*, v 178–205.

—, *Le théâtre grec. L'édifice, l'organisation matérielle, les représentations*, Paris, 1925.

NILSSON, M. P., *Zur Geschichte des Bühnenspiels in der röm. Kaiserzeit*, Lund, 1906.

—, *Griechische Feste von religiöser Bedeutung*, Leipzig, 1906.

—, 'Die alte Bühne und die Periakten', *Från filologiska föreningen i Lund*, 4 (1914), 1–14.

NOACK, F., 'Das Proskenion in der Theaterfrage', *Philologus* 58 (1899), 1–24.

—, Σκηνὴ τραγική. *Eine Studie über die scenischen Anlagen auf der Orchestra des Aischylos und der anderen Tragiker*, Tübingen, 1915.

O'CONNOR, J. B., *Chapters in the History of Actors and Acting in Ancient Greece*, Diss. Princeton, Chicago, 1908.

PARENTI, I., 'Per una nuova edizione della "Prosopographia Histrionum Graecorum"', *Dioniso*, 1961, 5–29.

13—S.H.H.D.

PÉLÉKIDES, CH., 'L'archonte athénien Polyeuktos (247/6)', *B.C.H.* 85 (1961), 53–68. (On the dating of the Soteria.)

PFISTER, 'Soteria', *R.E.*, 2e Reihe, iii 1223–8.

PICARD, CH., 'Statues et ex-voto du "Stibadeion" dionysiaque de Délos', *B.C.H.* 68–9 (1944–5), 240–70. Cf. *C.R.A.I.*, 1944, 136–41.

PICKARD-CAMBRIDGE, A. W., *The Theatre of Dionysus in Athens*, Oxford, 1946.

—, *Festivals = The Dramatic Festivals of Athens*, Oxford, 1953.

—, *Dithyramb, Tragedy, and Comedy*, 2nd ed. revised by T. B. L. Webster, Oxford, 1962.

PÖHLMANN, E., *Griechische Musikfragmente*, Erlanger Beitr. z. Sprach- und Kunstwissenschaft, viii, 1960.

POLAND, F., *Geschichte des griechischen Vereinswesens*, Leipzig, 1909.

—, 'Technitai', *R.E.*[2] v 2473–558.

POMTOW, J., editor of the Delphian inscriptions in *S.I.G.*, 3rd ed., 1915–24.

POUILLOUX, J., see ROUX, G.

PUCHSTEIN, O., *Die griechische Bühne. Eine architektonische Untersuchung*, Berlin, 1901.

REES, K., 'The Three-Actor Rule in Menander', *Clas. Phil.* 5 (1910), 291–302.

REICH, H., *Der Mimus*, i.1–2, Berlin, 1903.

REINACH, TH., editor of the Delphic Hymns in *F.D.* iii.2, pp. 150ff.

REISCH, E., *De musicis Graecorum certaminibus capita quattuor*, Diss. Wien, 1885.

—, 'Chor' in *R.E.* iii 2373–404.

—, see DÖRPFELD, W.

REPLAT, J., see BÉGUIGNON, Y.

RIBBECK, O., *Die römische Tragödie in Zeitalter der Republik*, Leipzig, 1875.

ROBERT, C., 'Zur Theaterfrage', *Hermes* 32 (1897), 421–53.

ROBERT, L., 'Pantomimen im griechischen Orient', *Hermes* 65 (1930), 106–22.

—, 'Notes d'épigraphie hellénistique, XXXVI. Sur les Sôteria de Delphes', *B.C.H.* 54 (1930), 322–32.

—, 'Études sur les inscriptions et la topographie de la Grèce centrale, I. Fêtes thébaines', *B.C.H.* 59 (1935), 193–9.

—, 'Recherches épigraphiques, II. Smyrne et les Sôteria de Delphes', *R.É.A.* 38 (1936), 5–23.

—, *Études épigraphiques et philologiques*, Bibl. de l'École des Hautes Études, fasc. 272, Paris, 1938.

ROSTOVTZEFF, M., *S.E.H.* = *The Social and Economic History of the Hellenistic World*, i–iii, Oxford, 1941.

ROTOLO, V., *Il pantomimo. Studi e testi*, Atti della Accad. di Scienze Lettere e Arti di Palermo, ser. 4, vol. 16, pt. 2, fasc. 1, 1955–6 (published 1957), pp. 221–347.

ROUSSEL, P., *I.G.* xi.4, *Inscriptiones Deli liberae, decreta foedera, catalogi, dedicationes, varia*, Berlin, 1914.

—, *D.C.A.* = *Délos colonie athénienne*, Bibl. des Écoles françaises d'Athènes et de Rome, fasc. 111, Paris, 1916.

—, 'La fondation des Sôtéria de Delphes', *R.É.A.* 26 (1924), 97–111.

—, LAUNEY, M., *I.D.*, *Dédicaces postérieures à 166 av. J.–C. (nos.2220–2528). Textes divers, listes et catalogues, fragments divers postérieurs à 166 av. J.–C. (nos. 2529–2879)*, Paris, 1937.

—, see DURRBACH, F.

ROUX, G., DUNANT, CHR., *B.C.H.* 75 (1951), 136–7. (On the theatre of Delphi.)

—, POUILLOUX, J., *Énigmes à Delphes*, Paris, 1963. (Latest plan of the sanctuary including the theatre.)

RUMPF, A., 'Classical and Post-Classical Greek Painting', *J.H.S.* 67 (1947), 10–21.

SCHACHTER, A., 'A Note on the Reorganization of the Thespian Museia', *Num. Chronicle* 7th s. 1 (1961), 67–9.

SCHNEIDER, K., 'Σκηνικοὶ ἀγῶνες' in *R.E.*, 2ᵉ Reihe, iii 492–513.

SCHOEFFER, V. VON, 'De Deli insulae rebus', *Berliner Studien* 9 (1889), Heft 1.

SCHRAMM, F., *Tragicorum Graecorum hellenisticae, quae dicitur, aetatis fragmenta*, Diss. Münster, 1929.

SCHULHOF, E., 'Fouilles de Délos', *B.C.H.* 32 (1908), 101–32. (On vase-festivals.)

SEGRE, M., 'L'asilia di Smirne e le Soterie di Delphi', *Historia* 5 (1931), 241–60.

SKUTSCH, F., 'Χοροῦ bei Terenz', *Hermes* 47 (1912), 141–5.

STILLWELL, R., *Corinth* ii, *The Theatre*, The Amer. School of Class. Studies at Athens, Princeton, 1952.

SUSEMIHL, F., *Geschichte der griechischen Litteratur in der Alexandrinerzeit*, i–ii, Leipzig, 1891–2.

TARN, W. W., *Antigonos Gonatas*, Oxford, 1913.

—, *Hellenistic Civilization*, 3rd ed. revised by the author and G. T. Griffith, London, 1952.

THOMPSON, M., *The New Style Silver Coinage of Athens*, Numismatic Studies no. 10, The American Num. Soc., New York, 1961. (On the poets Asklepiades and Poses.)

THOMPSON, M., 'Athens again', *Numismatic Chronicle*, 7th s., 2 (1962), 301–33. (Answer to D. M. Lewis, see above.)

TOEPFFER, J., 'Die attischen Pythaisten und Deliasten', *Hermes* 23 (1888), 321–32.

TURNER, E. G., 'Dramatic Representations in Graeco-Roman Egypt: How Long do they Continue?', *L'Antiquité Classique* 22 (1963), 120–8.

VALLOIS, R., 'L' "agalma" des Dionysies de Délos', *B.C.H.* 46 (1922), 94–112.

—, *Architecture = L'architecture hellénique et hellénistique à Délos*, Bibl. des Écoles françaises d'Athènes et de Rome, fasc. 157, Paris, 1944.

—, *Les constructions antiques de Délos, Documents*, Bibl. des Écoles françaises d'Athènes et de Rome, fasc. 157 bis, Paris, 1953.

VENINI, P., 'Note sulla tragedia ellenistica', *Dioniso*, 1953, 3–26.

VOLLGRAFF, G., 'Inscriptiones argivae', *Mnemosyne* N.S. 47 (1919), 252ff.

WEBSTER, T. B. L., *Studies in Later Greek Comedy*, Manchester Univ. Press, 1953.

—, *Greek Theatre Production*, London, 1956.

—, *Studies in Menander*, 2nd ed., Manchester Univ. Press, 1960.

—, *Monuments Illustrating Old and Middle Comedy*, *B.I.C.S.*, Supplement no. 9, 1960.

—, *Monuments Illustrating New Comedy*, *B.I.C.S.*, Supplement no. 11, 1961.

—, *Monuments Illustrating Tragedy and Satyr Play*, *B.I.C.S.*, Supplement no. 14, 1962.

—, 'Menander: Production and Imagination', *Bulletin of the John Rylands Library* 45 (1962), 235–72.

—, *Griechische Bühnenaltertümer*, Studienhefte zur Altertumswissenschaft no. 9, Göttingen, 1963.

—, 'Alexandrian Epigrams and the Theatre', *Miscellanea di studi alessandrini in memoria di Augusto Rostagni*, Torino, 1963, pp. 531–43.

—, 'Le théâtre grec et son décor', *L'Antiquité Classique* 32 (1963), 562–70.

WEINREICH, O., *Epigramm und Pantomimus*, Sitz.-Ber. d. Heidelberger Akad. d. Wiss., Phil.-hist. Kl., i, 1944–8, 1. Abh.

WEISSINGER, R. T., *A Study of Act Division in Classical Drama*, Iowa Studies in Classical Philology, 1940.

WEISSMANN, K., *Die scenischen Anweisungen in den Scholien zu Aischylos, Sophokles, Euripides und Aristophanes, und ihre Bedeutung für die Bühnenkunde*, Programm des k. neuen Gymnasiums in Bamberg, 1896.

WELLES, C. BRADFORD, *Royal Correspondence in the Hellenistic Period*, Yale Univ. Press, 1934.

WILHELM, A., *Urkunden = Urkunden dramatischer Aufführungen in Athen*, Sonderschr. d. Oesterr. arch. Inst. in Wien, 1906.

—, *Griechische Inschriften rechtlichen Inhalts, Πραγματεῖαι τῆς 'Ακαδημίας 'Αθηνῶν*, vol. 17, no. 1, Athens, 1951.

WILL, E., 'Le sanctuaire syrien de Délos', *Les Annales archéologiques de Syrie*, 1 (1951), 59–79.

WINNINGTON-INGRAM, R. P., see EITREM, S.

WÜST, E., 'Pantomimus' in *R.E.* xviii 833–69.

ZIEBARTH, E., *Das griechische Vereinswesen*, Leipzig, 1896.

—, 'Delische Stiftungen', *Hermes* 52 (1917), 425–41. (On vase-festivals.)

ZIEGLER, K., 'Tragoedia' in *R.E.*, 2e Reihe, vi 1899–2075.

GENERAL INDEX

The following abbreviations are used:

a. actor
c. comic
chd. chorodidaskalos
chor. choreut
d. didaskalos
fl. flautist
him. himatiomisthes

hypd. hypodidaskalos
ko. kitharode
k.-p. kithara-player
p. poet
s. satyric
t. tragic

INDEX OF ANCIENT AUTHORS
AND INSCRIPTIONS

INDEX OF SCHOLARS